The Handbook
of Investment
Performance Measurement
Second Edition

A User's Guide

The Spaulding Series

The Spaulding Series is a unique collection of publications, carefully selected and brought together by David Spaulding and The Spaulding Group management. These books, many original while others previously out of print, are designed to enrich any investment professional's, academic's, or investor's library by providing essential and fundamental resources and references.

Pension Funds: Measuring Investment Performance, by Peter O. Dietz (2004)

The Handbook of Performance Measurement, by David Spaulding (2005)

Readings in Fixed Income Performance Attribution (2007)

Classics in Investment Performance Measurement (2009)

The Handbook of Performance Attribution (planned for 2011)

The Handbook of Investment Performance Measurement
Second Edition

A User's Guide

David Spaulding, CIPM

TSG Publishing

Somerset, New Jersey

Library of Congress Cataloging-in-Publications Data
Spaulding, David.
   The Handbook of Investment Performance Measurement: calculating and evaluating investment risk and return, 2nd Edition / David Spaulding

TSG Publishing, Inc.
   A Division of **The Spaulding Group, Inc.**

ISBN 1-893813-31-1

TSG Publishing books are available at special quantity discounts to use as premiums, sales promotions, or training programs. For additional information, please contact The Spaulding Group, Inc., 33 Clyde Road, Suite 103, Somerset, NJ 08873; 732-873-5700; www.SpauldingGrp.com.

The Journal of Performance Measurement® is a registered trademark of The Spaulding Group, Inc.

AIMR-PPS® and GIPS® are registered trademarks of the CFA Institute (formerly, the Association for Investment Management and Research).

Cover design by Cybill Conklin

"I encourage performance practitioners (and investment practitioners) at all levels to read this text. It will confirm your understanding of the basics of performance and also introduce you to quite a few advanced topics. It's likely that you will find something that you didn't understand as well as you might be able to (I know I did). Besides, it's a fun read! I have often heard Dave refer to performance analysis as an 'evolving discipline.' I am sure that this is true. I am equally sure that this text will help that process to continue to move forward."

-Stephen Campisi

The role of performance measurement has grown considerably over the past several years. So has the demand for information resources to meet the needs of performance measurement professionals, both seasoned veterans and novices. This latest offering by David Spaulding builds upon his already successful and well regarded <u>Measuring Investment Performance</u> and <u>Performance Measurement Attribution</u>.

Not only has performance measurement's role in the financial industry grown, it has also evolved in response to the many demands that have been placed upon it by practitioners, portfolio management, customers, and regulators. During the eight years since his first book was published, Spaulding has devoted a great deal of time to both reflection and research. The result is a book that goes well beyond anything previously offered.

Performance measurement isn't limited to calculating rates of return (although there's plenty of discussion on this critically important area). It also includes benchmarks, risk measurement, performance attribution and the performance presentation standards. This invaluable handbook offers a great deal of valuable information on all of these topics, in an easy-to-read and comprehend fashion, with practical examples and exercises to reinforce the material.

Spaulding draws extensively from his firm's focus on performance measurement, as well as his own experience in consulting to numerous clients, conducting training throughout the globe, and interacting with other performance measurement professionals at conferences and meetings.

This guide looks at performance measurement and all of its complexities, providing the reader with a valuable text and reference. It's insightful, clearly written and illustrated. <u>The Handbook of Investment Performance</u> is an essential resource for anyone involved with performance measurement.

Other books by David Spaulding

Measuring Investment Performance (McGraw-Hill, 1997)

Investment Performance Attribution (McGraw-Hill, 2003)

TSG's Guide to the Performance Presentation Standards (The Spaulding Group, Inc., 1999) (uncredited)

TSG's Performance, Attribution, and Risk Measurement Reference Guide (The Spaulding Group, Inc., 2002) (uncredited)

TSG's Performance, Attribution, and Risk Measurement Reference Guide (The Spaulding Group, Inc., 2004) (uncredited)

Performance Measurement in Finance (Butterworth-Heinemann, 2002); contributing author

Readings in Fixed Income Performance Attribution (The Spaulding Series, 2007); co-editor and contributing author

Classics in Investment Performance Measurement (The Spaulding Series, 2009); co-editor and contributing author

Dedication

One of the unexpected benefits of writing a book is that the author is afforded the opportunity to dedicate it to someone. Over the years I've taken this role quite seriously and have chosen both family members and friends to acknowledge.

The first edition was dedicated to a friend of mine, Ian Harvey, who I had known for more than 40 years. Somehow we remained in contact for all those years. Ian and I met when I joined the Order of DeMolay, a Masonic organization for young men. A few years before the release of the earlier book, Ian had been diagnosed with cancer, and I thought the dedication would be a way to express how special he was to me. He and his family were quite touched by this gesture.

Sadly, Ian's battle with cancer came to an end four years ago. He is missed by many friends and especially his wife and children. This edition is therefore dedicated to Ian's memory.

This book is also dedicated to my grandson, Brady David Spaulding, born August 1, 2009.

Table of Contents

Foreword to Second Edition

Over the last 25 years, performance measurement has developed beyond recognition. We've seen the development of detailed attribution and risk analysis, the introduction of increasingly complex instruments and the varied challenges they raise for performance measurers, and, of course, the development of a whole range of additional investment strategies. As a result, performance measurement has been firmly moved from the dull back office to a more exciting and essential role, blinking in the bright sunlight in the middle office of asset managers. Performance measurement provides the key quality control of the investment decision process, enabling money managers to correctly understand their performance, communicate with clients and crucially determine how performance can be improved.

David Spaulding has been a key witness to these changes via his involvement through various consulting engagements, the Performance Measurement Forums and conferences, training courses, participation in the development of Global Investment Performance Standards (GIPS®) and via *The Journal of Performance Measurement®*. This exposure is clearly reflected in the 2nd edition of the Handbook of Investment Performance.

David writes in a refreshingly friendly and fun style in the context of the dry world of performance measurement. David has not simply regurgitated the work of others; he has clearly attempted to add value by presenting material in a fashion useful to both the expert practitioner and absolute beginner.

I may not agree with David on every subject, but that is the beauty of this book; David's thought processes are there in black and white and you are free to make your own judgment.

Over many years of professional collaboration I have come to value David's opinion on many subjects and this 2nd edition does not disappoint.

This publication is a great educational tool and valuable reference source for performance measurers in particular, but also other stakeholders in the investment decision process.

Carl Bacon
Deeping St James
May 2010

Foreword to First Edition

Performance measurement is a critical, yet underserved and underappreciated phase of the portfolio management process. This is a curious, yet so far persistent problem. Investment managers and clients understand the need for professionals who can construct effective investment strategies that deliver a high level of return with a minimum of risk. So, the good news is that the "architects' of the investment planning phase of portfolio management get the respect (and compensation) that they deserve. The news is also good for the analysts and traders who buy and sell the securities that turn a strategy into a portfolio of specific investments. In fact, the majority of most firms' resources go into this transactional phase, which generates lots of activity and the fees that go along with the search for the elusive "alpha" demand by active managers and the clients who hire them. The significance of these fees is not to be minimized. By some estimates, fees for active management in the investment industry are now in excess of $35 billion per year.

What are investors getting for the fees they pay? It would seem that this would be the burning question on the minds of most investors. One would also expect investment managers to be asking this question, along with other relevant ones, such as: "How much risk did I actually take?" And more importantly: "Did I get paid for the risk that I took?" "How well did I do, relative to the indexes that represent my strategy?" "How well did I do relative to comparable managers?" At this point the investment managers would want to know: "Who are the people in my firm who can give me these answers?" We might also expect the firm's management to have a few questions of their own, including "How do we tell our performance story effectively, so that we bring in new clients and retain the clients we already have?" And, "How can I know that I am complying with standards regarding the returns I show to potential and existing clients, so that I can prevent a costly inquiry by regulators that could irreparably harm the firm's reputation?"

These are all critical questions. Unfortunately, they go largely unanswered in many firms! Isn't it surprising that, given the importance of performance analysis as part of the portfolio management process, the staff of most performance measurement units are not closely aligned with the investment management function? In many firms, these groups work almost independently of each other, often never interacting at all. This is both a problem and an opportunity. For those firms that do not consider performance analysis to be a part of the portfolio management process, the loss of market opportunity and the risk of regulatory sanctions are very real threats. However, the firms that do not recognize the value of performance analysis enjoy a source of significant competitive advantage, from product development through marketing, sales, product delivery and client relationship management.

So, the critical question before the managers of performance analysis units is this: "How can I help to reposition my group so that it receives the recognition it deserves, along with the opportunity to participate in the portfolio management process?" I suggest that this process starts with repositioning the staff of the performance unit by first enhancing their knowledge of both the investment process and the science (and the art) of performance analysis. Sadly, many performance units are not only understaffed, but also wrongly staffed. Today's investment environment demands performance analysts who share the same investment and quantitative skills as those who develop strategies and make investments. There is no longer a place for performance analysts who considers themselves to be "second banana" to the investment "professionals," or who consider themselves part of the "back office." It is time for well-qualified investment professionals who specialize in the evaluation phase of the portfolio management process to step up and start delivering the value-added type of analysis that today's investment firms require. This demands an increased knowledge of investments and the markets in which they are traded. It also requires an increased knowledge of the analysis of performance.

Which brings us to this new book by David Spaulding, which is actually a complete rewrite of his first (and rather successful) book on performance measurement. If today's performance analyst is to gain the higher skills that the market demands, the question is "From where?" Well, regarding the knowledge of the investment process, there are many sources, including textbooks, academic courses and professional programs, such as the Chartered Financial Analyst (CFA) program. But, where does one go to study the analysis of investment performance? After all, even advanced programs such as the CFA merely scratch the surface of only a few of the topics required to provide top-quality performance analysis. So, with a dearth of available self-study materials available, what's a performance analyst to do?

And so we turn to this rather excellent text, which provides not only an overview of all of the relevant topics in performance analysis, but also provides a depth of knowledge and understanding that form a strong foundation for the performance specialist. Dave Spaulding has been widely acknowledged not only as an expert in performance as a practitioner, but also as an educator. I have come to appreciate his writings because he has a knack for explaining rather technical information in a very readable, almost conversational manner. This makes the information easier to understand and to apply to real life situations. So, for those who are learning about performance for the first time, this text will be an invaluable resource, one that I am sure you will find yourself reaching for time and again. For the experienced practitioner, you will find updates on critical areas of analysis, so that you will be up to date with the true "state of the art" regarding performance. And, everyone benefits from having a single text with all the necessary information on evaluating investment performance, gleaned from a variety of sources, including many recognized experts in the field world-wide. To get the same information, one would have to find and read several books, many articles, and attend quite a few expensive conferences to get the first-hand knowledge included in this single text.

And so I encourage performance practitioners of all levels (and investment practitioners) to read this text. It will confirm your understanding of the basics of performance, and also introduce you to quite a few advanced topics. It's likely that you will find something that you didn't understand as well as you might (I know I did). Besides, it's a fun read! I have often heard Dave refer to performance analysis as an "evolving discipline." I am sure that this is true. I am equally sure that this text will help that process to continue to move forward.

Stephen Campisi

Preface and Acknowledgments
Second Edition

It's now been thirteen years since I wrote my first book, <u>Measuring Investment Performance</u> and five years since the first edition of this book appeared. This rewrite actually began in 2008, but for a variety of reasons has required more time than we anticipated.

I will confess that almost immediately after the book was published I had an epiphany: we're generally calculating returns the wrong way. Such a drastic realization was quite a surprise. I would have liked to have yelled "stop the presses" but alas had to go forward with what had been written. But now that the first edition is (thankfully) sold out, I can offer my revised thinking on this subject.

Over the intervening years my beliefs about the way we calculate returns versus how we should have only been strengthened. And, I'm grateful that many others have begun to "see the light" as well, perhaps most notably Stefan Illmer and Steve Campisi. How we each arrived at this realization is unknown to me but what is known is that we're all passionate about this subject. We each have spoken on this subject at various conferences and user groups; Steve and Stefan even debated the topic with two rivals at the 2007 Performance Measurement, Attribution and Risk Conference (PMAR) and I debated Carl Bacon on it at PMAR Europe I in 2010. I've written various articles addressing this topic, and Steve and I coauthored an article (Spaulding & Campisi (2008)) that was placed as an opposing piece to one written by Carl Bacon (2008).

To my knowledge this is the first such book to devote so much attention to the subject of money-weighted returns. While much of the first edition has remained as it was written, the greatest changes deal with this subject. You'll see that we added a chapter on what I consider the characteristics of a "first class performance system." Clearly, this is a subjective assessment, but hopefully will provide you with some insights and things to think about.

Since the earlier edition, the industry continues to undergo change. I coined the "three Cs of Performance Measurement" a number of years ago, and "change" continues to be a staple of investment performance. In 2006 we witnessed the "convergence" of all "country versions of GIPS®" and the creation of a single standard. This rather momentous event is quite unique as it's virtually impossible to identify anything else 30-some nations agree on, especially something in writing. As a result, the AIMR-PPS® (as well as the many other country versions) is no more. And as this book goes to press, we are prepared for the upcoming inception date for the most recent changes to these standards.

We are witnessing even greater respect for our field. The Performance

Measurement Forum created a "blue ribbon committee" in 2004 to develop a certification program for performance measurers. Our basic objectives were (1) to recognize those in the industry who had achieved a high level of expertise and (2) to help promote performance measurement's role in the investment process. Shortly after we began, the CFA Institute announced a similar program, and since the industry doesn't need two certification programs, we abandoned our effort and publicized our support for what the CFA Institute was doing under the leadership of Philip Lawton (since replaced by Todd Jankowski). The CIPM (Certificate in Performance Measurement) is slowly achieving the objectives that we established. This is a great contribution to our industry.

Recently Carl Bacon introduced a revision to his first book (Bacon (2008)) and Christopherson, Cariño and Ferson (2009) introduced a new book. I encourage you (if you haven't already done so) to acquire copies of both as they are "must haves" in any serious performance measurer's library, as well as Bruce Feibel's text (2003).

Overview of what you'll find

You'll find within this text some expanded examples, further clarity on a few topics, and, as noted previously, expanded discussion on the use of money-weighting. I am sure that if I began work now on a third edition (which I will within the next three years), I'd think of more items to include, but this will have to wait; this book has taken long enough to get completed.

Acknowledgments

My list of those to whom I am indebted doesn't change a great deal from the list in the first edition. I do want to thank Carl Bacon for writing the foreword for this edition. I have come to love and respect Carl a great deal. And while we often find things to disagree about, at the core we agree about most things. Carl's contributions to the industry have been many and I'm grateful to be able to call him a friend.

A few things have changed on the personal side of my life. My wife and I have now been married more than 38 years, our older son, Chris, is now married (wife Monica), and they had their first child, Brady, in August of 2009. Our younger son (Douglas) is (in addition to working for our firm) completing his Masters in Fine Arts at Farleigh Dickinson University in creative writing, and Patrick Fowler and Jaime Fowler Puerschner's respective families have grown (two children, each).

And finally, thank you for acquiring and actually reading this book. If you uncover any errors, please let me know (DSpaulding@SpauldingGrp.com). And, if you have any questions or comments, feel free to send me a note.

Preface and Acknowledgments
First Edition

It's been eight years since I wrote my first book, *Measuring Investment Performance*. Since that time, a great deal has happened to the industry. For example:

- We now have global performance presentation standards, GIPS®
- The AIMR-PPS® is now part of these global standards, as a "country version of GIPS" or CVG
- Several other countries have adopted GIPS, created CVGs, or created translated versions of GIPS
- Attribution has become much more important to the industry and virtually a "must have" for any institutional investor
- *The Journal of Performance Measurement*® (*JPM*) has become the place to go for current thinking and development in investment performance
- Fixed income attribution has taken off, with many models developed in just the past five years
- In 1997, there were hardly any software vendors offering software supporting the presentation standards; today, there are many such systems available
- Consequently, we've seen a drop in the use of spreadsheets to manage composites
- Software vendors sell all over the world, and managers are willing to consider vendors from just about anywhere – the Internet and other technological developments have eliminated geographic boundaries
- The Investment Performance Council (IPC), a global organization with representatives from virtually every locale, has been created to oversee the presentation standards
- The Performance Measurement Forum has been created and serves investment performance measurement professionals throughout North America and Europe
- Vendors such as Russell/Mellon and Wilshire have revealed their previously secretive linking methods to achieve multi-period attribution
- Other vendors, such as Thomson/Vestek, have developed and presented their methods for linking attribution effects
- Various debates have raged regarding various controversial aspects of performance, including: geometric vs. arithmetic attribution, holdings-based vs. transaction-based attribution, and what constitutes a time-weighted or money-weighted return

- The Association for Investment Management and Research, which was formed in 1990 as a result of the merger of the Financial Analysts Federation and the Institute of Chartered Financial Analysts, has been renamed the Chartered Financial Analyst Institute (CFA Institute)
- AIMR (now the CFA Institute) has introduced one-day workshops on the standards[1]
- The Performance Measurement Forum has offered standards for performance attribution and for making adjustments to prior performance
- The European Investment Performance Committee (EIPC) has developed guidelines for performance attribution
- A France-based group, GRAP (Groupe de Réflexion en Attribution de Performance), has developed guidance on fixed income attribution
- The Foundation of Investment Performance Professionals has been created to support those that are engaged in this exciting field
- A Blue Ribbon Committee (BRC) was formed by the Foundation to develop a certification program for performance measurement professionals
- The CFA Institute has decided to develop a certification program for investment performance professionals

And, since that time, my firm introduced a training program which includes a course, Fundamentals of Performance Measurement, which is based on that first book. As a result of that class, my participation in the Performance Measurement Forum, and through a variety of other activities, my own knowledge of performance measurement has grown. I have also come to realize that there was much that could have been included in my first book.

That first book has now been sold out. And rather than have it reprinted, given all that has occurred over the past several years, I decided to start over. This is not a rewrite of the earlier book – it's a *new book from scratch*. It benefitted a great deal from the classes I teach and the other articles I've written over the years.

We decided to publish it as part of "The Spaulding Series," which we began in 2004 with the republication of Peter Dietz's *Pension Funds: Measuring Investment Performance*.

A growing knowledge base

Some say that to learn something well, write about it. I've also heard that to learn something well, teach it. Well, I've done both, and as a result I have learned, and continue to learn, more and more about this wonderfully exciting field of investment performance measurement.

If you read my first book, thank you. And thank you for now reading this one. This will hopefully provide you with additional insights into performance measurement. And if this is the first of my books that you've read, I hope you find it of interest and value.

Over the past several years, I've had the privilege to meet and get to know many individuals who have contributed to this segment of the investment industry. While I know I'm at risk of leaving someone off by naming some here, I feel obligated to pay tribute to them:

- Bob McAllister was my first teacher of performance measurement, and I still periodically reach out to him for his thoughts and ideas.
- Brian Singer and Denis Karnosky were the developers of the Karnosky-Singer model for global performance attribution. While I haven't met Denis, I've had the opportunity to get to know Brian, who serves on the advisory board of *JPM*. Even though Brian has never worked in performance, *per se,* he has contributed greatly to the profession.
- Jose Menchero has been a tremendous addition to the industry and has been responsible for developing techniques, such as his multi-period linking methodology, and for his other analytical work. Jose's prior life as a physics professor no doubt has contributed to his method of approaching analysis and has resulted in some great work, which *JPM* has had the privilege of publishing. Jose also contributes to the *JPM* as a member of the advisory board.
- As the first chairman of the IPC, John Stannard was a major contributor to the successful development and implementation of GIPS. He has also served as an advisory board member of *JPM* and as a contributing author.
- James (Jamie) Hollis, who I've had the privilege of knowing for almost 20 years, has contributed greatly to the development of the presentation standards as a former Chair of the AIMR-PPS Implementation Committee and today as the Chair of the IPC.
- As the current point person for the CFA Institute on the standards, Jonathan Boersma has played a key role in much of the development over the past several years.
- Stefan Illmer has become known as one who is always thinking of new approaches and ideas. His creativity is benefitting the industry tremendously.
- Claude Giguère is one of the leading authority's on performance measurement in Canada and has made significant contributions through his participation with GRAP and the BRC.
- Carl Bacon has become a leading performance measurement authority throughout Europe and the U.S. and a major contributor to the development of standards and ideas through his participation with the EIPC, IPC, BRC, and other initiatives. Carl is also a recent author, with the publication of *Practical Portfolio Performance and Attribution* (John Wiley, 2004).
- As the "benchmark king," Neil Riddles continues to be the leading authority on all facets of benchmarks.

- Bruce Feibel is contributing to the knowledge base of the industry, especially in the area of risk measurement, through the recent publication of his book *Investment Performance Measurement* (John Wiley, 2003).
- Leslie Rahl continues to be a (if not, the) leading authority on risk measurement.
- Herb Chain and Matt Forstenhausler are two of the industry's leading verifiers, and I've learned much from them through the training classes we conduct for the CFA Institute (formerly AIMR).
- In spite of not working formally in performance measurement for some time, Steve Campisi continues to play a role, through his own research and development efforts, especially in the areas of fixed income attribution and multi-period linking.

I have learned so much by having the benefit of interacting with these folks, with some on a fairly regular basis. Much of this book's content can be attributed to what I've learned from these individuals.

And many of these individuals also serve the industry through their volunteer efforts on the various committees and subcommittees. They, along with their fellow committee members, are owed a debt of gratitude for their commitment of time and talent.

When I wrote my first book, I realized that many others could have. And since then, both Carl Bacon and Bruce Feibel have done just that. So why do we need this revision?

Before I answer the question, let me point out something that I learned some time ago – a writer needs multiple books on style (I have four in my office) plus a few dictionaries (and I have four of these). Why so many style guides and dictionaries? Because they don't all agree, so to have multiple references, especially if you spend much time writing (as I do), is a requirement.

So, why a revision when there are other books available? First, as noted above, my first book has sold out, and to get the publisher to do a second printing, without some revision, wouldn't have made sense. And even though there are now two other books available (Carl's and Bruce's), we each have different approaches to writing and content. Your library should include their books, too, as a performance measurement professional should have multiple resources to refer to and to draw upon.

What's different

In addition to the content being different with this book, you'll also find exercises at the end of several of the chapters. I did this with my last book, *Investment Performance Attribution*, as I felt it enhanced the offering considerably. The exercises give you a chance to try out what you've read.

As I did with my first book, the solutions are in the book, and details are available at our website (www.SpauldingGrp.com). You'll also find corrections at our site, too.[2]

The explanations are much more detailed than what I offered earlier, too. I also eliminated some material which didn't contribute that much to the earlier book.

The style of writing (somewhat conversational) remains the same, as many of the readers of my earlier books have told me they find it helpful.

Overview of what you'll find

We begin with background on the subject of performance measurement (Chapter 1). Here, we explain the concepts and types of performance measurement and provide a brief history of how we got to where we are today. We then tackle the subject of money-weighted returns (Chapter 2) – what I previously referred to as dollar-weighting. Given the globalization of the industry, referring to something as "dollar-anything" doesn't seem fair or appropriate, so the more generic money-weighting term has taken over. We then move onto the subject of time-weighted performance, first discussing approximation methods (Chapter 3) and then exact or true methods (Chapter 4). We finish up the subject of returns by discussing multi-period performance (Chapter 5) and then discuss other issues related to returns (Chapter 6).

Chapter 7 deals with benchmarks and addresses the various types. You'll find that my covering of attribution is much greater than it was in the first book. Chapter 8 touches on just about all facets of this subject, although in not as much detail as my book on attribution. We next tackle a risky topic – risk measurement (Chapter 9). Again, there's more covered here than what we addressed in the first book.

We then shift gears and move into the topic of the presentation standards (Chapter 10). Again, you'll find a lot more here, including a roadmap to the standards. Given that we now have GIPS and multiple local versions (including the AIMR-PPS), most of the chapter speaks in general terms.

Given the complexity of the industry, it's become even more important for firms to have controls, policies, and procedures in place, so we address this in Chapter 11. And we wrap up with a discussion of the Performance Measurement Profession (Chapter 12); something that didn't really exist ten years ago.

In addition, you'll find a few appendices at the end of some chapters that provide additional in- depth discussion, as well as a list of references we feel you'll want to have access to.

Other acknowledgments

"Writing is an audacious act to begin with."
Thaisa Frank and Dorothy Wall

"Writing makes a person very vulnerable. It opens you to public criticism, to ridicule, to rejection. But it also opens conversation and thought. It stirs minds and touches hearts. It brings us into contact with our souls. Writing is the way I think things through."
Joan Chittister

In my first book, I thanked my many English teachers who would probably fall over if they knew I had written a book, given my less-than-stellar efforts in their classes. It didn't occur to me until after it was published that what I had actually written was a mathematics book. And given that my undergraduate degree is in math, and that what we found in it were a lot of numbers and equations, the feat was probably not that significant. I do, however, enjoy writing quite a bit. In addition to having written numerous articles over the past few years, I now write a monthly newsletter which is available on our Web site.

I also want to thank Patrick Fowler, Christopher Spaulding, Sue Kneller, Sabina Hastings, Jaime Fowler Puerschner, and Doug Spaulding for their support. I want to especially thank Doug, who handled the production side of this project.

I want to thank my book reviewers, who took the time to read through the manuscript and then provided me with corrections and ideas: Carl Bacon, Steve Campisi, Hiroshi Fujibayashi, Jennifer Cahill, Sandra Hahn-Colbert, Todd Juillerat, Corné Reniers, and Neil Riddles. I am very appreciative of the time they invested to review the manuscript, the errors they found, and the comments they offered. In spite of their best efforts and mine, as noted above, a few errors will no doubt slip through. I apologize for them in advance and assume full responsibility.

Thanks to Cybill Conklin for her wonderful cover design. Cybill has become our designer-of-choice and has contributed to several of our projects.

Thanks to my proofreader, Mary Meagher, for her expert review. Mary also serves as the proofreader for *JPM*.

Before closing, I must also thank my wife of 32 years, Betty, who continues to support me in all of my efforts.

And finally, thank you for acquiring and actually reading this book. If you uncover any errors, please let me know (DSpaulding@SpauldingGrp.com). And, if you have any questions or comments, feel free to send me a note.

[1] We were pleased to have been chosen to conduct these, through a consortium we formed with Deloitte & Touche and Ernst & Young.

[2] You may think it's premature to talk about corrections while I'm still writing, before the book has been published, but as the author of other books, I know that mistakes occur and therefore anticipate this to happen with this book, too, in spite of our best efforts.

Chapter 1 –
Performance Measurement - What's It All About?

"Managing money is about one thing: performance."
Barton Biggs. "Hedge Hogging"

One of the points I like to emphasize about investment performance measurement[1] is that it borrows ideas from many other disciplines. In fact, performance measurement is hardly limited to investments.

Performance measurement, in general, is a way to assess how well something or someone is doing. It falls into two general categories: subjective and objective.

Subjective assessments

There are countless examples of subjective performance measurement. Politicians continuously face this kind of review by their constituents and the media. Some actually go so far as to seek it out. A good example is former New York City Mayor Ed Koch, who was renowned for going about the city asking "How am I doing?" He wasn't expecting a numerical or quantitative rating; rather, he wanted people to say "You're doing a great job, mayor!" or "Mayor, we have a problem."

Performance reviews are another example. Many corporations and government agencies put their employees through periodic reviews. These exercises afford management the opportunity to let their staff know how they're doing and how they can improve. Such reviews are often tied to the salary adjustments that are made.[2]

When I was in the army I discovered quite a formal system to conduct reviews. A soldier would get a review at least once a year and often more often than that, as they could get one when they changed jobs or when their boss was replaced, as well as on other occasions.

The U.S. military isn't the only one that conducts such reviews. We discovered a list of comments from the Royal Navy and Marines (see Table 1-1), which offers some insights into the kind of remarks we might read in these reports. While you will no doubt find some of these comments humorous, the point is that they are entirely subjective. Depending on who is conducting the review, we might see very different comments.

Voters are often asked to voice their opinion about elected officials, and it is typical to see quite a mix of comments. While these are often influenced by the voter's political party affiliation vis-a-vis the official, there isn't necessarily a perfect correlation. The point is, one person might think the president or prime minister is doing a fantastic job, while someone else is ready to toss him out. When we conduct a subjective review, we are bringing along a lot of our biases and personal preferences.

• His men would follow him anywhere, but only out of curiosity.
• I would not breed with this officer.
• This officer is really not so much a has-been, but rather more of a won't be.
• When she opens her mouth, it seems that this is only to change whichever foot was previously there.
• He has carried out each and every one of his duties to his entire satisfaction.
• He would be out of his depth in a car park puddle.
• Technically sound but socially impossible.
• This officer reminds me very much of a gyroscope – always spinning around at a frantic pace but not really going anywhere.
• This young lady has delusions of adequacy.
• When he joined my ship, this officer was something of a granny; since then he has aged considerably.
• This medical officer has used my ship to carry his genitals from port to port, and my officers to carry him from bar to bar.
• Since my last report he has reached rock bottom, and started to dig.
• She sets low personal standards and then consistently fails to achieve them.
• He has the wisdom of youth and the energy of old age.
• This officer should go far – and the sooner he starts, the better.
• In my opinion, this pilot should not be authorized to fly below 250 feet.
• This man is depriving a village somewhere of an idiot.
• Works well under constant supervision and cornered like a rat.

Table 1-1: Royal Navy and Marine Fitness Reports, from the Internet[3]

Objective assessments

An alternative to subjective reviews would be objective or quantitative ones.

Here, we base our evaluation on statistics or other measurable qualities.[4]

In today's sports world we see many examples of this. In baseball, for example, hitters are judged on batting average, on-base percentage, slugging percentage, and much more. Pitchers are assessed on their win/loss record, earned run average, strikeouts, and more. And these statistics go into all kinds of detail, as we get a hitter's batting average against right-handed pitchers and left-handed pitchers, while there are runners in scoring position or when the bases are empty, and on and on.

In school, students are given examinations. Granted, if the test is of the essay form, then some subjectiveness will no doubt influence the score. If the test is one where the right answers are quite clear, then such a test falls into the objective category. As long as we use the same rules to measure performers in a particular field of review, we can't be charged with being unfair in our assessment.[5]

Why do we measure performance?

So, performance measurement isn't limited to the investment world. But why do we do it at all?

In general, we do it because we want to know *how well we're doing* or *how well someone else is doing*. We may then use the information to decide on promotions, raises, terminations, etc. And the individual being reviewed can use the feedback to chart a course for improvement, career change, etc.

Performance measurement system

In an ideal world, when we conduct any form of performance measurement, we would have a "system" to manage the process. By system I don't necessarily mean a computer system, but rather an organized process with the appropriate procedures and controls to ensure that the process is fair and uniform.

Such a system should possess the following characteristics:

1. Appropriate: Our evaluation method should be appropriate to the situation being reviewed. It should make sense. I recall an event that occurred more than 25 years ago when I had been looking to hire someone. After months of searching I found the ideal candidate. My boss, however, said "no." And why did he not want to hire him? Because he didn't like the man's handshake – he

felt it was "too strong." Was that an appropriate measure? I don't think so. In our classes I often ask students to list the criteria they use when deciding how much of a tip (gratuity) to leave the waiter/waitress after a meal; a typical

Criteria for a performance system
1. Appropriate
2. Consistent
3. Free from bias
4. Standardized
5. Understood
6. Have controls

response is "how good the meal was." But does it make sense to reward or penalize the waiter/waitress for the meal? Unless they're doubling as the cook, this criteria is probably inappropriate, yes?

2. Consistent: Our evaluation system should be consistent over time; we shouldn't change the rules for evaluation. Now, this doesn't mean we can't ever change the rules if we believe we have a better measure, but they shouldn't be changing on a regular or frequent basis; otherwise, it makes it difficult for the person being evaluated to improve.

3. Free from bias: Whoever is doing the evaluation shouldn't bring other factors into play which might affect their judgment. In the States, during the presidential election, there are usually a handful of debates. And after these debates, it's not unusual for the respective running mates to be asked how well they thought their fellow candidate had done. Does this really make sense? Do you think that the vice presidential candidate is going to criticize, in any way, his running mate? I recall a reporter asking George H.W. Bush (a.k.a. "Bush 41") how well he thought his son (George W. Bush) did during a debate. Don't you think his response would be a bit biased? What are the chances he'd publicly criticize his son's performance?

4. Standardized: Ideally, the methods should be standardized within an organization and, where appropriate, across similar organizations, as well. Getting back to our baseball example, we measure batting averages the same in the major league as in the minor leagues, in colleges, and across countries. This makes comparisons more comprehensive.

5. Understood: The process should be understood by all involved. I recall doing my first review in the army. I took the review questions literally. And so when I was asked how my sergeant had performed in a particular area, I thought "above average" seemed appropriate. I later came to find out that "above average" meant "average" or even "below average," as the reviews were typically inflated. Roughly 90% of those reviewed fell into the "top 10%" range! But no one had told me, and it hadn't occurred to me to ask for guidance. We need

to know as much about what's expected and how we'll be measured as possible. I've heard some say that rates of return often "don't make sense" and that they're not supposed to. Actually, they're always supposed to make sense...it has to do with the reader's understanding of what's presented that's key.

6. <u>Have controls</u>: Our system needs controls to ensure that the results have real value. When, for example, a portfolio manager is allowed to calculate her own performance,[6] we might wonder if this is appropriate. Because salaries and bonuses are often tied to the results of the system, it's critical that there are controls in place to ensure there's no cheating going on.

Investment performance measurement

There was a time when investment managers weren't measured subjectively. Or, if they were, that the metric was inappropriate. While pursuing his doctorate, Peter Dietz discovered lots of challenges in the world of investment performance measurement (Dietz (1966) and Dietz (2004)). As Dietz pointed out, "Most of the companies interviewed had developed some type of performance measure, but in no case were the users satisfied that their measures were at all adequate."[7] He went on to state "It was clear that the methods developed could not readily be compared with one another...Most of the methods attempted to arrive at some sort of rate-of-return figure. However, these figures were incompatible with one another. Some calculated return on cost, others on market values. Some included only ordinary income in the rate; others included realized gains and losses and/or unrealized appreciation."

One of his discoveries was that many pension funds weren't marked-to-market; that is, they weren't revalued to the current market prices. Rather, the holdings' values were at book price or the original price.[8] So, we buy a stock valued at $10 five years ago, and that's still the price on our records. There's no way to decide if it was a good purchase or not. As Dietz pointed out, "market value represents the true economic value, which is available to the investment manager at any point in time, whereas book value is arbitrary."[9]

Dietz also discovered that at times when a portfolio manager's performance was measured that the metric wasn't always appropriate. For example, often the Internal Rate of Return (IRR) was used. As we'll see in the next chapter, this measure is affected by external cash flows – something the manager often cannot control.

Some used average yield as a measure, which relies on the income realized. But, as Dietz pointed out, "A measure of performance based only on ordinary income is misleading, when trying to compare two or more funds. The fund invested in equities would have been unduly penalized."[10]

One of Peter's major contributions to the industry was encouraging the use of a reasonable metric for assessing the performance of an investment manager: a time-weighted rate of return.[11]

Money-weighting vs. time-weighting

The earliest reference we've found for the term "time-weighting" is from the Bank Administration Institute's standards (BAI (1968)): "The recommended rate is called 'time-weighted' because it is simply the weighted average of internal rates of return for the subperiods between cash flows with each weight being only the length of its corresponding subperiod."[12]

Today, do we actually *weight time* when we measure performance? As we'll shortly see, in the Modified Dietz and Modified BAI methods we weight the cash flow based on the amount of time it is present. But is that what we mean by *time-weighting*?[13]

How about *money-weighting*? Do we weight money? As we discuss in Chapter 2, the Internal Rate of Return weights money based on its timing (how's that for some added confusion?).

Long ago, the explanation I was given for the differences is: *money-weighting measures the performance of the fund*, while *time-weighting measures the performance of the manager*. The first time I heard this I was confused. While it took some time for the differences to sink in, I can fully understand if it's unclear to you. Hopefully, in the next few chapters the differences will be clear.

Another way to put it is that money-weighting is affected by cash flows, while time-weighting isn't (or is minimally) influenced by cash flows. We'll discuss methods to calculate both, as well as formulas to derive approximations to the time-weighted rate of return. There is no weighting of time with time-weighted returns. Rather, we're simply attempting to minimize (or eliminate) the impact of these flows, over which the manager has no control. But the term has stuck.

Which to use?

Recall that one of the criteria for a "performance system" noted above is appropriateness. Dietz's objection to the use of IRR was based upon two key points: (1) he was dealing with returns at the *portfolio* level and (2) he was concerned with those cases where *the client controls the cash flows*. Recognizing this is critically important. The reality is that <u>both</u> measures have value. We will address this in greater detail in Chapter 6.

The three C-words of Performance Measurement
Confusion
Controversy
Change

The three Cs of investment performance

There are three "C-words" which we can associate with the field of investment performance:

#1 <u>Confusion</u>: Much of what we deal with is confusing (we've perhaps already encountered a couple of these, including the use of the term "time-weighting" and the suggestion that Modified BAI and Modified Dietz are actually money-weighted measures). There are certain areas of performance where confusion is greater than others, but all seem to have aspects that many find confusing. Suffice it to say, there's lots to be confused about. In this book we'll try to clarify some of the more confusing points (and hopefully won't add to the list).

#2 <u>Controversy</u>: There are probably lots of reason for the controversy we find. First, the field of performance measurement is still relatively new and still being developed. Second, given the globalization of investment performance, there's bound to be some controversy as we go from one country to another. And, for some of the areas of performance measurement, there hasn't been enough research done to fully justify one approach's preference over another.

These first two C-words stem from the fact that much of what we're dealing with is *art,* not *science*. And just as with any art form, there are many approaches and concepts to performance measurement. We've succeeded in establishing a fair number of rules which are generally well acknowledged and understood, but we still manage to discover new areas of controversy and confusion on a fairly regular basis. The more we delve into investment performance, the more we find challenges.

#3 <u>Change</u>: Investment performance measurement is on a path of increased development. Even though some of the concepts have been around for over 40 years, we're still learning and expanding. Performance measurement is one of the most exciting areas of the investment industry.

If past performance is not an indication of future results, why measure it?

You're no doubt familiar with statements such as "past performance is not necessarily an indication of future results." If this is the case, why do we bother to measure performance and spend so much money and time on it? Well, the simple response is "do you have a better alternative?" Also, even though we can't guarantee that our past record will continue going forward, everyone wants to know what we did in the past.[14] People are constantly measured based on past performance. And investing shouldn't be any different.

The key, however, is to make sure that the way we measure is appropriate and that we provide information in a manner that has value. Thus, the development of the presentation standards, which we take up in Chapter 11.

Summary

Performance measurement is a concept that isn't peculiar to investment management. To avoid confusion, even our book title needed the qualifier "investment" so that we avoided a situation where someone who is interested in generic performance measurement or performance measurement relating to other disciplines or contexts won't be mislead.

As a discipline, investment performance measurement can date its start to the mid-1960s. Thus, it's still a relatively new idea. And given its dynamics, we find loads of confusion, controversy, and change taking place.

The coming chapters will serve to clarify some of the confusion and identify areas of controversy, as we move forward in this ever-changing area.

ENDNOTES

[1] We'll generally use the term "performance measurement" rather than the more cumbersome "investment performance measurement."

[2] There are no doubt numerous examples of where executives have reaped huge rewards, in spite of their firm's poor performance. John Plender's article, "What a performance," discussed "the poor link between corporate results and executive rewards"

(Plender, 1999): "eyebrows twitched in the U.K. fund management community when it emerged this week that [Martin Taylor, the former chief executive of Barclays] would receive a £1.6m package following his resignation – a reward that comes after a year in which Barclays' operating profits from continuing businesses were down 20 percent." More recently, Merrill Lynch's year-end 2008 bonuses were harshly criticized given the firm's huge loss. (Stempel (2009)) Dvorak (2009) went even further in addressing this topic. Oddly (perhaps), a U.S. senator suggested that recipients of bonuses from AIG "resign or commit suicide." (Reddy, et al (2009)).

[3] There are numerous Web sites that contain this table, with no original source identified.

[4] Actually, subjective reviews can include quantitative components (e.g., rate the individual on a scale from one to five); that's not what we mean here.

[5] Well, this isn't exactly true as some exams have been accused of being racially biased (e.g., the IQ test).

[6] We actually had a client where one of the managers did her own performance measurement calculation rather than rely upon what came out of the system. (We touch on this in Chapter 12.)

[7] Dietz (2004).

[8] While this may sound odd, the reality is that a few countries, not very long ago, had this same problem. Dietz wrote "It is interesting to note that several banks have argued that market value is not a true value because their funds are so big that they could not be liquidated at market price." Dietz's response: "This is a hollow argument, since nonmarketability [sic] is a risk the trustee has purposely taken in order to increase return." Dietz (2004).

[9] Ibid.

[10] Ibid.

[11] Dietz actually referred to it as an "average return."

[12] BAI (1968).

[13] Actually, one might argue that the Modified BAI and Modified Dietz are actually money-weighted returns; that the geometric linking of their intraperiod values results in an approximation to time-weighting. We discuss this later in Chapter 6.

[14] Having spent some time in politics, I know how our past record is important to the voter. They expect us to behave in a similar way to the past. Of course, in politics, we have greater control over our actions than in the world of investing.

Chapter 2 –
Calculating Money-weighted Returns

"The most relevant metric from an investor's perspective
is *dollar-weighted* rates of return[1]"

Alexander M. Ineichen

One term we often hear is money- or dollar-weighting.[2] In his seminal work, Peter Dietz discussed the problem with using money-weighted returns to measure the performance of investment managers: "One of the more sophisticated methods employed discounting procedures to give the actual rate that was earned on the contributions to give the current value of the fund. While this method gives an accurate rate of return, it cannot be used for comparative purposes, since it is influenced by the timing of cash flows into or out of the fund (contributions and withdrawals of cash and/or securities)."[3]

The Internal Rate of Return calculates a true money-weighted rate of return. Interestingly, the Modified Dietz and Modified BAI formulas provide an approximation for both the true time-weighted and true money-weighted returns! Confused? We'll clarify this as we move forward.

The IRR also goes by other terms, such as the discounted cash flow. It comes from the present value formula. The IRR is the annualized implied discount rate (effective compound rate) which equates the present value of all of the appropriate cash inflows with the sum of the present value of all the appropriate cash outflows accruing from it and the present value of the unrealized residual portfolio.[4] Another way to state this is that it's the rate of discount that equates the present value of the entire series of cash flows associated with the investment to zero.[5,6]

Present value is a concept that is familiar to many people and stems from the idea that a certain amount of money received today has greater value than it would if we were to receive the same amount in the future.[7] If, for example, we had a choice of getting $100 today or $100 a year from now, we'd probably take the money now, since we can invest the money we get today and have the opportunity to have more a year from now.

The present value formula is rather straightforward:

$$P_o = \frac{F_1}{(1+i)^t}$$

where

    P_0 = the present value

    F_1 = the future value or cash flow

    i = periodic growth rate

    t = number of periods or compounding periods

For example, what is the value today of a dollar we are to receive a year from now? To find this out we need an interest rate. Let's assume the rate we could earn on our money is five percent. Then, using the present value formula we have:

$$P_o = \frac{\$1}{(1+.05)^1} = \frac{1}{1.05} = 0.9524 = 0.95$$

As we can see, the result is 95.24 cents (which rounds to 95 cents). Why? Because if we were to invest 95 cents at 5% for one year, it would grow to $1. So, these are equivalent values – that is, $1 in one year has a present value of $0.95, and $0.95 has a future value in one year of $1, given an interest rate of five percent. We can confirm this by compounding our initial value by multiplying by 1.05.

What if we were to receive the dollar in five years; what would the present value be then?

$$P_o = \frac{\$1}{(1+.05)^5} = \frac{1}{1.2763} = 0.7835 = 0.78$$

If we were to invest 78.35 cents at 5% for five years it would grow to $1.00. We can see this by simply multiplying 78.35 by 1.05, five times. Try it.

Present values are used in various ways. For example, when undertaking a large development project, to validate the worthiness of the effort we might estimate our capital outlays as well as anticipated revenue over the life of the project. We could then bring all of these values back to today's dollar terms to decide if the project is worthwhile. Or, to compare one project with another.

In investments, analysts can use present values to aid in valuing a company's worth, based upon the company's anticipated earnings. A bond's price is partly derived from the present value of the future interest and principal cash flows.

The IRR can be derived from the present value formula by simply altering the meaning of our terms. We can show it as follows:

$$BMV = \frac{EMV}{(1+r)^t}$$

Here, our present value (P_0) is replaced by *BMV*, which stands for Beginning Market Value; our future value, F_1, is replaced by the ending market value (EMV); and our interest rate is replaced by *r*, which stands for the return or rate of return. We can shift the formula around a bit algebraically to solve for zero:

$$0 = BMV - \frac{EMV}{(1+r)^t}$$

This formula treats the ending market value as an outflow – that is, if we were to liquidate the portfolio. In the present value formula, we know the future cash flows and the interest rate, and solve for the present value. With the IRR, we know the beginning and ending market values and the cash flows; we are solving for the rate of return or *r*. Let's try a simple example.

We invest $1 million for one year. At the end of this period our portfolio is worth $1.1 million. What's our return? In this example we won't have any cash flows, so we're only dealing with the beginning and ending market values, and solving for *r*, our rate of return:

$$0 = 1 - \frac{1.1}{(1+r)}$$

Algebraically, we can change this formula to:

$$r = 1.1 - 1 = 0.1 = 10\%$$

Therefore, our return is found to be 10%, which probably isn't all that surprising. What if we continue to hold our investment for an additional year? During the second year we get a 40% return[8] and our investment grows to 1.54 million. What will our return then be?

$$0 = 1 - \frac{1.54}{(1+r)^2}$$

Again, employing some algebraic mastery we get:

$$(1+r)^2 = 1.54$$

We can take the square root of both sides,

$$\sqrt{(1+r)^2} = \sqrt{1.54}$$

$$1 + r = 1.241$$

which then yields our desired result:

$$r = 1.241 - 1 = 0.241 = 24.1\%$$

Thus, our return is 24.1 percent. Actually, this is the *annualized* return for the two-year period, not the *cumulative* return. Chapter 5 discusses these two terms in greater detail, but for now we'll just say that 24.1% is the return we would have gotten for each of the two years in order to obtain $1.54 million on our $1 million investment. To see this, simply multiply $1 by 1.241 two times.

Okay, that was simple, right? Well, when there are no cash flows IRRs are pretty easy to calculate, but when we introduce a flow or two (or more), we begin to see the challenge with the internal rate of return.

We have to expand our formula a bit to take into consideration cash flows:[9]

Internal Rate of Return

$$0 = BMV + \left(\sum_{j=1}^{n-1} \frac{F_j}{(1+r)^{t_j}} \right) - \frac{EMV}{(1+r)^{t_n}}$$

---

where F_j is the jth flow. There are $n-1$ flows because EMV is the last flow. We use t_n to represent the time at which we derive the ending market value.

Let's stay with our last example, but we'll make one slight change: at the start of the second year, after obtaining our initial 10% return (and having $1.1 million in our account), we add another $1 million, so we begin the second year with $2.1 million in our account. Again, we get a 40% return during this year, but since we started the year with the extra million dollars our portfolio is worth $2.94. What return does the IRR yield for the two-year period? If we substitute our beginning value (1 million), cash flow (1 million), and ending value (2.94 million) into the equation, we get:

$$0 = 1 + \frac{1}{1+r} - \frac{2.94}{(1+r)^2}$$

The following explains what these values represent:

In our earlier examples, where we were only dealing with the beginning and ending market value (i.e., no cash flow), isolating the r so we could solve for the return was fairly straightforward. But how do we isolate the r in this expression? We can't.[10]

We will solve for *r* using an iterative approach by trying various values for *r*, attempting to find by trial and error the value which will solve our formula. Table 2-1 shows how we found the solution, starting with 30.0% (0.3000) and going back and forth until we found the answer which came closest to zero (actually, close enough for us to feel comfortable with the solution), which is 28.61 percent.[11]

0.2800	-0.0132
0.2890	0.0063
0.2810	-0.0110
0.2850	-0.0023
0.2880	0.0042
0.2870	0.0020
0.2860	-0.0001
0.2865	0.0010
0.2862	0.0003
0.2861	0.0001

Table 2-1: Finding the solution to our second scenario

Now, let's compare these two scenarios (see Table 2-2). Even though the manager performed in an identical way during these two years for each of the scenarios (10% in year 1; 40% in year 2), we get a higher IRR or return for the second. Why? Because we had more money invested at the start of the second year. As the name suggests, the return is <u>money</u>-weighted. The return is dependent to a degree on the amount of money that's in the portfolio. Since there was more money invested when we got a 40% return, we get a higher IRR overall. With less money (as in scenario 1), we get a lower IRR.

Let's look at another example.[12] Table 2-3 shows five years of annual returns for a mutual fund.

What we're going to do is calculate the IRR, where a client invests $75,000 into the fund. What's key for our example is when the money is invested. Our

	Scenario 1	Scenario 2
Year 1	Began with $1 million	Began with $1 million
During Year 1	Earned 10%	Earned 10%
End of Year 1	Have $1.1 million	Have $1.1 million
Beginning of Year 2	$1.1 million	Cash flow of $1 million So $2.1 million
During Year 2	Earned 40%	Earned 40%
End of Year 2	$1.54 million	$2.94 million
IRR	24.10%	28.61%

Table 2-2: Comparing the Two Scenarios

	Annual Return
1996	-5.00%
1997	-15.20%
1998	3.10%
1999	30.75%
2000	17.65%

Table 2-3: Mutual Fund Annual Returns

client begins with an initial contribution of $5,000 at the start of the first year. He then makes additional deposits at the start of each subsequent year, increasing the contributions by $5,000 each time (i.e., year 2: $10,000, year 3: $15,000...).

Table 2-4 shows the investments, the beginning market values for the start of

	Annual Return	Cash Flows	BMV	EMV
1996	-5.00%	$5,000	$5,000.00	$4,750.00
1997	-15.20%	$10,000	$14,750.00	$12,508.00
1998	3.10%	$15,000	$27,508.00	$28,360.75
1999	30.75%	$20,000	$48,360.75	$63,231.68
2000	17.65%	$25,000	$88,231.66	$103,604.57

Table 2-4: Mutual Fund Annual Returns - Client # 1

each year, as well as the ending market values for each of these years.

Perhaps a brief explanation is in order. The cash flow column simply indicates the amount that is invested at the start of each of the years ($5,000 in 1996, $10,000 in 1997...). The BMV column shows the beginning market value at the start of each year, while EMV shows the market value at the end of each year. For the first year, the BMV is the starting cash flow ($5,000). But, for each succeeding year, we take the new cash flow (e.g., for 1997, $10,000) and add it to the ending market value (EMV) from the prior year (e.g., $4,750 from 1996).

Our total investment into the fund is $75,000 and we end up with $103,604.57, thus earning $28,604.57. Let's calculate the IRR.

We need to insert our beginning market value ($5,000), the cash flows for each of the other years, and the ending market value into our formula:

$$5,000 + \frac{10,000}{(1+r)} + \frac{15,000}{(1+r)^2} + \frac{20,000}{(1+r)^3} + \frac{25,000}{(1+r)^4} - \frac{103,804.57}{(1+r)^5} = 0$$

As with the second scenario of our earlier IRR example, we cannot isolate the r value, so we must solve the equation through iteration. Table 2-5 shows the steps we went through to find the answer. The idea behind this approach to find the solution is, through trial and error, to discover the return that yields the result closest to zero.

Trial	Result
14.00%	297.46
15.00%	-872.75
14.50%	-297.61
14.26%	-14.51
14.24%	9.29
14.25%	-2.61

Table 2-5: Finding the IRR for the Mutual Fund Client # 1

Our first attempt (14.00%) resulted in 297.46, so we need to find a return that yields a negative result so that we form a "boundary" around which the actual return lies. Our second attempt (15.00%) provided this for us (yielding a result of -872.75), so we know the answer lies between these numbers (14% and 15%). We find that 14.26% yields a negative result while 14.24 provides a positive. We stopped at 14.25%, since this seems to be as close as we can get to zero, unless we want to work with fractions of basis points, which isn't necessary.[13]

Now, let's look at a second client of this fund. Here, you'll see we again invest $75,000; we just change the order of our investments. We begin with $25,000 in the first year and work our way down during the subsequent years, reducing our cash flow each year by $5,000. Table 2-6 shows our values.

Since our ending market value is $103,893.77, we actually make a bit more money investing this way ($28,893.77 vs. $28,604.57), so we'd logically expect to see a higher return, yes? Let's calculate our IRR:

$$25,000 + \frac{20,000}{(1+r)} + \frac{15,000}{(1+r)^2} + \frac{10,000}{(1+r)^3} + \frac{5,000}{(1+r)^4} - \frac{103,893.77}{(1+r)^5} = 0$$

	Annual Return	Cash Flows	BMV	EMV
1996	-5.00%	$25,000	$25,000.00	$23,750.00
1997	-15.20%	$20,000	$43,750.00	$37,100.00
1998	3.10%	$15,000	$52,100.00	$53,715.10
1999	30.75%	$10,000	$63,715.10	$83,307.49
2000	17.65%	$5,000	$88,307.49	$103,893.77

Table 2-6: Mutual Fund Annual Returns - Client # 2

As we did before, through iteration (trial-and-error) we obtain our result (see Table 2-7). And this time, we find that our return is significantly lower: 9.12% vs. 14.25%, in spite of making more money this time. How can this be: earn more money but have a lower return?

Well, in addition to weighting the money, the IRR also takes into consideration the time the money was present (recall the IRR's relationship to the present value formula). That is, like the time value of money formula, it distinguishes between a dollar today and a dollar tomorrow, or, in our case, $25,000 being invested in year 1 versus $25,000 being invested in year 5. In this second situation, we began with a lot more money – thus, its weight counts for a lot more in our ending value. Our first client began with just $5,000 and managed to end up at almost the same amount at the end. This client's $25,000 contribution occurred at the start of the fifth year, whereas, with the second client the $25,000 was there right from the start.

Trial	Result
9.00%	-286.04
10.00%	1996.87
9.50%	873.22
9.25%	298.12
9.10%	-51.28
9.11%	-27.89
9.14%	42.21
9.13%	18.86
9.12%	4.50

Table 2-7: Finding the IRR for Mutual Fund Client # 2

Perhaps this will be clearer if we measure the value of all the contributions for both clients at the start of year 1, using an interest rate of 10 percent (see Table 2-8). In both scenarios we get a cash flow of $25,000 (at the start of year one for the first client, and at the beginning of year five for the second). From a present value basis, this $25,000 is only valued at $17,075 for the first case, but a full $25,000 in the second. Summing our present values the difference is quite clear, as we were able to achieve essentially the same gain in the first scenario with only $58,589, versus $66,507 for the second case. The IRR captures both the timing and size of the cash flow in its calculation.

	Year 1	Year 2	Year 3	Year 4	Year 5	Total
Client #1:						
Flow	$5,000	$10,000	$15,000	$20,000	$25,000	$75,000
PV	$5,000	$9,091	$12,397	$15,026	$17,075	$58,589
Client #2:						
Flow	$25,000	$20,000	$15,000	$10,000	$5,000	$75,000
PV	$25,000	$18,182	$12,397	$7,513	$3,415	$66,507

Table 2-8: Present Value Comparisons of Annual Cash Flows at 10% Interest Rate

These distinctions are what causes the IRR to generate different values, depending on the timing of the cash flows. The ending return is very much dependent on the amount of money that's present at any given point in time.

Alternative approaches to solve the IRR

The IRR is, as we noted above, an equation that usually doesn't have a direct solution; thus, we must engage in an iterative process to solve it. Over the years a variety of approaches have been suggested. We will briefly describe what we believe are the three most commonly used approaches to solve the IRR.

Bisection

The bisection method (also referred to as binary chopping and interval halving, or what I have also referred to as "bracketing"[14]) involves establishing a range such that we have two values that "bound" the zero line. We then begin to bisect the possible solutions until we're close enough to identify the solution within a basis point or less. Figure 2-1 provides a visual representation of the process.

For this example, let's use Client #2 from earlier, where the client makes a series of contributions into a mutual fund over a five year period, beginning with $25,000. Table 2-7 provided the results of our process. We'll repeat it but using a slightly different series of guesses for the solution. Recall that the equation we wish to solve is as follows:

$$25,000 + \frac{20,000}{1+r} + \frac{15,000}{(1+r)^2} + \frac{10,000}{(1+r)^3} + \frac{5,000}{(1+r)^4} - \frac{-103,893.77}{(1+r)^5} = 0$$

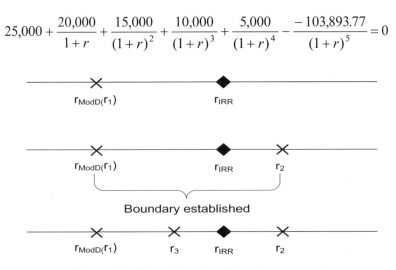

Figure 2-1: Visualizing the Bisection Approach

We begin by solving for the Modified Dietz. We will treat the first cash flow ($25,000) as our beginning market value. We therefore require weights for our subsequent cash flows. Since each flow occurs at the start of a year and we're dealing with a five year period, it isn't hard to figure them out (see Table 2-9 for the answers).

We can now calculate our return:

$$R_{ModDietz} = \frac{EMV - BMV - \sum_{i=1}^{n} c_i}{BMV + \sum_{i=1}^{n} w_i c_i} =$$

$$\frac{103,893.77 - 25,000 - (20,000 + 15,000 + 10,000 + 5,000)}{25,000 + (.8 \times 20,000 + .6 \times 15,000 + .4 \times 10,000 + .2 \times 5,000)} = 152.5341\%$$

This return (152.5341%) is <u>not</u> our starting point because it's the return for a five-year period. The IRR yields an annualized result so we need to convert the Modified Dietz result to its annualized equivalent, which is 8.8112%, or simply 8.81 percent. This will be our starting point to solve the IRR. When we substitute this number into our IRR equation we get a result of -733.40. We now need to find a return estimate which yields a result that's greater than zero, to "bound" the zero line. But should our next guess be above or below the Modified Dietz figure? We don't know, so we simply take a guess and if we're wrong, we will go in the other direction. How far above or below the Modified Dietz should we go? This, too, is a guess as there's no prescribed way to know. If our answer is taking us in the right direction (in this case, for example, higher than the result from Modified Dietz but still below zero), we keep moving in that direction.

Cash Flow	Timing	Weight
$20,000	Start of year 2	80%
$15,000	Start of year 3	60%
$10,000	Start of year 4	40%
$5,000	Start of year 5	20%

Table 2-9: Weights for Cash Flows

Table 2-10 shows the approach I took. As you can see, after I tried the Modified Dietz return I decided to add roughly 50 basis points and try 9.30%; for-

	Our Estimate	Result
Modified Dietz	8.8112%	(733.40)
	9.30%	413.86
	9.05%	(168.48)
	9.10%	(51.28)
	9.20%	182.01
	9.15%	65.55
	9.13%	18.86
	9.11%	(27.89)
	9.12%	**(4.50)**

Table 2-10: Solving for the IRR

tunately this yielded a positive result, so I knew I had established a boundary around the zero line. I now bisected the boundary (or essentially split the difference) and tried 9.05%, which resulted in a negative result, indicating that the boundary was now a bit tighter. I continued until it was within one basis point, resulting in the 9.12% solution.

As noted above, if I'm concerned that the line isn't linear and that perhaps the right answer might be 9.13%, I can take the analysis down to a tenth of a basis point, as I show in Table 2-11.

Our Estimate	Result
9.12%	(4.50)
9.13%	18.86
9.125%	7.18
9.124%	4.84
9.123%	2.51
9.122%	**0.17**
9.121%	(2.17)

Table 2-11: Continuing the Search

We can plot our equation as I've done in Figure 2-2. It appears that the equa-

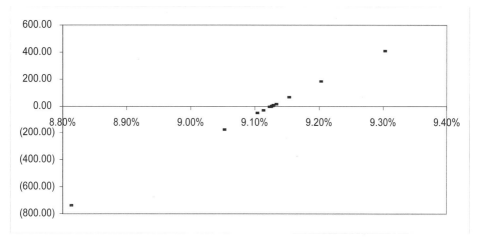

Figure 2-2: Graphing the IRR Equation

tion may be linear; this is easily confirmed by drawing a line between our end points, as shown in Figure 2-3.

The bisection method is rather simple to comprehend and not difficult to carry out, either manually or through programming. While it tends to be slower than some of the other methods, we are assured of finding the solution.

Newton-Raphson Method[15]

The Newton-Raphson (NR) method may be the most widely used approach to find roots. Essentially it involves finding the tangent at the initial guess in order to

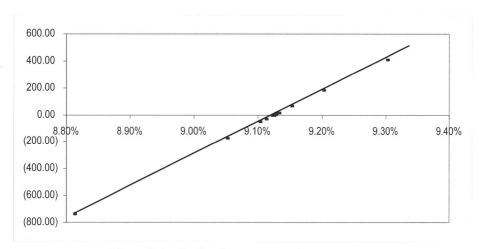

Figure 2-3: Confirming the Equation's Linearity

identify the subsequent guess, which is usually an improved estimate of the actual result. The tangent is the slope at the point of the curve, which is identified as the first derivative. The point where the slope intersects the x-axis yields our next estimate. Thus one might suggest that we're using calculus in order to derive the solution. The formula for the NR approach is:

$$r_{i+1} = r_i - \frac{f(r_i)}{f'(r_i)}$$

where:

    r_i = the most recent estimate for the return

    r_{i+1} = the next estimate which we are determining

    $f(r_i)$ is the IRR function

    $f'(r_i)$ is the derivative if the IRR function.

As Chapra & Canale (2005) pointed out, the NR approach is often very efficient but on occasion performs poorly. If, for example, the first prediction is a poor one, an excessive amount of attempts may be employed to converge on the solution. The ability to converge on the true return depends on the formula and the accuracy of the initial guess. The initial guess should be "sufficiently" close to the solution but even this isn't a guarantee the process will work. As a result, there are occasions when no answer will be found although one exists.[16]

The Secant Method[17]

One of the problems with the NR approach is finding the derivative, which isn't always easy. An alternative is the secant method. The approach requires two initial guesses. For the IRR we'd begin with the Modified Dietz; we then take a second guess, either slightly above or below this number. A line is then drawn between these two points; where it intersects the x-axis is where we'd find our next estimate. The formula for the secant method is:

$$r_{i+1} = r_i - \frac{f(r_i)(r_{i-1} - r_i)}{f(r_{i-1}) - f(r_i)}$$

The next estimate (r_{i+1}) is obtained from the prior two guesses (r_i and r_{i-1}).

As with the NR approach, the secant method is quite efficient but may encounter occasions where no solution is found.

Challenges with IRR

Obviously one of the challenges with the IRR is the fact that when we have multiple cash flows iteration is required. If there's a single flow or no flow, then we should be able to isolate the "r" and solve directly. But once we introduce multiple flows, it's mathematically impossible to do this, necessitating iteration.

In a recent article Bacon (2007) stated that the IRR is "notoriously difficult to calculate." While one might question whether or not he's employing a bit of hyperbole, nevertheless, through the years various individuals have attempted to come up with ways to solve the IRR in as efficient a manner as possible.[18] We've identified three methods above, all of which are in common use today.

The IRR offers a few other challenges. First, we may have the possibility of multiple solutions. If there are many flows, especially where we have inflows and outflows mixed throughout the period, we can have a polynomial equation for which multiple roots exist (i.e., where the curve crosses our zero-axis multiple times). One might therefore argue that all of the results are acceptable. While it's true that we can have multiple solutions (roots) that satisfy the equation, can we have multiple returns? This seems to be far from acceptable when reporting returns to a client. In addition, some of the results may actually be imaginary numbers which clearly wouldn't qualify.

To date there are no "rules" as to how to deal with this situation.[19] In fact, there is no way to necessarily know that there are, indeed, multiple solutions, although various articles have come down on both sides of this matter! Mao (1969), for example, suggests that "the existence of multiple IRR's [sic] is *prima facie* evidence that the investment is mixed."[21]

We sometimes hear about "Descartes' Rule of Signs" as a way to determine if multiple roots exist, but it appears that there is no guarantee.

When multiple solutions exist, which to choose? Again, there are no rules or guidance today, although one might consider the following:

- if there are two solutions, and one is positive and one negative, simply determine if a gain or loss was realized. If there's a gain for the period, then the positive solution would seem to be the correct result; if there's a loss, then the negative wins.

- calculate the return using Modified Dietz and choose the answer from the IRR that comes closest to what the Modified Dietz produces.

When to know you have the answer can also be a bit of a challenge. As we're going through our iteration, when do we stop? Must we continue until we have completely solved the equation (i.e., found a return that yields a result of zero)? I believe not. I think we can adopt a policy that we either (a) stop when we've narrowed the search between results that bound the zero axis (i.e., one result above zero and the other below) within one basis point such that we can determine which is closer (e.g., 9.11% results in -27.89; 9.12% results in 4.50; we'd choose 9.12%) or (b) stop when we've narrowed the search between results that bound the zero axis within one-tenth of a basis point (e.g., 9.122% yields a solution of 0.17; 9.121% yields -2.17[22]). The rule a firm establishes to "know when to stop" can also be referred to as its "termination criterion."[23]

The flip side of multiple solutions is "no solution." That is, the approach might not find a solution even though one exists. As noted above, some methods are more sensitive to this possibility than others.

The IRR cannot find a solution equal to or below -100 percent. There are occasions when one can actually lose more than 100% of their investment (*e.g.*, in a margin account when securities were shorted).

Control of cash flows and the BAI standards

Let's return to our earlier example. Who decided to add the million dollars at the start of year 2? Probably the client. And, because of the action of the client, we earned more money. Not bad, right? Well, what if instead of adding money the client took money away at this point; what would we have earned? Less, right? Assuming our manager performed at the same 40% rate for year 2, his return would have been lower. Is that fair? Most people would say "no." It was the client's decision, not the manager's.

For the mutual fund examples, each of our clients invested the same amount of money; they just varied the timing of their contributions and as a result had very different returns. Should the manager be penalized or rewarded based upon the client's timing of flows? Again, most people would say "no." That's what Dietz said.

In 1968, the Bank Administration Institute in the United States published the first standards for calculating returns (BAI (1968)). A major point they raised was that money-weighted (they called it "dollar-weighted") is inappropriate for measuring the performance of the investment manager, since she doesn't control the cash flows. And, recognizing how the timing and magnitude of flows can have a direct impact on the resulting return, the BAI advocated using time-weighted rates of return. We will take up time-weighting methods beginning in the next chapter. The key point to mention at this time is that time-weighting eliminates or reduces the effect of cash flows, while money-weighting doesn't.

The BAI standards were followed shortly thereafter by two other sets of standards: the Investment Council Association of America (ICAA (1971)) and the U.K. Society of Investment Analysts (Society of Investment Analysts (1972)) published standards based on what the BAI had done.

It's worth noting that the BAI standards were partly based on the work of Peter O. Dietz, who published his doctoral thesis in 1966 (Dietz (1966)). In it, Dietz lamented the then-common practice to evaluate the performance of pension fund managers. What Dietz found was a total absence of consistency, the occasional failure to revalue portfolios (marked-to-market), and the use of the IRR. This groundbreaking work served the industry well and has resulted in some of us thinking of Dietz as the "father of investment performance measurement."

It was common in the 1970s and 1980s for firms to say that their performance was "BAI" or "ICAA" compliant, which essentially meant they calculated time-weighted rates of return.

Is there any benefit to the IRR?

It appears that once the BAI, ICAA, and (U.K.) Society of Investment Analysts' standards were published, little was done with the IRR because it is universally agreed that it is an inappropriate way to calculate returns for investment managers. In financial literature there's little written about it other than to point out its shortcomings.

So, since we can see that the IRR can yield inconsistent results, depending on the timing of flows, does it have any use? Well, actually, yes. But to discuss this we need to first tackle the subject of time-weighted returns, which we do in the next couple chapters. We will contrast money- and time-weighted returns in Chapter 6.

Summary

In this chapter we discussed money-weighting and the use of the internal rate of return. We showed how the IRR can yield different results, depending on the size and timing of cash flows and the amounts in the portfolio, thus the use of the terms money-weighting and dollar-weighting. We explained that because the client usually controls cash flows, the IRR is generally recognized as an inappropriate way to judge a manager's performance.

Exercise

A portfolio begins with $1.00 million. At the end of the first year, it has grown by 10% and ends the year at $1.10 million. The client decides to withdraw $600,000, so the portfolio begins the second year at $500,000. During the second year, the portfolio's value increases to $700,000, or by 40 percent. Calculate the IRR.

ENDNOTES

[1] Ineichen (2003).

[2] We'll use the more generic money-weighting, since not all currencies are dollar-based.

[3] Dietz (2004).

[4] IPC (2003,1).

[5] Mao (1969).

[6] Copeland, *et al.* (2005)

[7] Of course this assumes that we can invest this money and get interest on our investment; this wouldn't necessarily be the case during a period of disinflation.

[8] To see this, simply multiply 1.10 by 1.40; you'll get 1.54.

[9] While there are more complex ways to show the IRR, some using integral calculus

(see, for example, Kelly & Tippett (1989)), the approach shown here is more common.

[10] While with some work it is actually possible to solve this particular problem, the reality is that as we add cash additional flows we will reach a point when finding an algebraic solution isn't possible. If you wish to investigate this further we suggest you investigate the Abel-Ruffini theorem, which can be found on the Internet.

[11] This approach is referred to as "bisection." We discuss a few alternative methodologies later in this chapter.

[12] This example is taken from a short article that Mark Kritzman wrote for the *Financial Analysts Journal* (Kritzman (1993)).

[13] Technically, one could argue that we're assuming that the formula is linear when in reality it may not be, so taking our trial to yet another level might be worthwhile, but we'll stop here.

[14] When I was a Field Artillery officer in the 1970s I learned this approach as a way to hit a target. The Forward Observer plots the target using a map and communicates its coordinates to the Fire Direction Center, which provides instructions to the Battery (essentially direction and elevation). When the first round is seen, the observer then makes adjustments (add/drop, right/left) in such a way that subsequent rounds "bracket" the target, so that fairly quickly the target is hit. Little did I realize that this approach would serve me later in life.

[15] Much of this material was Chapra & Canale (2005).

[16] See Chapra & Canale (2005) for further discussion.

[17] Here, too, I used Chapra & Canale (2005) as a principle resource.

[18] See, for example, Fisher (1966) and Kaplan (1967).

[19] I am chairing a group (IRR Working Group) that is attempting to establish such guidance.

[20] See, for example, Mao (1969), Chapra & Canale (2005), Jean (1968), Hazen (2003), Longbottom & Wiper (1978), Greynolds, et al. (1980), and Zhang (2005).

[21] Mao (1969).

[22] The reason we'd resort to fractions of a basis point is because the curve might not be linear; in reality, we could simply calculate the result at the midpoint between the two results that are a basis point apart and that bound the zero line in order to confirm which is correct.

[23] See, for example, Chapra & Canale (2005).

Chapter 3 –
Calculating Approximate Time-weighted Returns

In the last chapter we discussed how money-weighted returns are generally inappropriate to evaluate the success of an investment manager because of the effect cash flows have on them. In this chapter we discuss what time-weighting is and a few ways to derive approximations to the true or exact time-weighted rate of return (TWRR).

The expression "time-weighting" comes from the BAI standards (BAI (1968)). The term "time-weighting" came from a return method which weighted the time to derive the return. To our knowledge, this is not an approach which is in use today. Nevertheless, the term "time-weighting" has remained. As you'll see, we actually weight the cash flow (money-weight?) in our approximation methods. But this weighting is over a time period (time-weight?). So there is bound to be confusion.

The key distinction between time- and money-weighting is that time-weighting eliminates or reduces the effect of cash flows, while money-weighting is strongly affected by them.

Another way to view the difference:

Money-weighting measures the performance of the portfolio
while
time-weighting measures the performance of the portfolio manager.

If you're like me, the first time you hear these statements you'll be confused. It's kind of hard to see the difference. It sounds like we're essentially saying the same thing, right? Well, we will hopefully make the differences clearer before we're done.

Let's start by looking at a basic formula to calculate performance:

$$ROR = \frac{EMV - BMV}{BMV}$$

where
ROR = Rate of Return
EMV = Ending Market Value

BMV = Beginning Market Value

You may already be familiar with this formula. It's quite intuitive and easy to understand.

When we calculate the numerator (EMV ! BMV), what are we producing? We are calculating the amount that was earned (or lost) during the period: our profit or loss. So if we started with $100 and ended with $150, we earned $150 minus $100, or $50, right? And we place this amount over the amount we began with to derive our return:

$$ROR = \frac{\$150 - \$100}{\$100} = \frac{\$50}{\$100} = 0.50 = 50\%$$

We typically show the return as a percentage, often to two decimal places (or, to the basis point, where a basis point is 1/100th of a percentage point [i.e., 100 basis points = 1 percentage point]).[1]

Let's try another example: we begin with $200 which grows to $250. We therefore earn $250 minus $200, or again $50. And the return is:

$$ROR = \frac{\$250 - \$200}{\$200} = \frac{\$50}{\$200} = 0.25 = 25\%$$

Note that even though we earned the same amount in this example as we did in the first, our return is lower. Why? Because of the *base* upon which we measure our performance. The *base* is our beginning market value. This is a critical component of our return analysis. Let's discuss this a bit further.

Two friends go to a casino and spend a few hours gambling. While they were there they played at different tables. At an agreed-upon time our two gamblers meet for their trip home. One turns to the other and asks "How did you do tonight?" The response: "I won $50!" And the second friend responds: "Wow, so did I! I guess we both had a good night."[2]

They both won $50, so on the surface it may appear that they did equally well. But did they? If we had gone around the casino that night, we would have found one of the friends playing at a table with a minium bet of $10, where his bets were typically between $10 and $20. The second was playing at a table with a minimum of $100, where his bets ranged from $100 to $200. In other words, the second gambler was making much bigger bets than the first. So was their performance the same? Hardly. I would suggest that the friend who spent the night making relatively small bets did much better than the other. Make sense?

What if we started with $200 but lost $50? What happens with our equation then? Let's see:

$$ROR = \frac{\$150 - \$200}{\$200} = \frac{-\$50}{\$200} = -0.25 = -25\%$$

As we see, the formula shows that we lost 25% of our money, which is what it should report. Another way to calculate performance is simply:

$$ROR = \frac{EMV}{BMV} - 1$$

This formula is derived algebraically from our earlier one:

$$ROR = \frac{EMV - BMV}{BMV} = \frac{EMV}{BMV} - \frac{BMV}{BMV} = \frac{EMV}{BMV} - 1$$

Let's try it with our first example, where we began with $100 and ended with $150:

$$ROR = \frac{150}{100} - 1 = 1.50 - 1 = 0.50 = 50\%$$

We see that we get the same result. So either formula works in an equivalent fashion.

Both of these formulas are quite simple to use and accurately yield our rate of return, providing one thing: there are no cash flows. If there are cash flows, these equations won't work because they don't account for cash flows. In spite of this, we'll see these formulas reappear shortly.

What are cash flows?

At the portfolio or fund level, cash flows are contributions or withdrawals of cash and/or securities into (or out of) a portfolio. At the sub-portfolio level, they are purchases, sales, and income (see Figure 3-1 for a graphical representation; we discuss sub-portfolio returns in Chapter 6). To distinguish between these two types of cash flows we can refer to those at the portfolio level as "external cash flows," since the monies come in from outside (or leave) the portfolio. Sub-portfolio cash flows can be referred to as "internal cash flows" because they're generated internally, within the portfolio. For brevity, we will generally simply say "cash flow," except when we're specifically addressing the sub-portfolio case.

Figure 3-1: Cash flows A common question is "what about income?" In other

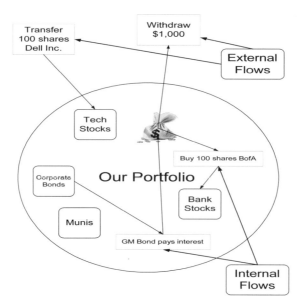

Figure 3-1: Cash Flows

words, what about dividends and interest that the portfolio may have received? They are not considered cash flows; they are simply included with the market values. And the general rule is that we should *accrue* for income; at a minimum, accrue for interest on bonds and ideally accrue for dividends on stocks. This shows a more accurate picture of your portfolio's market values.[3]

Well, what if the income is withdrawn, as is frequently the case with mutual funds? Then it's treated as an outflow. Ideally, you would still accrue it up until the point that it's realized as cash.

Calculating returns with cash flows; the Original Dietz

Peter O. Dietz developed a method early on which yields an approximate TWRR. It has been called both the "midpoint method" and the "Original Dietz" method (Dietz called the result an "average return"). It assumes that cash flows occur at the midpoint or middle of the period over which we're measuring the return. So, if we're calculating performance for the month of June, we'd assume that the flow occurred on the 15th.

The formula will look somewhat familiar to you:[4]

$$ROR = \frac{EMV - BMV - C}{BMV + 0.5 \times C}$$

where

   EMV = Ending Market Value
   BMV = Beginning Market Value
   C = Cash Flows

This is essentially the formula we showed at the start of this chapter, with the exception of the "-C" in the numerator and the "+0.5 x C" in the denominator. These additional terms are used to handle the cash flows.

Our earlier formula

$$ROR = \frac{EMV - BMV - C}{BMV + 0.5 \times C} \qquad ROR = \frac{EMV - BMV - C}{BMV + 0.5 \times C}$$

Handling cash flows

Let's start with the numerator. What we're doing here is arriving at the same thing we got the first time we used the formula (without the "-C"): the amount we earned. An example will probably help. We begin with $100, end with $120, and had a $14 contribution during the period. So the numerator is:

$$EMV - BMV - C = 120 - 100 - 14 = 6$$

We earned $6 during the period.

Now, let's look at the denominator. Again, this is the *base* upon which we will measure performance. It's simply:

$$100 + 0.5 \times 14 = 100 + 7 = 107$$

The 0.5 in the denominator means that we're assuming that the cash flow occurred at the midpoint of the period. Therefore, we're using the starting value plus half of the cash flow as our base. We're saying that the manager had use of this cash flow for half of the period. Putting the numerator and denominator together, we can calculate our return:

$$ROR = \frac{120 - 100 - 14}{100 + 0.5 \times 14} = \frac{6}{107} = 0.056075 = 5.61\%$$

We show that we earned $6 during the period and that we're using half of the cash flow ($7) as part of our base over which this gain is measured, resulting in a return of 5.61 percent.

Let's try another example: we begin with $200, end with $220, and have a $10 contribution:

$$ROR = \frac{220 - 200 - 10}{200 - (0.5 \times 10)} = \frac{10}{205} = 0.04878 = 4.88\%$$

Let's try a case where we have a *large* cash flow, where *large* is often defined as 10% of the market value. Here, we begin with $100 and have a cash flow of $50. Our ending market value is $170. What's our return?

$$ROR = \frac{170 - 100 - 50}{100 + 0.5 \times 50} = \frac{20}{125} = 16\%$$

We will return to the topic of large cash flows shortly.

There is an alternative way to express the Original Dietz:

$$ROR = \frac{EMV - 0.5 \times C}{BMV + 0.5 \times C} - 1$$

This formula is similar to a formula we introduced at the start of this chapter:

$$ROR = \frac{EMV}{BMV} - 1$$

If we try the case where we start with $100, end with $120, and have a $14 cash flow:

$$ROR = \frac{120 - 0.5 \times 14}{100 + 0.5 \times 14} - 1 = \frac{113}{107} - 1 = 5.61\%$$

As you see, we get the same result as with the earlier version of this formula; while it may not be obvious, these are equivalent representations of the formula. I have become used to using the earlier version we discussed since I think it better represents what's really happening – I think it's more intuitive.

For many years the Original Dietz was a favorite of money management firms: it was simple to implement, easy to understand, and produced a fairly accurate picture of the manager's performance. While the GIPS standards don't necessarily apply to the entire performance measurement universe, they disallowed the use of the Original Dietz method for periods after January 1, 2005.[5]

Improving the accuracy of our results

We are always striving to improve the accuracy of our results. I attended a workshop in the late 1980s sponsored by the ICAA where the subject of improving accuracy was discussed.[6] We realized that with every step toward improvement there is a corresponding cost associated with our effort. We need to determine whether or not the incremental improvement in accuracy is worth the increased cost. For some, the difference in accuracy is so slight that it isn't justified; for others, it may be mandatory.

One way to improve accuracy is to shorten the time periods over which we measure our performance. For example, several years ago some firms only valued their portfolio annually; can you imagine this? So, if we used the Original Dietz, we would assume that all of our flows occurred around July 1 – the middle of the year. If the flows occurred toward the extremes (January/February or November/December), you can imagine how this *assumption* began to fall apart. So, if we shorten the measurement period, our accuracy will improve. And this is what firms did, initially to a quarter and then to a month. Today, we're seeing many firms shorten their measurement period to a day, which means the exact methodology, which we address in the next chapter. The cost is increased fees for pricing and a more complex system.

Another challenge is the presence of large cash flows, which is often thought of as 10% or more of the market value.[7] Studies have been done to demonstrate how large flows can cause huge distortions in the return.[8] To deal with this situation we can *day-weight* our flows, which means instead of assuming that the flow occurs at the middle of the period, we weight it based upon when it actually occurs. We will now discuss a couple ways to accomplish this.

The Modified BAI

We tell people that if the word "modified" is modifying a formula name (please excuse the pun), then it's probably something from the CFA Institute (formerly AIMR), as this has been the only source we've seen for its use.[9] The term generally means that the cash flows have been *day-weighted*.

Day-weighting means that we *weight* the cash flow's participation in the denominator by the number of days the flow is present in the portfolio. The general formula for the weighting is quite simple:

$$W_i = \frac{CD - D_i}{CD}$$

where
    W = weight
    CD = number of Calendar Days in the period
    D − day of the flow

i = the number of the flow

The subscript *i* is used to allow us to reflect the presence of more than one flow in the period. Let's try a simple example: what if our flow occurs on the 3rd of June; what will our weighting factor be?

$$W = \frac{30 - 3}{30} = \frac{27}{30} = 0.90$$

Since June has 30 days in it, our CD equals 30. Our result, 0.90, is the equivalent of saying that our cash flow was present in the portfolio for 90% of the month.

What if the flow occurs on the 27th of December? Our weighting factor would be:

$$W = \frac{31 - 27}{31} = \frac{4}{31} = 0.129$$

Since December has 31 days, our CD becomes 31, and we see that our money was only present for about 13% of the month.

The BAI suggested three formulas, with the ideal one being the "exact" method. The second was called the "linked IRR," which is the same as the Modified BAI formula. The third used a time-weighting technique to link returns, which has essentially been abandoned by the industry.

The Modified BAI is considered a reasonable approximation, as long as the flows and/or market volatility aren't excessively large. It bears a striking resemblance to our IRR because it *is* the IRR:

$$EMV = \sum_{i=1}^{n} F_i (1 + R)^{W_i}$$

where

    EMV = the ending market value
    F = the amount of the cash flow
    R = the return
    W = our weighting factor
    i = the number of flows
    n = the total number of flows in the period

Like the IRR, this formula is solved using iteration. The difference is that this formula requires that the portfolio be revalued on a regular basis, at least quarterly and ideally monthly. As with Modified Dietz (which we discuss below), linking these IRRs results in the approximation to the exact time-weighted return.

Let's measure the performance for the month of June, where our beginning market value is $100 and our ending market value is $120; our portfolio has a single cash flow of $14 which occurs on the 3rd of the month. As we just saw, our weighting factor for this flow is 0.90. Like the IRR, this formula requires iterative processing to solve. Our formula for this problem is as follows:

$$120 = \left(100 \times (1+R)\right) + \left(14 \times (1+R)^{0.90}\right)$$

As we did for the IRR, we can shift the EMV (120) to the right, so that we'll be solving for zero:

$$0 = \left(100 \times (1+R)\right) + \left(14 \times (1+R)^{0.90}\right) - 120$$

A brief explanation may be in order. There are two flows that we're considering:

- the initial value ($100), which is in the portfolio at the start of the month, and is present for the full month, thus; the factor (1+R) being raised to the power of 1
- the cash flow ($14), which came in on the 3rd

As you can see from Table 3-1, our solution is 5.33 percent.

Guess	Result
.01000	5.2539
0.0500	-0.3715
0.0600	0.7538
0.0550	0.1911
0.0530	-0.0339
0.0535	0.0223
0.0533	-0.0002
0.0532	-0.0114
0.0534	0.0111

Table 3-1: Solving the Modified Dietz Problem

Modified Dietz

We don't believe Peter Dietz ever referred to this formula as being *modified*; he simply called it *day weighting*.[10] Again, we credit the CFA Institute for this qualifier.

The formula looks almost the same as the Original Dietz:

$$ROR = \frac{EMV - BMV - C}{BMV + W \times C}$$

Here we have substituted our weighting factor, W, for the 0.5 we had earlier with the Original Dietz; this is the only difference. As we said earlier, the Original Dietz assumed that the flows were present for half of the month, thus the 0.5; here we're day-weighting the flow so we use the percent that the flow was actually in the portfolio.

Let's calculate the return for the example we just did using the Modified BAI, where we're calculating the return for June, with a flow of $14 on the 3rd, and our BMV is $100, EMV is $120:

$$ROR = \frac{120 - 100 - 14}{100 + 0.90 \times 14} = \frac{6}{112.6} = 0.05329 = 5.33\%$$

As you can see, we get the same result as we did with the Modified BAI.

When we calculated the return for this situation earlier using the Original Dietz, our return was 5.61%; it's been lowered by almost 30 basis points. Why? We have increased the denominator with a larger portion of the cash flow (the money was available longer); with the Original Dietz we used only half of the flow; with the Modified Dietz we recognize the full time the flow was present and thus we're saying to the manager "We know you earned $6, but it appears that a larger portion of the flow probably contributed to this gain, so to assume half of the flow would be incorrect."

What if the flow had occurred on the 27th of the month? Our weighting factor is:

$$W = \frac{30 - 27}{30} = \frac{3}{30} = 0.10$$

Here we see that the money was only present for 10% of the time. So let's calculate our Modified Dietz using this weight:

$$ROR = \frac{120 - 100 - 14}{100 + 0.10 \times 14} = \frac{6}{101.4} = 0.059172 = 5.92\%$$

Our return, 5.92%, is much higher than we previously calculated. Why? Because we only had use of the cash flow for a very short period – we're only using 10% of it or $1.40 in our denominator, so most of the $6 gain is attributable to the beginning market value of $100.

We said that large cash flows could impact the accuracy of our return. Previously, we discussed the case where we begin with $100 and have a cash flow of $50. Our ending market value is $170. Using the Original Dietz we calculated a return of 16 percent. What if the flow occurs on June 5? What's our return? We begin by calculating our weighting factor:

$$W = \frac{30 - 5}{30} = \frac{25}{30} = 0.8333$$

Now we can use the Modified Dietz formula to derive our return:

$$ROR = \frac{170 - 100 - 50}{100 + 0.8333 \times 50} = \frac{20}{141.665} = 0.1412 = 14.12\%$$

This is a rather significant difference, isn't it? The large flow, coupled with its timing (fairly early in the month) results in an almost 200 basis point decrease in return. Clearly, our Original Dietz failed to provide us with much accuracy in this case.

An alternative weighting factor

The way we've been calculating our weighting factor so far assumes that the flow occurred at the *end* of the day. For example, when the flow occurs on the 27th of a 30-day month, our numerator is 30-27 or 3, which refers to the 28th, 29th, and 30th.

What if the flow occurred at the *start* of the day? We need to add one to the numerator, and our formula becomes:

$$W_i = \frac{CD - D_i + 1}{CD}$$

Looking at the example with the flow on the 27th of June, we get:

$$W = \frac{30 - 27 + 1}{30} = \frac{4}{30} = 0.13333$$

Our weight has gone from 10% to

Weighting Factors
Start of Day: $$W_i = \frac{CD - D_i + 1}{CD}$$
End of Day: $$W_i = \frac{CD - D_i}{CD}$$

13.33% to reflect this additional day.

The Generalized Modified Dietz

What if we have more than one cash flow in a period? We need to represent our Modified Dietz formula in a broader way to better handle these situations, what we refer to as the "Generalized Modified Dietz" formula:

$$ROR = \frac{EMV - BMV - \sum_{i=0}^{n} C_i}{BMV + \sum_{i=0}^{n} \left(W_i \cdot C_i \right)}$$

Here we introduce a Riemann summation in the numerator (the capital Greek letter Sigma, or Σ) to sum up our cash flows, and a similar summation in the denominator to add up our weighted cash flows.

Here's an example: our portfolio begins the month of July with $1,000. On the 5th, an inflow of $100 occurs; on the 12th, another inflow of $50 takes place. And then, on the 28th, an outflow of $75 occurs. Our portfolio's ending market value is $1,100. What's our return?

Let's begin by calculating our three weighting factors. First, for the flow that occurs on the 5th:

$$W_1 = \frac{31-5}{31} = \frac{26}{31} = 0.8387$$

Next, the flow on the 12th:

$$W_2 = \frac{31-12}{31} = \frac{19}{31} = 0.6129$$

And finally, our flow on the 28th:

$$W_3 = \frac{31-28}{31} = \frac{3}{31} = 0.0968$$

Now let's enter our data into our formula; first the specific values we're dealing with:

BMV = $1,000

EMV = $1,100

F₁ = $100

F₂ = $50

F₃ = !$75

> **Generalized Modified Dietz**
>
> $$ROR = \frac{EMV - BMV - \sum_{i=0}^{n} C_i}{BMV + \sum_{i=0}^{n} \left(W_i \cdot C_i \right)}$$

$W_1 = 0.8387$

$W_2 = 0.6129$

$W_3 = 0.0968.$

And now, the formula:

$$ROR = \frac{1,100 - 1,000 - (100 + 50 + (-75))}{1,000 + (0.8387 \times 100 + 0.6129 \times 50 + 0.0968 \times (-75))} =$$

$$\frac{25}{1107.255} = 0.2258 = 2.26\%$$

The formula acts the same as the simple case with a single flow, with the exception that we're summing up the cash flows in the numerator and the weighted flows in the denominator. Since it's common to have multiple cash flows in a period, this is a handy formula to use to get a good approximation of the true return.

How accurate is the approximation?

In this chapter, we discussed three ways to calculate an approximate time-weighted rate of return: Original or midpoint Dietz, Modified BAI, and Modified Dietz. All are affected by cash flows to some extent, with the Modified BAI and Modified Dietz doing a better job of addressing them.

As cash flows become large, we begin to see these formulas' accuracy diminish. We therefore recommend that you consider *revaluing* the portfolio when large flows occur. Most people consider "large" to mean cash flows greater than 10% of the market value.

We will address ways to gain even greater precision in our next chapter.

The Modified Dietz and money-weighting

Some have suggested that the Modified Dietz is actually a *money-weighted* rate of return, not a *time-weighted* return, and that time-weighting is achieved by linking (which we'll take up in the next chapter).

Summary

In this chapter we introduced the concept of approximate measures of rates of return. We also discussed what cash flows are and how they can be dealt with in our formulas. We addressed three rather popular ways to derive performance: Original Dietz, Modified BAI, and Modified Dietz.

Exercises

1. We begin the period with $100 and end with $80. What's our return?

2. We begin the period with $100, end with $80, but had a -$25 cash flow on the 5th of the month (31-day month). Calculate the return using both the Original Dietz, Modified BAI, and Modified Dietz. Assume end-of-day treatment of the cash-flow.

ENDNOTES

[1] Our representation of a return can be done in various ways: percent (5%), decimal (0.05), or basis points (500 bps). They're different ways to express the same thing.

[2] Actually, any time you walk away with any of the casino's money you had a "good night."

[3] And I want to emphasize that you would accrue in both the denominator and numerator. In 1997, the AIMR-PPS was revised and emphasized this point; the earlier 1993 edition mandated accruals for fixed income, but apparently some firms only accrued in the numerator: how convenient as this would inflate the returns. We didn't understand the basis for any confusion but will emphasize here that if you accrue, accrue both your beginning and ending market values by the appropriate amounts.

[4] Dietz (2004), page 53.

[5] AIMR (1999), paragraph 2.A.2.

[6] "Accuracy vs. Cost in Performance Measurement," September 15, 1988. ICAA Computer/Systems Seminar. New York.

[7] In reality, for some firms 10% is too high and a lower threshold (perhaps 5% or 7.5%) is deemed more appropriate.

[8] See Lerit (1996).

[9] Here, we're speaking specifically of Modified BAI and Modified Dietz. The term "modified" is used elsewhere (e.g., modified duration), so this statement is not entirely accurate.

[10] Dietz and Krischman (1983), page 623.

Chapter 4 –
Calculating Exact Time-weighted Returns

In this chapter we introduce various ways to derive *true* or *exact* measures of rates of return. For many firms, approximation measures are inadequate. Why? There can be various reasons, including:

- market volatility
- large cash flows
- portfolio turnover

Under these circumstances, even the best approximation method begins to lose its accuracy and, for many firms, becomes unacceptable for reporting performance.

To improve performance, we turn to exact methods of time-weighting rates of return. In each case, as you will see, we are required to revalue the portfolio more frequently.

The move to daily returns

From the very beginning of the introduction of time-weighted returns there's been a recognition that using an approximation method is less than ideal. For example, the Bank Administration Institute identified the "Exact Method" as the best way to calculate returns (BAI (1968), pages 19-21). However, the BAI was also quite aware of the challenges the industry faced at that time in implementing such an approach. First, most firms repriced portfolios on a monthly or quarterly (and in some cases, annual) basis; most firms relied entirely on the clients' custodians for record keeping, as portfolio accounting software wasn't typically an available option; and computers were quite expensive and it would be several years before the advent of the personal computer.

That being said, the investment industry has been moving to daily rates of return for some time. There are two main reasons for this:

#1 – to improve the accuracy of our monthly returns

#2 – to provide daily returns to our management and/or clients.

Accuracy for daily returns requires accurate market values, meaning:

- accurate pricing
- accurate exchange rates
- timely and accurate processing of trades
- timely and accurate processing of corporate actions[1]
- timely capture and processing of cash flows

Moving to daily processing without having this level of accuracy will not yield a more accurate return; it may actually result in a much less accurate return.

Today, some firms calculate daily returns during the month, even though each day's accuracy cannot be assured. These returns are therefore seen as *indicative* of what's going on but should be understood as being *subject to change*. Following the month-end reconciliation and the application of any required changes to the portfolio, returns can be rerun.[2]

BAI Exact Method

We discussed in the last chapter how the BAI standards call for time-weighting. How did they propose to do this? They actually proposed three methods: the linked IRR, which is an approximation method; their "time-weighting" approach, which provides an alternative way to link returns (by weighting the time); and the exact method.[3]

In this approach, we revalue the portfolio whenever a cash flow occurs, and calculate a new IRR from that cash flow point until the ending measurement point or the next cash flow. We *link* these individually derived values together. We discuss linking in Chapter 5, so if you want to take a look at the linking methodology before continuing, please do so.

Let's take a look at an example we discussed in Chapter 2 and apply the BAI method to it. To refresh your memory, we begin with $1 million. At the end of the first year, it rises to $1.10. We then add another $1 million, so we begin the second year at $2.10 million. And at the end of that year our portfolio has risen to $2.94. Let's calculate the IRR up until the first cash flow:

$$1.00 - \frac{1.10}{1+r} = 0$$

We can isolate our r and arrive at our solution as follows:

$$1 + r - 1.10 = 0$$
$$r = 1.10 - 1 = 0.10 = 10\%$$

Now, to calculate the IRR for the second year, we begin with $2.10:

$$2.10 - \frac{2.94}{1 + r} = 0$$

And this becomes:

$$2.10 \times (1 + r) - 2.94 = 0$$
$$1 + r - \frac{2.94}{2.10} = 0$$
$$r = \frac{2.94}{2.10} - 1$$
$$r = 1.4 - 1 = 0.40 = 40\%$$

If we link these two period returns together, we get 54%, which annualizes to 24.10 percent.[4] If you recall from Chapter 2, when there was no cash flow, this was the IRR result we got. So we see how the *linked IRR* or BAI method provides us with a return that isn't influenced by the cash flow. This method calculates an exact time-weighted rate of return.

Modified Dietz

In Chapter 3 we referred to the Modified Dietz as an *approximation* formula. Well, it is. But if we shorten the period to a single day, when we have a flow we can achieve an *exact* rate of return.

The formula is essentially as we introduced it previously:

$$ROR = \frac{EMV - BMV - C}{BMV + W \times C}$$

The key difference here is what we mean by the weighting factor.

Previously it was calculated from the days in the month. But here we're dealing with a single day. Do we figure out what *time* the flow occurred and weight it based on the number of hours in our trading day? Hopefully not.[5] We generally assign one of three values to W:

• Start-of-day treatment: W = 1.0 (we want to include the entire flow amount)

- Mid-day treatment: W = 0.5 (we want to include half of the flow amount)
- End-of-day treatment: W = 0 (we don't want to include any of the flow amount)

This weighting occurs in the denominator and essentially means that if we treat the flow as a start-of-day flow, then whatever appreciation that's achieved will be measured against a base consisting of

Modified Dietz weights for exact TWRR
Start-of-day treatment: W = 1.0
Mid-day treatment: W = 0.5
End-of-day treatment: W = 0

the beginning market value plus the entire cash flow. If we do end-of-day, then we're not using any of the flow, and the gain (or loss) is being attributed entirely to the beginning market value. And, with the mid-day approach, we're using half the flow.

Let's take the case where we begin the day at € 100, end at €110, and have a cash flow of € 5. What's our return?

If we assume start-of-day, it is:

$$ROR = \frac{110 - 100 - 5}{100 + 1.0 \times 5} = \frac{5}{105} = 0.04762 = 4.76\%$$

And, end-of-day yields:

$$ROR = \frac{110 - 100 - 5}{100 + 0 \times 5} = \frac{5}{100} = 0.05 = 5\%$$

In general, we should be able to determine when the flow occurred. If we learn early in the day about the flow, then it's a start-of-day flow and we should be charged with the entire amount; if we don't hear about it until so late in the day that we can't invest it, then we get charged with zero. The midpoint is considered a way to balance the weighting out. One could argue that it *approximates* the treatment of the flow because we don't revalue when it occurs. The mid-day return is:

$$ROR = \frac{110 - 100 - 5}{100 + 0.5 \times 5} = \frac{5}{102.5} = 0.04878 = 4.88\%$$

Not surprisingly, this return falls midway between the start- and end-of-day returns.

Many firms who have traditionally used the Modified Dietz on a monthly basis as an *approximation* method find the conversion to exact made easier by simply continuing with this formula but adjusting the meaning of the weighting factor.

True Time-weighted ROR

Another way to derive our daily returns is to use the True TWRR formula, which is quite similar to a measure we introduced in Chapter 3:

$$ROR = \frac{EMV}{BMV} - 1$$

The distinction on a daily basis is that we have to calculate this ratio during the entire period, revaluing the market values, as appropriate, for cash flows. The True TWRR formula is:

$$ROR = \prod_{i=1}^{n} \left(\frac{EMV_i}{BMV_i} \right) - 1$$

The Greek capital letter pi ($\prod$) acts in a similar way to the Riemann sum's sigma (Σ), except that instead of adding, we're multiplying (it's the product function). Here, we multiply the various days in a

True Time-weighted ROR
$ROR = \prod_{i=1}^{n} \left(\dfrac{EMV_i}{BMV_i} \right) - 1$

period, where each day we have its beginning and ending market values.

Using our last scenario, if we assume that the cash flow occurred at the end of the day, we'd have the following:

$$ROR = \frac{105}{100} - 1 = 0.05 = 5\%$$

The cash flow (€5) will be added to the ending market value (€105) and used as the starting value for the next day's return calculation. In this way, the entire day's appreciation of €5 is attributed to the day's starting value (€100), without any involvement of the cash flow.

If we do start-of-day treatment for the cash flow, we'd have:

$$ROR = \frac{110}{105} - 1 = 1.04762 - 1 = 0.4762 = 4.76\%$$

To employ this approach for a mid-day treatment, we actually use a version of the Original Dietz, which we briefly discussed in Chapter 3:

$$ROR = \frac{EMV - 0.5 \times C}{BMV + 0.5 \times C} - 1$$

So, for our example we have:

$$ROR = \frac{110 - 0.5 \times 5}{100 + 0.5 \times 5} - 1 = \frac{107.5}{102.5} - 1 = 1.04878 - 1 = 0.04878 = 4.88\%$$

As you can see, we get the same results as we got using the Modified Dietz approach.

Let's try this method for a month. We will revalue the portfolio when cash flows occur. We begin the month at €100. Part way through the month, we get a contribution of €7. At the start of the day in which the flow occurs, our market value is € 101. At the end of this day, the market value (with the cash flow) is € 110. At the end of the month our portfolio is valued at €112. Let's calculate the return for the month.

If we assume start-of-day treatment for our cash flow, the return is as follows:

$$ROR_{SOD} = \frac{101}{100} \times \frac{110}{108} \times \frac{112}{110} - 1 = 1.01 \times 1.0185 \times 1.0182 - 1 = 1.0474 - 1 = 4.74\%$$

Let's consider each of these factors for a moment. The first (101/100) represents the return from the beginning of the month up until the end of the day preceding the day of the flow. What we are actually reporting is a one percent gain for that day, since 1.01 - 1 = 0.01, or one percent.

The second factor[6] (110/108) is the return for the day of the flow. On that day our market value started at 101; because it's start-of-day treatment for the cash flow, we add the flow (7) to this value, which yields 108. On that day, our market value closed at 110, thus our ratio. And, we find that on this day our return is 1.85% (1.0185-1).

The third factor picks up the remainder of the month (from the close of the day with the cash flow through month end). Since we achieved a market value of 110 on the day of the cash flow and ended the month at 112, our ratio (112/110) captures the return, which is 1.82% (1.0182-1).

After we multiply these three factors and subtract 1, we have the return for the month (4.74%).

If we assume end-of-day treatment, we have:

$$ROR_{ROD} = \frac{101}{100} \times \frac{103}{101} \times \frac{112}{110} - 1 = 1.01 \times 1.0198 \times 1.0182 - 1 = 1.04873 - 1 = 4.87\%$$

Our first factor is the same as for start-of-day.

Because we're assuming end-of-day treatment, then the second factor, which represents the day of the flow, does not show the flow yet, as we're not including it in our return calculation. Thus, we have the beginning value as the numerator (101) and the day's ending market value without the benefit of the cash flow (103). Our return on this day is 1.98% (1.0198-1).

The third factor handles the remainder of the month, picking up the cash flow (7 + 103) and going to month-end, for a return of 1.82% (1.0182-1).

The key distinction between these two methods is the day of the flow, where we know that there was a gain of €2. The question is, to what do we attribute this gain? To the start-of-day value (or, the prior day's ending market value) without or with the cash flow? If we use start-of-day and include the flow, the denominator will be larger and reduce that day's return from 1.98% (for end-of-day) to 1.85 percent.

Here the cash flow is relatively small. If the flow is very large, which can happen, the differences between start- and end-of-day treatment can be huge. Appendix 4-B provides further discussion on this.

Another example

Recall that in Chapter 2 we had a situation involving a mutual fund with cash flows over a five-year period. Let's calculate the return using the True Daily method. We'll use the scenario described in Table 2-4, which we repeat here (Table 4-1).

Our portfolio has been revalued following each cash flow. This is what we require to calculate an exact time-weighted return.

	Annual Return	**Cash Flows**	**BMV**	**EMV**
1996	-5.00%	$5,000	$5,000.00	$4,750.00
1997	-15.20%	$10,000	$14,750.00	$12,508.00
1998	3.10%	$15,000	$27,508.00	$28,360.75
1999	30.75%	$20,000	$48,360.75	$63,231.68
2000	17.65%	$25,000	$88,231.66	$103,604.57

Table 4-1: Mutual Fund Annual Returns - Investor # 1

Our return is found to be 27.52 percent:

$$R = \left(\frac{4750}{5000}\right)\left(\frac{12508}{14750}\right)\left(\frac{28360.75}{27508}\right)\left(\frac{63231.68}{48360.75}\right)\left(\frac{103604.57}{88231.66}\right) - 1 = 27.52\%$$

You will be given the opportunity to calculate the return for the second investor as an exercise at the end of this chapter.

Revaluing Every Day

We refer to these methods as daily but so far have only been revaluing them at the time of cash flows. What if we were to revalue every day; wouldn't that yield even greater accuracy? For many, this seems to make intuitive sense, but let's see.

Let's use the True Daily method to calculate the return for the period shown in Table 4-2, where there are no cash flows.

Day	Market Value
0	100
1	101
2	102
3	103
4	104
5	105
6	106
7	107
8	108
9	109
10	110

Table 4-2: Revaluing Daily

We can see that our return is derived as follows:

$$ROR = \frac{101}{100} \times \frac{102}{101} \times \frac{103}{102} \times \frac{104}{103} \times \frac{105}{104} \times \frac{106}{105} \times \frac{107}{106} \times \frac{108}{107} \times \frac{109}{108} \times \frac{110}{109} - 1$$

Now recall for a moment what you were most likely taught when you were around eight or nine, when studying fractions; your teacher probably told you about cancelling out common terms in the numerator and denominator. See the common terms above? We can cancel them, too.

The 101 in the numerator of the first term and the 101 in the denominator of the second, for example, can be cancelled out:

$$ROR = \frac{\cancel{101}}{100} \times \frac{102}{\cancel{101}} \times \frac{103}{102} \times \frac{104}{103} \times \frac{105}{104} \times \frac{106}{105} \times \frac{107}{106} \times \frac{108}{107} \times \frac{109}{108} \times \frac{110}{109} - 1$$

Continuing along, we can cancel the other common terms:

$$ROR = \frac{\cancel{101}}{100} \times \frac{\cancel{102}}{\cancel{101}} \times \frac{\cancel{103}}{\cancel{102}} \times \frac{\cancel{104}}{\cancel{103}} \times \frac{\cancel{105}}{\cancel{104}} \times \frac{\cancel{106}}{\cancel{105}} \times \frac{\cancel{107}}{\cancel{106}} \times \frac{\cancel{108}}{\cancel{107}} \times \frac{\cancel{109}}{\cancel{108}} \times \frac{110}{\cancel{109}} - 1$$

When we're done, we're left with the ending market value divided by the beginning market value:

$$ROR = \frac{110}{100} - 1 = 10\%$$

So, there is clearly no difference between *daily* rates of return and simply *revaluing portfolios at the time of cash flows*. However, given that we usually don't know when a flow will occur, we would most likely reprice our portfolios daily.

Repricing vs. revaluing

Is repricing the same as revaluing? I would say "no." To me revaluing means reconciling the portfolio to ensure its holdings match the "official books and records"[7] for the account. Most firms reconcile monthly. This doesn't preclude the ability to reconcile daily positions, however, as a firm can adjust daily figures to reflect accurate positions during their monthly reconciliation process.

If we limit revaluing to simply repricing, we run the risk of the account having incorrect data, which in turn may jeopardize the accuracy of the return.

Exact vs. True Daily

As noted above, the BAI suggested the use of the "exact" method. How does this differ from daily? It doesn't. The BAI's exact method required the firm to revalue for cash flows and to calculate the IRR between these valuation points. This eliminates the impact of cash flows.

We can easily demonstrate this algebraically. We begin with the IRR formula as shown in Chapter 2, for the case when there are no cash flows:

$$BMV = \frac{EMV}{(1+r)^t}$$

Since we're dealing with a single time period, our "t" equals one.

$$BMV = \frac{EMV}{1+r}$$

We divide both sides by BMV:

$$\frac{BMV}{BMV} = 1 = \frac{EMV}{(1+r)BMV}$$

We next multiply both sides by (1 l r):

$$1+r = \frac{EMV(1+r)}{BMV(1+r)} = \frac{EMV}{BMV}$$

Finally, we subtract 1 from each side:

$$r = \frac{EMV}{BMV} - 1$$

This shows that the BAI's exact method is the same as the daily method.

Unit Value method

The Unit Value approach is the third exact measure we'll discuss.[8] This approach is quite different than what we've discussed so far. Here we create two terms - unit values and number of units - which are used to facilitate the calculation of the return.

This approach is similar to the way we calculate the return for a mutual fund. In the case of a mutual fund, we have a Net Asset Value (NAV) and number of shares.

As with a mutual fund's NAV, where the initial value is *defined*, we *define* a unit value at the start. Let's use the example we just dealt with where our beginning market value is €100. Let's define our unit value as 10.[9]

Next, we figure out *how many units* we have (where units are like shares). This formula is quite straightforward:

$$NumberOfUnits = \frac{MarketValue}{UnitValue}$$

Applying this to our example, we calculate ten units to start.

$$NumberOfUnits = \frac{100}{10} = 10$$

Since each of these units are valued at €10, and since we have 10 of them, our portfolio has a market value of €100.

The day before the cash flow, our portfolio has grown to 101. From a unit value perspective we still only have 10 units, but our unit value has changed. To calculate our unit value we use this formula:

$$UnitValue = \frac{MarketValue}{NumberOfUnits}$$

$$UnitValue = \frac{101}{10} = 10.1$$

The inflow of €7 is treated as a purchase of units. Since our new unit value is 10.1, we can purchase 0.693 units, so we now have a total of 10.693 units.

$$NumberOfUnits = \frac{7}{10.1} = 0.693$$

When our market value increases to 110, our unit value becomes 10.287.

$$UnitValue = \frac{110}{10.693} = 10.287$$

We close the month with a market value of 112. Our end-of-month unit value becomes 10.474.

$$UnitValue = \frac{112}{10.693} = 10.474$$

You may have noticed that we have not yet discussed returns; we now can. The return formula for the unit value method is similar to that for the true value method, except we use the unit values:

$$ROR = \frac{EUV}{BUV} - 1$$

where

EUV = Ending Unit Value
BUV = Beginning Unit Value

For example, what's the return from the beginning of the month until our cash flow?

$$ROR = \frac{10.1}{10.0} - 1 = 1.00\%$$

We can calculate the return for the entire period by comparing the ending unit value (10.474) with the beginning period unit value (10.00):

$$ROR = \frac{10.474}{10.000} - 1 = 4.74\%$$

One nice feature of the unit value approach is that we can actually *read* the inception-to-date return from the ending unit value, providing we use a beginning unit value like 1, 10, 100, etc. In our case, the ending unit value is 10.474; if we subtract 10 and multiply by 10, we get 4.74 – our return!

	Start	Market Change	Inflow	Revised Market Value	Market Change	Market Change
Market Value	100	101	7	108	110	112
Unit Value	10	10.100	10.100	10.100	10.287	10.474
# of Units	10	10	0.693	10.693	10.693	10.693
ROR		1.00%			1.85%	4.74%

Table 4-3: Summary of Unit Value Process

Table 4-3 summarizes the data elements we calculated for the portfolio using the unit value approach.

While the unit value method yields the same return as the true daily method, it has the added disadvantage that it requires the creation of data elements (units and unit values) which only serve the purpose of calculating the return, which we can do just as easily directly from the market values.

When wondering why the unit value method hasn't been as widely used as some of the other methods, we come to two possible reasons:

#1 – It needs these additional data fields. While data storage today is quite inexpensive, there was a time when it wasn't
#2 – It's not terribly intuitive

Revaluing for large cash flows

We discussed Modified Dietz in the previous chapter. Like the Modified BAI, this formula is an approximation to the true or exact time-weighted rate of return. For some time we've recognized that its accuracy is dependent on (a) the size of cash flows and (b) the volatility of the market; when we encounter large flows and/or volatile markets, the accuracy diminishes. For example, let's consider the following (please refer to Table 4-4).[11]

Case #1: No cash flow				Case #2: 5% cash flow			
	Portfolio ROR	BMV	EMV		Portfolio ROR	BMV	EMV
1st half	1%	$1,000.00	$1,010.00	1st half	1%	$1,000.00	$1,010.00
2nd half	5%	$1,010.00	$1,060.50	2nd half	5%	$1,060.50	$1,113.53
C =	$ -	*Modified Dietz equals the True Time-weighted ROR*		C =	$50.50	*Modified Dietz approximates the True Time-weighted ROR*	
Mod D =	6.05%			Mod D =	6.15%		
True =	6.05%			True =	6.05%		
Difference =	0.00%			Difference =	0.10%		
Case #3: 10% cash flow				Case #4: 25% cash flow			
	Portfolio ROR	BMV	EMV		Portfolio ROR	BMV	EMV
1st half	1%	$1,000.00	$1,010.00	1st half	1%	$1,000.00	$1,010.00
2nd half	5%	$1,111.00	$1,166.55	2nd half	5%	$1,262.50	$1,325.63
C =	$101.00	*Modified Dietz's error is beginning to grow*		C =	$252.50	*Modified Dietz's approximation is unacceptable*	
Mod D =	6.24%			Mod D =	6.49%		
True =	6.05%			True =	6.05%		
Difference =	0.19%			Difference =	0.44%		

Table 4-4: Impact of Cash Flows on Modified Dietz Return

We've taken a month and split it in half. During the first half we have a 1% return; during the second half our return is five percent. In case #1 (upper left quadrant of table) we have no cash flows; as a result, our Modified Dietz return matches the true, exact rate of return (6.05%). In case #2, we introduce a 5% cash flow as we start the second half of the month; as a result, the Modified Dietz return is slightly different as it *approximates* the true return, while the true return method has eliminated the impact of the result. As we can see we're off by 10 basis points (upper right quadrant). In case #3 (lower left quadrant), we introduce a 10% cash flow which results in a 19 basis point difference, while in case #4 (lower right) we have a 25% cash flow which causes a 44 basis point difference.

This exercise shows the impact of large flows, especially with volatile markets. Consequently, we recommend that firms adopt a policy to revalue their portfolio when large flows occur. The GIPS Standards mandates this change effective

January 1, 2010.[12] While there was consideration to mandate revaluation for all external cash flows, this was modified to apply to only "large external cash flows," where the firm decides what "large" represents.

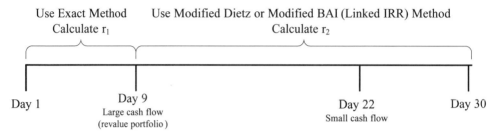

Figure 4-1: Mixing Return Methods for Large and Small Flows

This begs the question "what do we do for cash flows that don't qualify as "large"? Modified Dietz or Modified BAI are acceptable under these circumstances. One might also wonder what would be done if during a month both large and small flows occur. In these cases, the firm may employ both the Exact as well as an approximation method. As shown in Figure 4-1, we would calculate multiple returns for the s bounded by the large flows and month-ends. These flows are then linked to arrive at the monthly return. Linking is taken up in the following chapter.

Concluding remarks

The industry has been moving to daily rates of return for some time. The only way you can have accurate daily returns, however, is if you have accurate data. And assuming you do, you can see that we have a variety of ways to accomplish this, each yielding essentially the same returns as the other methods. So selection of one method over another is essentially a matter of preference.

In this chapter we introduced a variety of ways to calculate exact rates of return. We also contrasted exact with the money-weighted return (IRR) and approximation methods. In addition, we discussed the impact of large flows when using an approximation method and the revaluing of portfolios when large flows occur.

Exercises

1. Calculate the daily return using the Modified Dietz method for the following situation:

We begin the day with €100.
At the end of the day, our portfolio has grown by €10.
A cash flow of €5 occurred.
Our end-of-day market value is €115 (starting value €100, plus the cash flow €5, plus our portfolio's appreciation €10).

Assume start-of-day treatment for the cash flow.

2. Calculate the return using Modified Dietz for #1, using end-of-day treatment for the cash flow.

3. Calculate the Unit Value for the situation described in exercise 1.

4. Calculate the True Daily return for the mutual fund example as shown in Table 2-6 in Chapter 2.

Appendix 4-A - Timing Processing of Flows is Important

Cash flows have been the greatest challenge to performance measurement, and it hasn't gotten any easier. In fact, it's probably more of a challenge today than it was 20 years ago.

Let's use an example to demonstrate this point:

BMV = €100,000
C = €500,000
MV on day of flow
    Before the flow, MV = €105,000
    At the end of the day, without the flow, the MV = €135,000
    At the end of the day, with the flow, the MV = €635,000
EMV = €640,000.

To summarize what we are showing, the portfolio begins the month with

€100,000. An extremely large cash flow of € 500,000 occurs. At the start of the day, the portfolio's value was €105,000 (i.e., it had gained €5,000 since the start of the month).

On the day of the cash flow, the portfolio appreciated by €30,000.

The portfolio ends the month with a market value of €640,000.

The question is, is the cash flow a *start-of-day* flow or an *end-of-day* flow?

This is a question we always need to be prepared to address, but especially when large flows occur. Most firms establish policies on cash flows, either treating them as start- or end-of-day events.

Applying this question of start- or end-of-day to this example, what we're essentially asking is "should the €30,000 appreciation in market value be attributed entirely to the start-of-day value of €105,000, or did the cash flow contribute?"

Let's see how the returns will vary. First, the start-of-day approach:

$$ROR_{SOD} = \frac{105,000}{100,000} \times \frac{635,000}{605,000} \times \frac{640,000}{635,000} - 1 = 11.07\%$$

As you can see, the appreciation (€30,000) is being attributed to the start-of-day value (€105,000) plus the cash (€500,000). Now, let's look at the end-of-day solution:

$$ROR_{EOD} = \frac{105,000}{100,000} \times \frac{135,000}{105,000} \times \frac{640,000}{635,000} - 1 = 36.06\%$$

Here, we show the appreciation being entirely attributed to the start-of-day value (€105,000).

Now, look at the return differences. Quite amazing, right? Which is correct? It may be tempting to say the second (36.06%), but that would not be a good policy to follow. Rather, you should investigate to decide.

What would you look at? Perhaps find out when you were notified of the flow. If it was discovered in the morning, then start-of-day seems the right way to go.[13]

Or, look at the transaction activity that day – see if any of that new money was spent.

You could also look at the index that's associated with the portfolio. If you tend to manage in a manner that's similar to the index, the return the index got might give a hint as to what is correct here.

Let's look at one more example, this time from an outflow perspective:

BMV = €10,000,000

C = - €7,000,000

MV on day of flow

Before the flow, MV = €10,010,000

At the end of the day, without the flow, the MV = €9,800,000

At the end of the day, with the flow, the MV = €2,800,000

EMV = €2,750,000

On the day of the flow, the portfolio lost €210,000. The question is, what base do we use to measure this drop? If we use the start-of-day approach, then the very large cash flow came out before the drop:

$$ROR_{SOD} = \frac{10,100,000}{10,000,000} \times \frac{2,800,000}{3,100,000} \times \frac{2,750,000}{2,800,000} - 1 = -10.40\%$$

But, if we use the end-of-day method, then the flow occurs after the drop in value occurred, so the base is larger:

$$ROR_{EOD} = \frac{10,100,000}{10,000,000} \times \frac{9,800,000}{10,100,000} \times \frac{2,750,000}{2,800,000} - 1 = -3.75\%$$

Once again, we show a fairly significant difference in returns.

Do flows of such magnitude happen? Yes. And sometimes they happen as out-flows, which can also cause some challenges in figuring out what the correct treat-ment is.

You should have a policy on how to treat flows in general. And, when large flows occur, we suggest you do some checking to make sure the treatment is appropriate. We suggest that as a default you consider having inflows treated as start-of-day and outflows as end-of-day.

Appendix 4-B – Clariying the differences[14]

I don't know about you, but at times I've been confused about the differences between the IRR, BAI, and Modified BAI. Because I have the benefit of teaching a class on performance measurement and often get involved with various writing projects, I decided to reflect on the differences and attempt to make the differences as clear as possible. First, the term "BAI" is a rather broad term and I would argue that it simply means that the firm is using *one* of the methods that the BAI offered. Second, the "Modified BAI" formula is the same as the "Linked IRR." And, as discussed above, the BAI's Exact Method is the same as the Daily ROR formula.

The IRR is a *money-weighted* (or dollar-weighted) rate of return. Like the Modified and Original Dietz methods, the Modified BAI (or Linked IRR) is an *approximation* to the true, daily time-weighted rate of return (or exact method).

I created this diagram (Figure 4-B-1) as a way to try to demonstrate the differences. The squares at each end represent the two end points for our measurement period (inception date and most recent ending or reporting period). The triangles represent month-end points, and the circles show cash flows.

Internal Rate of Return

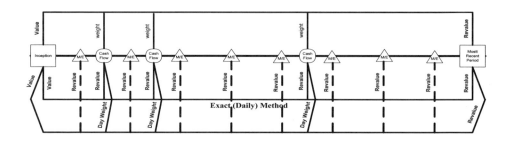

Modified BAI / Linked IRR / Modified Dietz

Figure 4-B-1: Graphical Representation of Various Rates of Return

The Internal Rate of Return

We'll begin with the Internal Rate of Return. The IRR formula is:

$$\frac{EMV}{(1+R)^T} + \left(\sum_{t=1}^{T-1} \frac{-C_t}{(1+R)^t} \right) - BMV = 0$$

As mentioned above, the IRR is a money-weighted return. As you can see from the graphic, with this method (represented by the dashed lines) we value the portfolio at only two points: the inception and the ending point. The cash flows that occur are included in the formula, based on when they occurred. The IRR is based on the *time value of money* or *present value* formula. The return (R) is found through an iterative process (trial and error).

The GIPS Standards have provisions which address private equity and venture capital.[15] In this market, the manager controls the cash flows, therefore the *money-weighted* return is required. These standards require *since inception IRR*. That's what we show here.

BAI Exact Method

As noted above, the Exact Method is the same as the true daily. The BAI (Bank Administration Institute) actually came up with a couple ways to calculate a time-weighted rate of return. With this method, we calculate multiple IRRs, over *variable time periods*, depending upon the timing of cash flows. Whenever a cash flow occurs, we revalue the portfolio and calculate a return using the IRR from the previous valuation point to that one. These individual returns are then linked to create a return that spans the entire period.

The return we get with this method is a *true, exact time-weighted rate of return.*

Modified BAI (Linked IRR) method

The Modified BAI formula is:

$$EMV - BMV \times (1+R) - \sum_{i-1}^{n} C_i \times (1+R)^{W_i} = 0$$

It is identical to the "Linked IRR" as defined by the BAI. With this approach, we calculate multiple IRRs, but on a set and *regular basis*; for example, quarterly or monthly. These IRRs are linked to span a broader (e.g., year) period. The cash flows are weighted, just like they are in the Modified Dietz formula (note the "W_i"; it's the same as we use in the Modified Dietz).

$$R = \frac{EMV - BMV - \sum_{i=1}^{n} C_i}{BMV + \sum_{i=1}^{n} W_i \times C_i}$$

As you can see in our graphic, revalue at month-ends, and day-weight the cash flows.

Like the Modified Dietz, this method yields an *approximate* time-weighted rate of return. And, its accuracy (again, like the Modified Dietz) is partly dependent on the relative size of the cash flows.

Comparison Summary

So, there you have it:

- Internal Rate of Return - money-weighted; revalue at the two end points
- BAI Exact - true time-weighted; revalue for every cash flow
- Modified BAI, Modified Dietz - approximation to the true time-weighted; revalue monthly or quarterly, time-weight the cash flows.

ENDNOTES

[1] A corporate action is an action of the corporation which effects the security. For stocks, examples can be stock splits, reverse splits, spinoffs, name changes, cash and stock dividends, and mergers; for bonds, it can be a call, interest payments, and defaults.

[2] We're also aware that a few firms use the Modified Dietz for their monthly returns rather than rerun the daily return process.

[3] BAI (1968), page 21.

[4] We will discuss both linking and annualization in Chapter 5. For now, you'll have to trust me on the calculation if you're not already familiar with the formulas; or, you can go visit the chapter now.

[5] There actually are some firms that use fractional weighting, from 0.0 to 1.0, to try to be somewhat precise as to when flows occur. Unfortunately, I would argue that this is shifting the exact approach to an approximation method since they aren't revaluing the portfolio at the time of the flow; nor would I encourage them to.

[6] A mathematically inclined reader may recognize that we could have simply had the ratio 112/108, since the 110 in the numerator of the second factor arithmetically cancels with the 110 in the denominator of the third factor. I include this extra, albeit superfluous, factor to emphasize the difference in treatment between the start- and end-of-day approaches.

[7] The term "official books and records" usually refers to the records as reflected by the account's custodian.

[8] For further information on the unit value approach, see Sieff (1966).

[9] While we can pick any value as the starting point, it's quite common to begin with a round number such as 10 or 100.

[10] Recall, for example the elimination of the first two numbers in the year for date fields in order to save space, which at the time may have saved the industry millions of dollars in data storage, only to cause the expenditure of billions of dollars when we had to put those two characters back in ("Y2K").

[11] I want to credit Jose Menchero for first coming up with an example like this as a

way to demonstrate the impact of flows.

[12] CFA Institute (2005), paragraph 2.A.2.b, page 10.

[13] Some may want to qualify this by saying "just because we heard about the flow, unless we acted on it we don't need to consider it." My view is that you're responsible for the money when you become aware of it, whether or not you do anything with it (that's an investment decision, which could help or hurt you).

[14] This section is taken from a newsletter which appeared in June 2004 (Spaulding, 2004, 1, pages 1-2).

[15] See www.cfainstitute.org/standards/pdf/venture_capital.pdf.

Chapter 5 –
Multi-period Performance Measurement

When we calculate rates of return they are usually for a given period: a day or month, for example. However, we often want to extend these periods to cover longer periods. In this chapter we discuss two concepts relating to multi-period rates of return: geometric linking and annualization.

Geometric linking

Let's say that we have calculated our returns for January, February, and March, as shown in Table 5-1.

Month	ROR
January	1.5%
February	2.3%
March	0.6%

Table 5-1: Monthly Returns

It isn't unusual for us to want the return for the first quarter. How can we achieve this?

A logical response might be to simply *add* the numbers together (1.5 + 2.3 + 0.6 = 4.4). This is referred to as *arithmetic linking*. While it's simple to do, it fails to take into account the compounding which is going on from period to period.

The preferred and generally accepted way to achieve the return for a period which spans multiple periods for which we've derived returns is geometric linking, as it takes into consideration compounding. You're probably familiar with compounding from an interest-earned perspective; that is, as we earn interest on an investment, interest earned on subsequent periods is not only earned on the initial amount but also on any interest that was previously earned. If, for example, we invested $100 and earned 5% interest during the first year, we earn $5; we end up with $105. If we earn 5% during the second year, we're not earning another $5 but 5% on the initial $100 plus 5% on the interest earned during the prior period ($5). This interest-on-interest is compounding. The same thing happens with returns. And we want to reflect this as we go across periods; that is, to ensure that our returns build upon one another.

The approach to link is a very simple five-step formula:

Step 1: convert the return percentages to decimals (can be accomplished by dividing by 100)
Step 2: add 1 to each of these numbers
Step 3: multiply the numbers
Step 4: subtract 1
Step 5: convert this number to a percentage (by multiplying by 100)

A common question that arises at this point is, why do we add one to each period return? This is how we achieve our compounding. Let's digress for a moment and look at a totally different scenario: salary increases. Let's say you join a firm and are paid £20,000 per year. At the end of the first year, you're given a 10% increase. What's your new salary? Well, 10% of £20,000 is £2,000, right? So, we could simply add this value on to our base salary to arrive at our new salary of £22,000. Or, we could multiply our base (£20,000) by our increase (10%) plus 1 (1.10), which gets us to our £22,000.

$$SalaryAfterRaise = Base + Increase = 20,000 + 2,000 = 22,000$$
$$SalaryAfterRaise = Base \times (1 + \% Increase) = 20,000 \times (1.10) = 22,000$$

It's now a year later, and you're given a 12% raise. What's your new salary? The increase isn't against the base, but your current salary of £22,000. To arrive at our adjusted salary, we can use either of the approaches as above to discover it's now £24,640. The increase this time isn't just against the original base (20,000) but also takes into consideration the earlier raise you got (2,000).

Over this time period, you've gotten two increases. If we were to take your starting salary and the two increases, how can we arrive at your current salary? By compounding:

$$SalaryAfterTwoRaises = 20,000 \times 1.10 \times 1.12 = 24,640$$

Now, back to our linking example.

Table 5-2 shows the application of the geometric linking process to our example. And, as you can see, our geometric return for the quarter is 4.46%, six basis points higher than what we achieved using the arithmetic approach.

Let's try another example.

Month	ROR	Step 1	Step 2	Step 3	Step 4	Step 5
January	1.5%	0.015	1.015			
February	2.3%	0.023	1.023			
March	0.6%	0.006	1.006			
Quarter				1.0446	0.0446	4.46%

Table 5-2: Linking the Monthly Returns

Table 5-3 shows the returns for four quarters, and we want to calculate the annual return.

Quarter	ROR
1st	2.45%
2nd	1.17%
3rd	-1.01%
4th	1.65%

Table 5-3: Quarterly Returns

We once again apply our four steps, as shown in Table 5-4.

Quarter	ROR	Step 1	Step 2	Step 3	Step 4	Step 5
1st	2.45%	0.0245	1.0245			
2nd	1.17%	0.0117	1.0117			
3rd	-1.01%	-0.0101	0.9899			
4th	1.65%	0.0165	1.0165			
Year				1.0429	0.0429	4.29%

Table 5-4: Linking the Quarterly Returns

And, we see that our return for the year is 4.29 percent.

Table 5-5 shows a situation where we have five annual returns, and we want the return across the five-year period.

Table 5-6 shows the step-by-step application of our geometric linking formula to derive the five-year return of 3.94 percent.

Year	ROR
1	3.57%
2	4.57%
3	-2.23%
4	1.78%
5	-3.56%

Table 5-5: Yearly Returns

Years	ROR	Step 1	Step 2	Step 3	Step 4	Step 5
1	3.57%	0.0357	1.0357			
2	4.57%	0.0457	1.0457			
3	-2.23%	-0.0223	0.9777			
4	1.78%	0.0178	1.0178			
5	-3.56%	-0.0356	0.9644			
Five Year Return				1.0394	0.0394	3.94%

Table 5-6: Linking Five Years of Returns

Cumulative returns

Geometric linking results in *cumulative* rates of return. For example, our last example yielded a five-year cumulative return of 3.94 percent. We will address annualization of returns below.

Linking across mixed time periods

One thing about geometric linking is that we use the same five-step formula, regardless of the length of time for the subperiods we're linking. The only key rule is that these subperiods must be continuous.

For example, what if we have returns for the subperiods shown in Table 5-7?

How do we link these? The same as we linked returns when the periods were the same (see Table 5-8).

So, the return for this mixed time period is 6.62 percent.

Subperiod	ROR
3rd Quarter, 2000	-3.45%
4th Quarter, 2000	1.45%
2001	6.83%
2002	1.89%

Table 5-7: Linking Mixed Time Periods

Subperiod	ROR	Step 1	Step 2	Step 3	Step 4	Step 5
3rd Quarter, 2000	-3.45%	-0.0345	0.9655			
4th Quarter, 2000	1.45%	0.0145	1.0145			
2001	6.83%	0.0683	1.0683			
2002	1.89%	0.0189	1.0189			
Across time period				1.0662	0.0662	6.62%

Table 5-8: Linking Across Mixed Time Periods

Month	ROR
January	1.5%
February	2.3%
March	0.6%
April	1.0%

Table 5-9: Monthly Returns

The ability to link variable length periods strikes some people as odd, so let's explore this a bit. We'll use a simple example. In Table 5-2, we linked three monthly returns to arrive at a quarterly return. What if we wanted to link a fourth month onto this, as shown in Table 5-11; how would we proceed? You have two options: you can link the four months together or link the fourth month onto the quarterly return.

Table 5-10 shows how we can link the four months; as you can see, we get a cumulative return of 5.50 percent. Table 5-11 shows the linking of April with the first quarter's return. As you can see, we get the same result.

Month	ROR	Step 1	Step 2	Step 3	Step 4	Step 5
January	1.5%	0.015	1.015			
February	2.3%	0.023	1.023			
March	0.6%	0.006	1.006			
April	1.0%	0.010	1.010			
Cumulative ROR				1.0550	0.0550	5.50%

Table 5-10: Linking the 4 Months' Returns

Month	ROR	Step 1	Step 2	Step 3	Step 4	Step 5
Quarter	4.46%	0.0446	1.0446			
April	1.0%	0.010	1.010			
Cumulative ROR				1.0550	0.0550	5.50%

Table 5-11: Linking the Quarter and One-month Returns

If you think about what's going on in this process, this shouldn't be too difficult to grasp. When we link subperiods (e.g., months) to get to a longer period (e.g., a quarter), we're doing this through multiplication. And so, when we then link that quarter with an even longer period (e.g., a year), that year was arrived at by linking quarters or months, which was also done through multiplication.

Let's try another mixed-time period example, where we began managing money for a portfolio on June 16, 2001. It's now February 8, 2003 and we want to provide our client with a return from their inception date through last night. Table 5-12 shows the returns for the various subperiods for which we've calculated returns.

Table 5-13 reflects the application of our five-step geometric linking to achieve our client's inception-to-date return of 1.87 percent.

Gaps in our time period

Sometimes we may run across a situation where we have a return for several time periods and then there's a gap. Perhaps we had a month where our client withdrew all of their money and then gave it back to us a month later. This gap

Subperiod	ROR
June 16- June 30, 2001	1.02%
3rd Quarter, 2001	1.16%
4th Quarter, 2001	-2.15%
2002	1.10%
January 2003	0.35%
January 31- February 7, 2003	0.42%

Table 5-12: Client's subperiod Returns

Subperiod	ROR	Step 1	Step 2	Step 3	Step 4	Step 5
June 16-June 30, 2001	1.02%	0.0102	1.0102			
3rd Quarter, 2001	1.16%	0.0116	1.0116			
4th Quarter, 2001	-2.15%	-0.0215	0.9785			
2002	1.10%	0.0110	1.0110			
January 2003	0.35%	0.0035	1.0035			
January 31 - February 7, 2003	0.42%	0.0042	1.0042			
Inception-to-date				1.0187	0.0187	1.87%

Table 5-13: Linking the Client's subperiod Returns

means that we have to break our performance up into two periods, the period *before* the gap and the period *after* the gap. Can we link across these gaps?

In the earlier edition of this book I offered what I believed to be the standard response to this question: "no." But after giving this much thought I concluded that in reality an argument can be made to link across periods. I commented on this in our firm's monthly newsletter ("Performance Perspectives") in April 2005 (Spaulding (2005, 3)). At the time I was focusing on returns at the sub-portfolio level, using timeweighted returns. I have since rethought the notion of using time-weighting for sub-portfolio returns and address this in Chapter 6. Regardless, I believe it's acceptable to allow such linking, but some caution is needed. In addition, the firm that employs this should state the criteria (e.g., the maximum length of a gap that would be permitted).

Annualizing returns

Often we want to express an average return to more simply represent our investing. We may be tempted to take a simple average; that is, to divide the cumulative return by the number of years in the period. There are two reasons why this wouldn't be a good idea. First, a simple average doesn't take into consideration compounding and could result in an inflated number. Also, the number could easily misrepresent reality.

Here's an example that shows why simple averages are not a good idea.

Fund	Year 1	Year 2	Year 3
A	-5%	-5%	40%
B	20%	5%	5%
C	100%	10%	-80%

Table 5-14: Input for Simple Averages

First, what is the average for these three funds?

$$ROR_A = \frac{(-5\%) + (-5\%) + (40\%)}{3} = \frac{30\%}{3} = 10\%$$

$$ROR_B = \frac{(20\%) + (5\%) + (5\%)}{3} = \frac{30\%}{3} = 10\%$$

$$ROR_C = \frac{(100\%) + (10\%) + (-80\%)}{3} = \frac{30\%}{3} = 10\%$$

You may not be surprised to see that all three funds yield the same average. What's the geometric returns for these funds? You can validate this on your own and will see that the results are as shown in Table 5-15.

Fund	Year 1	Year 2	Year 3	Simple Average	3-Year Geometric ROR
A	-5%	-5%	40%	10%	26.35%
B	20%	5%	5%	10%	32.30%
C	100%	10%	-80%	10%	-56.00%

Table 5-15: The Simple Average and Geometric Returns

In the foreword to my second book, Gary Brinson referred to the past practice of using simple averages which resulted in misleading information.[1] So the industry has apparently known for some time that simple averages, while easy to derive and comprehend, are inappropriate for representing performance results.

So how do we accomplish this? By annualization.

Annualization is an "average" that takes into consideration the effects of compounding. It essentially strips out the compounding.

I like to use the analogy of decaf coffee, which decaffeinates the coffee; i.e., it removes the caffeine. In a similar way we want to decompound the return; that is, to remove the compounding.

Annualization provides the annual return we would have obtained had we had the same return for each year over which the cumulative return spans. That is, if we perform geometric linking on the annualized returns for the number of periods represented, we should end up with the compounded result we began with.

Like geometric linking, we use a five-step formula to annualize returns. And, interestingly, four of the steps are identical to those in geometric linking; it's only the middle step which is different. The steps:

Step 1: convert the cumulative return percentage to a decimal by 100
Step 2: add 1
Step 3: take the nth root, where "n" is the number of years the cumulative return covers
Step 4: subtract 1
Step 5: convert this number to a percentage

What do we mean by an nth root?

Well, let's first recall the meaning of square roots. The mathematical solution yields a number when multiplied by itself will yield the original number. For example, the square root of 4 is 2, since 2 times 2 equals four.

$$\sqrt{4} = 2$$
$$2 \times 2 = 4$$
$$2^2 = 4$$

The square root of 25 is 5, for the same reason:

$$\sqrt{25} = 5$$
$$5 \times 5 = 25$$
$$5^2 = 25$$

Let's demonstrate one more root – the cube or third root. The same idea applies here, but this time we want the number which when multiplied three times yields the value within the root sign. For example, the cube root of 8 is 2, since 2 times 2 times 2, or 2 to the third power, equals eight.

$$\sqrt[3]{8} = 2$$
$$2 \times 2 \times 2 = 8$$
$$2^3 = 8$$

Note that within the symbol we have a "3." When we did the square root, by convention we don't have to show a "2," since the 2 is assumed unless something else is there.

But we're talking about the nth root. We use "n" because we don't know what the time period will be. Therefore, to show this we simply say the nth root. Again, the n represents the number of years for which the period covers.

Let's begin with a simple example. Recall in Chapter 2 that we calculated an IRR of 54% for a two-year period. We said at that time that the annualized return was 24.10 percent. Let's prove it:

Step 1 (convert cumulative return to a decimal): 0.54
Step 2 (add 1): 1.54
Step 3 (take the nth root). Since we're talking about two years, we are taking the second or square root.

$$\sqrt{1.54} = 1.2410$$

Step 3 therefore yields 1.2410
Step 4 (subtract 1): 0.2410
Step 5 (convert to a percent): 24.10 percent

We can validate this by simply geometrically linking this number two times, since it's supposed to represent the return we should have obtained for two years to produce a cumulative return of 54%:

Step 1: convert to a decimal (24.10% becomes 0.2410 and there will be two of them)
Step 2: add 1 (1.2410)
Step 3: multiply (1.2410 × 1.2410 = 1.54)
Step 4: subtract 1 (0.54)

Step 5: convert to a percent (54%)²

We earlier calculated a five-year cumulative return of 3.94 percent. Let's find the annualized return for this period. Applying our five-step formula, we get:

Step 1 (convert percent to a decimal): 0.0394
Step 2 (add 1): 1.0394
Step 3 (take the nth root)

What's *n* for this example? Since we're working on a five-year cumulative return, *n* is five. So, we take the fifth root of 1.0394.

$$\sqrt[5]{1.0394} = 1.0078$$

At this point, you may be wondering *how* did I figure this out. Good question.

I have two choices. First, I have a calculator that has an nth root function, which often comes in handy.

An alternative approach is to use MS/Excel. Here, I use the POWER function. You see, there is an equivalent way to use the power of our number and that's to raise our value to the transposition of our number of years or to the 1/n power. So, since we're talking about five years, it's 1/5.

$$1.0394^{1/5} = 1.0078$$

Step 3 therefore results in the value 1.0078
Step 4 (subtract 1): 0.0078
Step 5 (convert to a percent): 0.78%

Recall that we spoke earlier about taking a simple average of our five-year cumulative return. This would have yielded 0.79% (3.94 ÷ 5). We show that this number overstates the real annualized return.

The annualized return is an "average" which takes into account the compounding effect. It also represents the number which, if we had this return for each of the five years, would have yielded our previously derived cumulative return. Let's try it out. Table 5-16 shows the steps and math needed to geometrically link 0.78% five times.

Is this a *mathematically rigorous* test to prove our annualization formula? No. But it at least should give you some comfort that the methodology we use works.

Now, let's try a rather interesting example. Recall that earlier in this chapter

Years	ROR	Step 1	Step 2	Step 3	Step 4	Step 5
1	0.78%	0.0078	1.0078			
2	0.78%	0.0078	1.0078			
3	0.78%	0.0078	1.0078			
4	0.78%	0.0078	1.0078			
5	0.78%	0.0078	1.0078			
Five-year return				1.0394	0.0394	3.94%

Table 5-16: Testing Out Our Annualized Return

we linked returns for a mixed period and got a result of 6.62 percent. Let's annualize this.

Step 1 (convert to a decimal): 0.0662
Step 2 (add 1): 1.0662
Step 3 (take the nth root)

What's the root now? Well, we had two quarters and two years, so our time spans 2.5 years, so our root has to be 2.5.

$$\sqrt[2.5]{1.0662} = 1.0260$$

Step 3 therefore yields a result of 1.0260.
Step 4 (subtract 1): 0.0260
Step 5 (convert to a percent): 2.60%

Our annual return is therefore 2.60 percent. Although we can't geometrically link 2.5 times, we can still validate this result by raising it (converted to a decimal and adding 1) to the 2.5 power. Try it!

Here's an interesting example to consider, which is probably quite realistic. We earlier calculated a cumulative return for a portfolio which began on June 16, 2001 and ended on February 7, 2003. The geometrically linked value was 1.87 percent. The first two steps are easy:

Step 1: 0.0187
Step 2: 1.0187

But how do we do step 3? What's *n*? What *number of years do we have?* This is a bit tricky at first, but it really isn't too difficult. How many years are here? It's best to break this up into time periods and calculate the number of days:

June 16 - June 30, 2001: 15 days
3rd quarter (July is 31 days; August is 31 days; September is 30 days): 92 days
4th quarter: 92 days
2002: 365 days
January 2003: 31 days
February 1- February 7, 2003: 7 days.

The total number of days is 602. The number of years is 602 / 365 or 1.65. So, our root is 1.65.

$$\sqrt[1.65]{1.0187} = 1.0113$$

Step 3: 1.0113
Step 4: 0.0113
Step 5: 1.13 percent

Our annualized inception-to-date return is 1.13 percent.

Any odd time period like this needs to be broken up into days. If it spans a leap year, you may optionally divide the number of days by 365.25.[3]

Annualizing for periods less than a year

We have a manager who had a great January – his return was 8.78 percent. We want to annualize this.

Step 1: 0.0878
Step 2: 1.0878
Step 3: n = 1 month, so it's 1/12 (one twelfth of a year)

$$\sqrt[1/12]{1.0878} = 2.7453$$

Step 4: 1.7453
Step 5: 174.53 percent

Not bad. But, also not good, because you're not supposed to annualize for periods less than a year. Recall that I said earlier that instead of taking the nth root, you could raise the number to the $1/n^{th}$ root. What does that do when we have a time period of 1/12? It raise the number to the 1/(1/12) root, or 12th root! We are assuming that we'll continue to perform in this manner for the remainder of the year. We are violating a basic tenet of performance measurement, that "past performance is not an indication of future results." But, when we annualize a return of less than a year, that's essentially what we're doing.

Consequently, we have a rule, which was formally stated in both the GIPS and AIMR-PPS standards,[4] that you cannot annualize returns for periods less than a year. It's misleading. You are projecting a return for a shorter period onto a longer period, which is entirely the opposite of what we do when we annualize returns of periods greater than a year.

Is there an exception to this rule? You might say, yes. When we are dealing with money markets, it's not unusual for a short-term return to be annualized. But this is only done to provide an annual equivalent of what we're getting over a short period. This, to my knowledge, would be the only case where we would see this practice legitimately employed.

Chapter summary

In this chapter we introduced two very basic concepts within performance measurement: geometrically linking and annualization. Geometric linking is used to accumulate the returns of subperiods so that we can have a longer period cumulative return. Annualization produces an "average" which takes into consideration compounding for cumulative returns of one year or longer.

These two concepts are so essential that we suggest you memorize their formulas (or, at least have them readily available) because they are often called upon.

Exercises

1. Geometrically link the five annual mutual fund returns for Table 2-4 in Chapter 2.

2. Annualize the five-year cumulative return from above.

3. We have a cumulative return of 13.98% which spans the period June 30, 2000 through September 30, 2002. What's the annualized return?

ENDNOTES

[1] Spaulding, (2003, 2), page vii.

[2] Note: you may get a return of 54.01 percent. If you do, it's because of rounding.

[3] We hope to reach some consensus on the appropriate method for handling periods that involve leap years. As of this writing no such consensus yet exists.

[4] AIMR (1999), page 9; AIMR (2001), page 18.

Chapter 6 –
Time- Versus Money-weighted Returns

"If everybody agrees on something, you can be sure it's wrong!"
Anthony De Mello

"Every great idea starts out as a blasphemy"
Bertrand Russell

We've addressed time- and money-weighting separately; in this chapter we contrast them in great detail and provide you with some things to consider.

Over the past several years I have developed an increasing fondness for money-weighting such that I've concluded that in most cases it should be the preferred methodology, not time-weighting. While some might consider such a statement blasphemous, I'm pleased to report that (a) I'm not alone and (b) the movement to convert performance measurement professionals to this position is meeting with success.

Recall from Chapter 1 that money-weighting measures the performance of the account while time-weighting measures the performance of the manager. We've already learned why Peter Dietz, the Bank Administration Institute, etc., adopted the position that time-weighting is the ideal approach: because managers don't control the cash flows at the portfolio level, the client does. In deference to Dietz and the various groups that established standards in the mid-1960s and early 1970s, performance measurement was generally done at the portfolio level, so this linking of control of flows to the choice of methodologies was completely understandable. However, today we've gone well beyond portfolio-level returns and yet have failed to take the "cash flow control" issue into consideration when deciding on how to calculate returns.

In this chapter we will contrast the two methods and offer guidance on when each should be used.[1]

In the early years of performance measurement (e.g., 1960s and 1970s), the IRR was much more common. In fact, many authors felt that it was superior to time-weighting.[2] Hymans and Mulligan, in what is arguably the first book on performance measurement, referred to the IRR as the "true rate of return."[3]

Many people think that TWRR is the only way to go, with some suggesting it's "the industry standard." To support this, they often cite the AIMR-PPS or GIPS standards, even if the standards don't apply to their situation. Bacon, for example, has made his disdain for the IRR known for some time.[5] As a result, there's loads of confusion. Hopefully, this chapter will offer some clarity (and establish some ground rules, too).

Over the years I've occasionally read articles critical of time-weighted returns. The criticism is usually because the numbers occasionally don't make much intuitive sense. Mathematically, they're correct, but understanding what they mean can be a challenge.

I penned an article in 1998 that took a look at one such (albeit exaggerated) situation where the numbers didn't make a lot of sense (Spaulding (1998), I use this example in an introduction to performance class and never fail to get curious looks when I reveal the return figure. Time-weighting can be confusing and non-intuitive, often because we're using the wrong measure. And that's the point of this chapter. It is my contention that there are many (perhaps most) occasions when money-weighted returns should be preferred. I hope to convince you of this.

Bottom line – what's the real difference

The reason that Peter Dietz, the BAI, the ICAA, the AIMR-PPS, etc., encouraged (or required) the use of time-weighted returns is because money managers usually don't control cash flows.[6] And, if they don't control the flows, you can end up with different better (or worse) results because of the timing and size of the flows. Such situations are undesirable; thus we prefer TWRR which eliminate (if a true, exact return method is used) or reduce (if an approximation method is used) the effect of the flows. Fine. So in those cases where a money manager isn't controlling the flows, TWRR is the best way to operate. But that's it! For just about every other circumstance, we should use the MWRR. When we discuss money-weighting we usually mean the IRR, and this is what we'll use for most of this chapter; we will address a proxy for money-weighting later on. Let's look at some of these other circumstances and discuss why there's a value in having the MWRR.

Personal rates of return

Some mutual fund companies offer their clients "personal rates of return" along with time-weighted returns. We saw an example in Chapter 2 which showed examples of two individuals who each invested $75,000 into the same fund; while their exact TWRR are the same their MWRR are quite different: the MWRR took into consideration the impact of their contributions. Many investors find this information of value.

We provide another example in Appendix 6-E which you might find even more interesting.

Institutional returns

Note that I would advocate providing the money-weighted return along with the TWRR for institutions, too. This way, the institutional client can see how their individual portfolios did as a result of their contributions and withdrawals, along with how the manager performed. But I would suggest that institutions go well beyond that.

Question: how should an institution (e.g., a pension fund) measure their overall portfolio's performance? Answer: IRR. The institution controls the cash flows. The institution decides the asset allocation mix and when to add money, reduce money, rebalance, etc. And these events impact the performance of their portfolio. But if we use TWRR, we won't see the impact.

Ron Ryan is a big fan of liability-related indices in order to reflect how a fund is doing relative to an index that takes into account their anticipated expenses (Ryan (1997)). I agree with him. However, if the fund is measuring their performance using TWRR, then they aren't really getting the correct picture because they've eliminated the effect of the cash flows. Consequently, they may lose money and show a positive return (or the opposite situation may occur). The proper measure is the IRR.

Sub-portfolio returns

Consider this situation: we have a discretionary investment manager whose client decides when to add money to their account or make withdrawals. Therefore, the client controls the cash flows, and TWRR is the return-measure-of-choice to calculate the manager's return. Agreed.

However, once the manager gets the money, who decides when to overweight one sector and underweight another? Or, who decides when to make additional purchases of a security or to reduce their position? Answer: the manager. And these purchases and sales and weighting decisions are called *internal cash flows*. Thus, these cash flows are controlled by the manager and therefore should be measured by using IRR.

Let's look at an example. A portfolio contains several equity securities, including XYZ Industries. At the end of April there are 100 shares, with each share valued at $10 per share. When the stock price dips to $8.00 on the fifth of the month, the manager decides to purchase another 100 shares. Ten days later the price is now $6.00 per share. Since the manager is quite bullish about this stock, he decides to purchase another 200 shares. Five days after that, the price has hit $4.00 per share. Once again, the manager sees this as a tremendous buying opportunity and purchases 500 shares for his client. With but a few days left in the month, the price of the stock rises quickly and ends the month at $11 per share. So, what's the return on this stock as it sits in this portfolio? You (hopefully) don't need a calculator for this one, as you should be able to figure it out in your head. The answer is quite simple: 10 percent. While you may be nodding your head, you no doubt realize that some will question this, since it doesn't make sense when we consider those additional purchases during the month that the manager made. Need some proof? Well, let's use the following true daily rate of return formula:

$$R = \prod_{i=1}^{n} \frac{EMV_i}{BMV_i} - 1$$

and revalue the portfolio whenever a cash flow occurs:

$$R = \frac{800}{1000} \times \frac{1200}{1600} \times \frac{1600}{2400} \times \frac{9900}{3600} - 1 = \frac{1100}{1000} - 1 = 10\%$$

Remember, we're using time-weighted rates of return. And time-weighting eliminates the effect of cash flows. Therefore, those additional purchases meant nothing, as we simply compare the *starting* ($10) and *ending* ($11) values for the stock.

The only problem I have with this recommendation (to use money-weighting at the sub-portfolio level) is that the internal flows aren't always completely independent of the client. If a client adds cash to the portfolio, the manager must invest it. Thus, some of the purchases are in response to external flows. This being said, I'd still prefer to see money-weighted returns being employed here. And for this example, the result I came up with is 192.14 percent. Please see Appendix 6-B for the math.

Not convinced yet? Let's consider yet another example. Have you ever encountered a situation like the one shown in Table 6-1?

	Equities	Bonds	Cash	Total
ROR	2.32%	-0.85%	3.24%	6.01%

Table 6-1

At first, it appears a bit nonsensical. How can our portfolio's return exceed the returns of each of its components? If you've seen this, and even if you understand what's going on, explaining it can be a challenge. Let's look at the full year's portfolio and activity to uncover what's occurred (please refer to Table 6-2).

	Equities	Bonds	Cash	Total
BMV	10,000.00	10,000.00	80,000.00	100,000.00
ROR	-2.00%	-1.50%	0.80%	0.29%
EMV 1Q	9,800.00	9,850.00	80,640.00	100,290.00
ROR	-3.00%	-2.00%	0.80%	0.15%
EMV 2Q	9,506.00	9,653.00	81,285.12	100,444.12
Rebalance				
BMV	60,000.00	30,000.00	10,444.12	100,444.12
ROR	3.50%	1.20%	0.80%	2.53%
EMV 3Q	62,100.00	30,360.00	10,527.67	102,987.67
ROR	4.00%	1.50%	0.80%	2.94%
EMV 4Q	64,584.00	30,815.40	10,611.89	106,011.29
	Equities	Bonds	Cash	Total
ROR	2.32%	-0.85%	3.24%	6.01%

Table 6-2

Our portfolio began the year with €100,000. Our manager decided to allocate the funds as follows: 10% to equities, 10% to bonds, and the balance (80%) to cash. This strategy was apparently a wise one, given the returns for the first quarter (-2%, -1.5%, and 0.80%, respectively).

Sensing that both the equity and bond markets would remain in a less-than-desirable state, she did not alter the allocation as the second quarter began. Again, wise move, since equities and bonds had even worse quarters (-3% and -2% respectively) while cash continued to chug along at its 0.80% return.

As we begin the second half of the year, our manager decides to take a bold step and shift the balance in favor of equities, followed by bonds. And the equity market picked up, with a return of 3.50%, while bonds also did better, achieving a +1.20% return. No changes to the allocation for the fourth quarter, and we see further improvement, with equities achieving a 4% return and bonds getting to 1.50 percent.

When we geometrically link the four quarterly returns for our three asset classes, as well as our portfolio, we get the returns shown in Table 6-2. In other words, the manager does not get much credit for the cash allocation decision. But if the manager controls these decisions, what we'd consider *internal* cash flows, then is the time-weighted return the appropriate measure? After all, the portfolio's overall gain is attributable to these decisions, and the only way to really uncover them is to evaluate our performance by considering these flows. Thus, the argument (again) for using money-weighted returns at the sub-portfolio level. If we were to calculate the returns using the Internal Rate of Return, we obtain the results shown in Table 6-3.

	Equities	Bonds	Cash	Total
MWRR	11.84%	2.33%	3.24%	6.01%

Table 6-3

Do these returns make more sense? I would suggest that they do. Hope you agree.

The retail market

What type of returns should clients of brokerage firms get when the client accounts are non-discretionary, TWRR or MWRR?

Well, who controls the cash flows? The client. And who makes the investment decisions? Again, the client. Therefore, the answer seems pretty obvious to me: MWRR.

Several brokerage firms we deal with offer both methods. And software vendor Albridge Solutions, whose primary market is the brokerage community, previously used the Modified Dietz as an approximation to the IRR; they have since moved to the IRR. They also offer time-weighted returns but reported to me that most of their clients have adopted the money-weighted method.[7]

One huge advantage of MWRR over TWRR for retail clients is that there's less explaining to do. In volatile markets it's not unusual to find situations where a client lost money but had a positive return. This can be a challenge for the client to comprehend, especially since the return method is wrong to begin with.

However, a MWRR or IRR return won't result in these scenarios and will provide returns that are much more intuitive.

Are there occasions when time-weighting make sense for the retail investor? Yes; depending on how much involvement the client's financial planner has with their investment decisions, the TWRR can be an effective measure of that advice. However, to understand how they did with their investing, where they control the decisions and the flows, IRR is ideal.

Attribution

Steve Campisi raised the question about using money-weighted returns with attribution (Campisi (2004, 1)). He and I wrote a subsequent article addressing this in greater detail (Spaulding & Campisi (2007)); in the same issue, Bacon offered an alternative view (Bacon (2007)).

With attribution we are measuring the effect of the manager's decisions and to see how they contribute to the account's excess return. Since these decisions often involve various levels of allocation and selection, they fall into the "internal cash flow" arena and therefore call for money-weighting. But does anyone do this? Perhaps, but if so it isn't widespread.

But to use a TWRR return, we don't see how the manager's decisions paid off. For example, please refer to the example we discussed earlier, where the manager purchased XYZ Industries. If we use a TWRR and if the index also holds this security, the returns will be identical, even if the manager purchased additional shares of XYZ when the market was down. Does this make sense?

One of my favorites quotes comes from Brinson: "performance attribution, while still new, is still an evolving discipline."[8] Hopefully it will evolve further to reach a broad level of acceptance for money-weighted attribution.

Modified Dietz – Money-weighted?

In the first edition of this book I addressed the question about Modified Dietz being money-weighted.[9] At the time I was taking a somewhat middle-of-the-road position as the topic hadn't been completely vetted, and although it had been discussed in various forums, it hadn't been addressed in writing in much detail. I was also concerned that given the fact that most people viewed Modified Dietz as time-weighted, to suggest that in reality it's money-weighted would merely add confusion to an already confusing topic. I've since concluded that it's better to be clear on this matter:[10] Modified Dietz is money-weighted and is actually an approximation of the IRR. You may now question what we presented earlier when we said that Modified Dietz is an approximation of the exact time-weighted return. Well, it's that, too; it depends on how it's employed.

In Chapter 4 we provided Figure 4-B-1 as a graphical aid to help contrast time- and money-weighted returns. We've replicated it here (see Figure 6-1) with some slight modifications to reflect Modified Dietz as both time- and money-weighted. The key distinction:

*   when we chain-link Modified Dietz returns, we approximate a true TWRR (Exact Method)
*   when we only value the portfolio at the start and end of the period and weight the cash flows, we approximate a true MWRR (or IRR).

How good an approximation *is* the Modified Dietz return for the IRR? I'd say that in many cases it's quite close; so close, in fact, that many firms have adopted it rather than the IRR. The reason? It's easier to calculate. Recall that the IRR is an iterative process requiring a trial-and-error procedure to derive the solution. The Modified Dietz formula, however, involves a direct solution and is thus easier to program and easier to calculate.

But, as with the case where we use Modified Dietz to approximate the exact time-weighted rate of return, when large flows occur its accuracy can diminish.

Consider Scenario 2 from Chapter 2, where we began with $1 million, added another $1 million at the start of year 2, and ended with $2.94 million. Table 6-5 compares the results we get using Modified Dietz and the IRR. As you can see the results are quite similar (27.54% vs 28.61%). [11]

BMV	1
CF	1
EMV	2.94
W	0.5
RORModD	27.54%
IRR	28.61%

Table 6-4: Scenario from Chapter 2

	Client #1	Client #2
CF_1 (BMV)	5,000	25,000
CF_2	10,000	20,000
CF_3	15,000	15,000
CF_4	20,000	10,000
CF_5	25,000	5,000
EMV	103,804.57	103,893.77
ROR_{ModD}	12.76%	8.79%
IRR	14.25%	9.12%
Linked	82.30%	52.37%
	1.82	1.52
	12.76%	8.79%

Table 6-5: Clients #1 and #2 from Chapter 2

Internal Rate of Return / Modified Dietz (as MWRR)

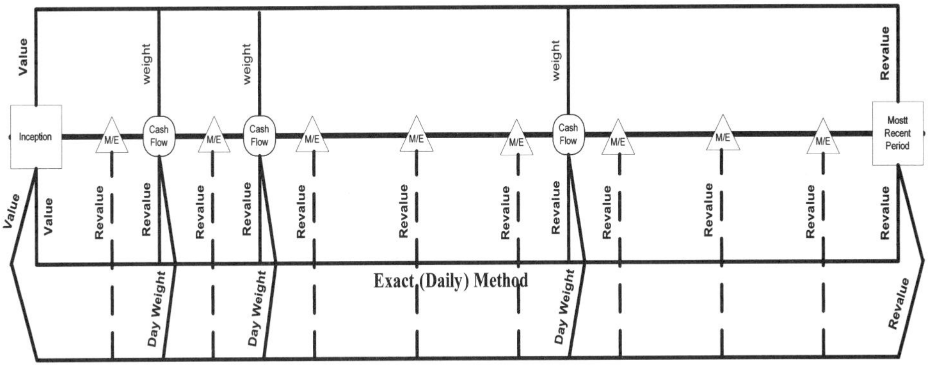

Modified BAI / Linked IRR / Modified Dietz (as TWRR)

Figure 6-1: Contrasting Time- and Money-weighted Returns

Likewise if we compare the results we obtain from the mutual fund examples in Chapter 2 (Client #1 and Client #2), we find the returns to be quite similar (see Table 6-5).[12]

There are occasions when the returns aren't as close. Here's such an example and the data we'll use:

- Length of period: 90 days
- Beginning market value: $99,450
- Ending market value: $343,610

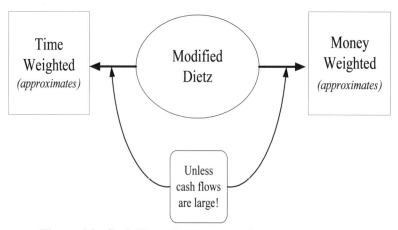

Figure 6-2: Cash Flows Impact Modified Dietz's Accuracy

- Cash flow: $500,000
- Date of cash flow: 62nd day.

Recall that the Modified Dietz formula is:

$$ROR = \frac{EMV - BMV - C}{BMV + W \times C}$$

Let's calculate the weighting factor:

$$W = \frac{CD - D}{CD} = \frac{90 - 62}{90} = 0.31111$$

We can now calculate the Modified Dietz return:

$$R = \frac{343,610 - 99,450 - 500,000}{99,450 + 0.31111 \times 500,000} = -1.0033 = -100.33\%$$

So how did we manage to lose more than 100% of our money? By my calculations, we had a total investment of $599,450 ($99,450 + $500,000) and ended with $343,610, meaning we lost $255,840. Hardly a 100% loss.

What do we get if we calculate the IRR? The IRR formula is as follows:

$$0 = -BMV - \frac{C_i}{(r+1)^{t_i}} + \frac{EMV}{(r+1)}$$

The interpretation of the signs is rather simple: we measure the result from our investments (putting money into the portfolio, which is equivalent to money coming out of our pocket) versus the amount we end up with (which is money coming back to us). Recall that because the IRR won't provide a direct solution if there are multiple cash flows, we must solve it for the IRR ("r") iteratively.

Table 6-6 provides the solution. As you can see, I used the "bracketing" or "bisection" method to arrive at the solution.[13] You'll also see that my first guess (which typically is the solution from Modified Dietz) resulted in an error. And why is this? Because the IRR does not support returns at or below -100%, which seems to be a deficiency, because there are obviously cases when one <u>can</u> lose more than 100 percent.[14] We find that the solution is -76.19 percent. Makes more sense, yes? And, the error of more than 24% (which is also more than a 100% loss) is both extreme and nonsensical.

Guess	Result
-100.33%	#NUM!
-99%	22,328,600.07
-80%	103,354.65
-60%	(180,379.68)
-70%	(100,059.91)
-75%	(24,349.91)
-77%	18,346.55
-76%	(4,139.98)
-76.50%	6,798.28
-76.25%	1,255.60
-76.10%	(1,999.07)
-76.20%	164.88
-76.15%	(920.00)
-76.18%	(269.77)
-76.19%	**(52.56)**

Table 6-6: Solving for the IRR

While the Modified Dietz is a fantastic formula that works well most of the time, there are occasions when it seems to fail us. So beware!

Solving for the IRR

Since the Internal Rate of Return requires iteration, various approaches have been developed to find the solution. Three of the most commonly used are bisection, Newton-Raphson, and Secant. We briefly discussed these in Chapter 2 and will go into greater detail below.

Common practices

When it comes to the IRR there aren't a lot of "common practices" today, although we hope that with the publishing of the IRR Standards Working Group's white paper, many will be adopted.

One practice that's common is to begin the process with the result we obtain using the Modified Dietz formula. As noted above, the Modified Dietz is an approximation to the IRR and is often identified as the "first order approximation." Essentially the situation is that we need to pick "some number" to start with, and the Modified Dietz at least "gets us in the neighborhood" of what the result is.

Summary

Hopefully this chapter has provided you with some ideas about money-weighting and has demonstrated some compelling reasons to use it. When trying to decide which to use, begin with the question "who controls the cash flows?" Also ask, "what are we trying to measure?" These should serve as guides as to which approach, if not both, to calculate and report.

Appendix 6-A – Calculating the IRR for the first example

Table 6-A-1 shows how each investor made their respective purchases during the month. We also show the days in each month as well as the weights. We use this information to calculate our returns.

Month	NAV	Investor #1	Investor #2	Days	Weights
Jan	10	1,000	1,000	31	
Feb	11			28	
Mar	12			31	
Apr	8		800	30	0.671233
May	14	1,400		31	0.586301
Jun	9			30	
Jul	11			31	
Aug	15	1,500		31	0.334247
Sep	9		900	30	0.252055
Oct	10			31	
Nov	9			30	
Dec	11			31	
Total Investment		3,900	2,700	365	
EMV =		3,300	3,300		
Gain/Loss		(600)	600		

Table 6-A-1: Investor Details

We're going to calculate the Internal Rate of Return for each investor. But to do that we need to perform an iterative process in an attempt to find the correct return. The Modified Dietz can be used as the first approximation to what the actual IRR is, so let's begin with that. And to do that we need to come up with the weight (since we're dealing with *weighted flows*). Since we're only valuing the portfolio twice (at the start and end of the year), the weight is for the full year. For example, Investor #1 purchased 100 shares on May 31. What weight does this represent? If you look at the "Days" column in the table, you see the number of days leading up to and including May (31, 28, 31, 30, 31). We add these together, to get the *day of the cash flow* (the result is 151). Our formula for the weight is:

$$W = \frac{CD - D}{CD} = \frac{365 - 151}{365} = 0.586301$$

You can see that this value is in the "Weights" column, along with the respective weights for the other three cash flows. We can now calculate the Modified Dietz for both investors. Here's the math for Investor #1:

$$ModDietz_{\#1} = \frac{EMV - BMV - \sum C}{BMV + \sum W \times C} =$$

$$\frac{3300 - 1000 - (1400 + 1500)}{1000 + (0.586301 \times 1400 + 0.334247 \times 1500)} = -25.84\%$$

You're invited to calculate it for Investor #2. The answer is 34.02 percent.

Now that we have these values, we can derive the respective IRRs. We need to take into consideration the timing of cash flows. We raise them to a power that reflects the timing. For simplicity, I used the month that the flow occurred, rather than days. For Investor #1:

$$IRR_{\#1} = 1,000 + \left(\frac{1,400}{(1+r)^{5/12}}\right) + \left(\frac{1,500}{(1+r)^{8/12}}\right) - \left(\frac{3,300}{1+r}\right) = 0$$

We now have to find the *r* which will satisfy this equation. Table 6-A-1 shows the process I went through, beginning with the Modified Dietz return we just calculated.

As you can see, the return that came closest to solving this equation (i.e., to get a value of zero) was -24.86 percent. That's our solution.

We invite you to try it for Investor #2. You should get the result 35.16 percent.

Investor #1 IRR	
-25.84%	(33.2)
27.00%	947.9
-26.00%	(38.9)
-25.50%	(21.6)
-25.00%	(4.6)
-24.00%	28.6
-24.90%	(1.2)
-24.80%	2.1
-24.85%	0.5
-24.86%	**0.1**
-24.84%	0.8
-24.87%	(0.2)

Table 6-A-2: Iterative Process to Find the IRR

Appendix 6-B – Calculating the IRR for the third example

The input is shown in Table 6-B-1.

	XYZ Industries		
	# Shares	Price	MV
30-Apr	100	10.00	1,000
5-May	100	8.00	800
15-May	200	6.00	1,200
20-May	500	4.00	2,000
31-May	900	11.00	9,900

Table 6-B-1

I solved for the IRR by using this formula:

$$IRR_{XYZ} =$$

$$1,000 + \left(\frac{800}{(1+r)^{5/31}} \right) + \left(\frac{1,200}{(1+r)^{15/31}} \right) + \left(\frac{2,000}{(1+r)^{20/31}} \right) - \left(\frac{9,900}{(1+r)} \right)$$

As you know, the IRR is solved iteratively (i.e., by trial-and-error). As noted above, a   rule-of-thumb is to start with the result you'd obtain by using the

Modified Dietz formula (which serves as the "first order" approximation to the IRR). The result using the Modified Dietz is 163.33 percent.

My trial-and-errors appear in Table 6-B-2.

Test	Result
163.33%	(253.17)
165.00%	(236.86)
170.00%	(189.27)
200.00%	59.79
180.00%	(99.68)
190.00%	(16.90)
195.00%	22.16
193.00%	6.72
192.00%	(1.10)
192.50%	2.82
192.30%	1.25
192.10%	(0.31)
192.15%	0.08
192.13%	(0.08)
192.14%	**0.00**

Table 6-B-2

And, as you can see, I hit the mark with 192.14 percent. By using the IRR, as opposed to the TWRR, we present a return that reflects the additional purchases (i.e., internal cash flows) that the manager made.

Appendix 6-C – Calculating the IRR for the second example

Here are the formulas I used to calculate the IRR:

$$IRR_{Equities} = 10,000 + \left(\frac{50,494}{(1+r)^{1/2}} \right) - \left(\frac{64,584}{1+r} \right) = 0$$

$$IRR_{Bonds} = 10,000 + \left(\frac{20,347}{(1+r)^{1/2}} \right) - \left(\frac{30,815.40}{1+r} \right) = 0$$

$$IRR_{Cash} = 80,000 + \left(\frac{-70,841}{(1+r)^{1/2}} \right) - 10,661.89 = 0$$

The solutions are found via an iterative process; I use the Modified Dietz return as the starting point. Table 6-C-1 shows what I went through to get the results.

Equities		Bonds		Cash	
Trial	**Result**	**Trial**	**Result**	**Trial**	**Result**
11.60%	-72.02883	2.32%	-1.32469147	3.26%	8.963381877
12.00%	48.059536	3.00%	130.6307451	4.00%	330.9397921
11.80%	-12.439163	2.50%	33.52922498	2.00%	-546.860076
11.90%	17.841984	2.40%	13.98079733	3.00%	-104.5214368
11.85%	2.7093715	2.38%	10.06595408	3.10%	-60.6687378
11.83%	-3.3481303	2.35%	4.190460651	3.20%	-16.88463166
11.84%	**-0.31906**	2.34%	2.231101359	**3.24%**	**0.60984409**
		2.33%	**0.2713111**	3.25%	4.981753909
		2.31%	-3.64956283	3.23%	-3.762749196

Table 6-C-1

Appendix 6-D – When the numbers don't make sense

Let's be realistic: the returns don't always seem to make sense.

In Chapter 2 we showed some examples of money-weighted returns that did-n't look correct – returns that weren't intuitive. Can this happen with time-weighted returns, too? Yes.

Let's go over an example to demonstrate this.[15]

	Activity	Position	Market Value
1 January	Account opens with €1,000 Purchase 1,000 shares of STAR at €1 per share	1,000 shares of STAR @ €1/share	€1,000
30 June		1,000 shares of STAR @ €100/share	€100,000
1 July	€1,000,000 inflow Purchase 1,000 DOG @ €1,000 per share	1,000 shares of STAR @ €100/share 1,000 shares of DOG @ €1,000/share	€1,100,000
31 December		1,000 shares of STAR @ €100/share 1,000 shares of DOG @ €100/share	€200,000

Table 6-D-1: Portfolio Activity

Table 6-D-1 shows the situation we'll be considering. As you can see, the client invests €1,000 and the manager purchases 1,000 shares of a one stock, which is valued at €1 per share, for a starting market value of €1,000.

Six months later, the stock has increased its share price considerably, to €100 per share, meaning our account is now valued at €100,000. Seeing this, the client decides to now invest €1 million.

The manager takes the additional funds and invests it entirely in another security, DOG, which is priced at €1,000 per share. So, the portfolio begins the second half of the year valued at €1.1 million.

Six months go by, and we find that STAR hasn't changed in price, but DOG has dropped to €100 per share, meaning the portfolio is now valued at €200,000. This also means that the portfolio has lost €801,000.

Before we calculate the return, think about this situation for a moment: our client began with €1,000, which grew to €100,000; the client then added €1 million. The account value at year-end is €200,000, reflecting a €801,000 loss.

So, our return will be what? Positive or negative? A large number or a small number?

Let's find out. Let's begin by calculating the return for the first half of the year:

$$R = \frac{100,000}{1,000} - 1 = 9,900\%$$

Since we began with €1,000 and ended with €100,000, our return is exceptional: 9,900 percent.

Now, let's look at the second half of the year:

$$R = \frac{200,000}{1,100,000} - 1 = -81.82\%$$

A disappointing -81.82% because we lost €900,000 in the period.

When we geometrically link these values, what do we get?

$$R = \left[\left(\frac{9,900\%}{100} + 1 \right) \times \left(\frac{(-81.82\%)}{100} + 1 \right) - 1 \right] \times 100 = 1,718.18\%$$

If you're like most people, this figure seems a bit odd. First, that it's positive, given the fact that we've lost so much money. Second, because it's so large! How can this be? Does this make any sense at all?

If we were to use the Internal Rate of Return, we'd get a result of approximately -96%[16] – doesn't this make more sense, given our tremendous loss?

At this point, you may be questioning the reason why we encourage the use of TWRR...I know I did. But let's take this example and change the numbers around a bit (see Table 6-D-2).

In this example, our client begins with €1 million, all invested in STAR, which, as before, increases its share price from €1 to €100, meaning our portfolio ends the first half of the year valued at €100 million. However, instead of adding money, our client withdrawals €98.9 million, leaving €1.1 million, which is then split between STAR and DOG. At the end of the year, STAR remains at €100 per share, and DOG has slipped from €1,000 to €100 per share.

Let's calculate our returns, starting with the first half of the year:

$$R = \frac{100,000,000}{1,000,000} - 1 = 9,900\%$$

Here, our portfolio increased from a starting value of €1 million to €100 million, yielding a return of 9,900 percent. For the second half of the year we have:

$$R = \frac{200,000}{1,100,000} - 1 = -81.82\%$$

Our portfolio started the second half with €1,000,000, but lost €900,000, ending the year at €200,000, which gives us a return of -81.82 percent.

	Activity	Position	Market Value
1 January	Account opens with €1,000,000 Purchase 1,000,000 shares of STAR at €1 per share	1,000,000 shares of STAR @ €1/share	€1,000,000
30 June		1,000,000 shares of STAR @ €100/share	€100,000,000
1 July	Withdrawal of €98.9 M (leaving €1.1 M in the account) Sale of 999,000 shares of STAR (leaving 1,000 shares) Purchase of 1,000 DOG @ €1,000/share	1,000 shares of STAR @ €100/share 1,000 shares of DOG @ €1,000/share	€1,100,000
31 December		1,000 shares of STAR @ €100/share 1,000 shares of DOG @ €100/share	€200,000

Table 6-D-2: Portfolio Activity

And, geometrically linking these numbers we get:

$$R = \left[\left(\frac{9,900\%}{100} + 1 \right) \times \left(\frac{(-81.82\%)}{100} + 1 \right) - 1 \right] \times 100 = 1,718.18\%$$

This is identical to our first example. You may be wondering at this point what's going on. After all, in our first case our client lost €800,000, while in this case our client made over €98 million.

What's going on is time-weighting.

Did our manager perform any differently for these two portfolios? No. In both cases, she began with the entire portfolio invested in STAR, which increased from 1 to €100 per share. And, in each case, she began the second half of the year with 1,000 shares invested in both STAR and DOG.

What's the difference between these two cases? It is the amount of money available at any point in time as a result of the contributions and/or withdrawals. And who is responsible for this, the manager? No. The client. And since the client controls the cash flows, we cannot hold the manager responsible for them.

In our first example, our client happened to make a huge contribution, just as the market was about to turn; in the second case, the client wisely (or because of sheer good luck) withdrew a significant portion of his funds before the market turned bad.

The time-weighted rate of return captures the manager's decisions. And, as we've already said, the manager performed exactly the same in both cases, so why shouldn't her return be identical?

Saying this, I wouldn't want to be the one to get the phone call from the first client inquiring into how we could dare to report a 1,718.18% return when he lost money, but that's another matter.

We hope that this material has enhanced your understanding of these concepts.

Appendix 6-E – Personal rates of return

Let's look at an example which might be a bit more realistic. We have two investors who both purchase shares in a mutual fund, whose monthly net-asset-values (NAVs) are as shown Figure 6-E-1.

Both investors begin by buying 100 shares at the end of the year's NAV ($10). Investor #1 makes two subsequent purchases of 100 shares each, one at the end of May (with an NAV of $14) and the other at the end of August (NAV of $16). The second investor also makes two additional purchases of 100 shares each, but hers are at the end of April (NAV of $8) and September (NAV of $9). We can see that the fund's NAV closes the year at $11.

Table 6-E-1 summarizes the contributions and profits/losses of each investor.

Our second investor seems to adhere to the adage *buy low, sell high*; we can't say this for our first, who made purchases at the peaks of the NAV during the year. Consequently, the first investor shows an unrealized loss of $600 while the second shows a gain.

Since time-weighting eliminates the affect of cash flows, we should get the same result for the fund and the two investors. From the following, we can see that we do:

$$ROR_{Fund} = \frac{EMV}{BMV} - 1 = \frac{11}{10} - 1 = 10\%$$

$$ROR_{\#1} = \prod_{i=1}^{n} \frac{EMV_i}{BMV_i} - 1 = \frac{1,400}{1,000} \times \frac{3,000}{2,800} \times \frac{3,300}{4,500} - 1 = 10\%$$

$$ROR_{\#2} = \prod_{i=1}^{n} \frac{EMV_i}{BMV_i} - 1 = \frac{800}{1,000} \times \frac{1,800}{1,600} \times \frac{3,300}{2,700} - 1 = 10\%$$

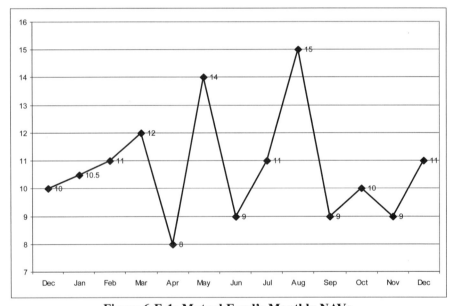

Figure 6-E-1: Mutual Fund's Monthly NAVs

Here's an opportunity to introduce the dollar-weighted or money-weighted return: the Internal Rate of Return or IRR. We'll begin with Investor #1.

Table 6-E-2 shows the purchases of each investor, as well as the days in each month. We need these days to derive our weighted cash flows in the Modified Dietz formula. Recall from Chapter 3 we introduced the weighting factor, which we use with the Modified Dietz formula. Here we'll use the Modified Dietz as our

	Investor #1	Investor #2
Initial Investment	$1,000	$1,000
April Purchase	-0-	$800
May Purchase	$1,400	-0-
August Purchase	$1,500	-0-
September Purchase	-0-	$900
Total Contributions	$3,900	$2,700
End of Year Market Value	$3,300	$3,300
Profit/Loss	-$600	$600
Time-weighted ROR	10%	10%

Figure 6-E-1: Investor Activity

starting point to solve for the IRR. For Investor #1, we begin with a purchase of 100 shares of the fund, with an NAV of $10 ($1,000). There are two subsequent cash flows ($1,400 and $1,500). The ending market value is $3,300. We calculate the Modified Dietz for the full year, weighting the flows from the beginning of the year:

$$W_{\#1,1} = \frac{CD - D}{CD} = \frac{365 - (31 + 28 + 31 + 30 + 31)}{365} = \frac{214}{365} = 0.586301$$

$$W_{\#1,2} = \frac{365 - (31 + 28 + 31 + 30 + 31 + 30 + 31 + 31)}{365} = \frac{122}{365} = 0.334247$$

We can now calculate the Modified Dietz for Investor #1:

$$ModifiedDietz_{\#1} = \frac{EMV - BMV - \Sigma C}{BMV + \Sigma W \times C} =$$

$$\frac{3,300 - 1,000 - (1,400 + 1,500)}{1,000 + (0.586301 \times 1,400) + (0.334247 \times 1,500)} = -25.84\%$$

We will use this value as our starting point to derive our IRR. In Chapter 2, we introduced the following formula to derive the IRR:

$$0 = BMV + \left(\sum_{j=1}^{n-1} \frac{F_j}{(1+r)^{t_j}} \right) - \frac{EMV}{(1+r)^{t_n}}$$

Table 6-E-3 shows the iterations I went through to find the solution. You can see that we get closest to zero with a return of -24.86 percent.

Month	NAV	Investor #1	Investor #2	Days in month
December	10	1,000	1,000	
January	10			31
February	11			28
March	12			31
April	8		800	30
May	14	1,400		31
June	9			30
July	11			31
August	15	1,500		31
September	9		900	30
October	10			31
November	9			30
December	11			31
Total Investment		3,900	2,700	
Ending Market Value		3,300	3,300	
Gain / Loss		- 600	+600	

Table 6-E-2: Investments and Data for IRR and Modified Dietz

We find the IRR for Investor #2 the same way. We first calculate the weights for our flows:

$$W_{\#2,1} = \frac{365 - (31 + 28 + 31 + 30)}{365} = 0.671233$$

$$W_{\#2,2} = \frac{365 - (31 + 28 + 31 + 30 + 31 + 30 + 31 + 31 + 30)}{365} = 0.252055$$

We can now solve the Modified Dietz for this investor:

$$ModifiedDietz_{\#2=} \frac{3,300 - 1,000 - (800 + 900)}{1,000 + (0.671233 \times 800) + (0.252055 \times 900)} = 34.02\%$$

Our formula for finding the IRR is:

$$IRR_{\#2} = 1,000 + \left(\frac{800}{(1+r)^{4/12}}\right) + \left(\frac{900}{(1+r)^{9/12}}\right) - \left(\frac{3,300}{1+r}\right) = 0$$

Again, we will use the Modified Dietz solution as our starting point. Table 6-E-4 shows our iterations to obtain the result: 35.16 percent.

For an investor who's interested in how his portfolio performed, the IRR is often a better representation, although the time-weighted return, in spite of its occasional lack of intuitiveness, is best to present the performance of the manager.

Trial	Result	Trial	Result
-25.84%	-33.2	34.02%	-14.2
-26.00%	-38.9	20.00%	-212.2
-25.50%	-21.6	35.00%	-2.0
-25.00%	-4.6	36.00%	10.2
-24.00%	28.6	35.50%	4.1
-24.90%	-1.2	35.20%	0.5
-24.80%	-2.1	35.10%	-0.8
-24.85%	0.5	35.15%	-0.1
-24.86%	0.1	35.19%	0.3
-24.84%	0.8	35.18%	0.2
-24.87%	-0.2	35.16%	0.0

Table 6-E-3: Finding the IRR Solution for the Investor #1 **Table 6-E-4: Finding the IRR Solution for the Investor #2**

ENDNOTES

[1] Some of what's shared in this chapter originally appeared in Spaulding (2005, 2).

[2] See, for example, Eadie (1973) and Green (1989).

[3] Hymans & Mulligan (1980).

[4] See, for example, Hayes (2000). We find "Time-weighted return: The industry standard, time-weighted return gives equal weight to each time period covered in the report, regardless of the differences in the amount invested. The logic is that money managers have no control over cash flow. The Association for Investment Management and Research requires time-weighted reporting in its presentation standards." This article is geared for registered representatives (financial planners) who deal in the retail market; why do they care about the AIMR-PPS?

[5] See, for example, Bacon (2007) and Bacon (2007/2008).

[6] In those cases where the manager controls the flows (e.g., venture capital / private placement management), then the IRR is the appropriate measure.

[7] This was reported to me in a phone conversation.

[8] Brinson et al.(1986), page 40.

[9] Spaulding (2005, 1), pages 33-39.

[10] See for example Spaulding (2004, 1).

[11] Because this is a two-year period, the Modified Dietz return we derive is a cumulative one; to compare it with the IRR we must annualize it.

[12] Here we're dealing with a five-year period, so the cumulative return we obtain using the Modified Dietz again needs to be annualized in order to compare it with the IRR.

[13] One of the goals of the IRR Standards Working Group we formed (see last month's issue) will be to identify the preferred method to arrive at the solution; other options include Newton-Raphson and Secant.

[14] This, too, will be addressed by the IRR Standards Working Group.

[15] This example is taken from Spaulding, 1998.

[16] You're invited to try this using what we discussed in Chapter 2. However, I think you'll find it difficult, unless you know the answer (96%) right away. I used the Excel XIRR function, which gave me a result of 95.97 percent. Using the method from Chapter 2, I found that 96.00 gave me the best result.
Note: if you calculate the return using Modified Dietz, you'll get -159.88%, emphasizing why revaluing the portfolio for large cash flows makes sense.

Chapter 7 –
Return on Leverage & Derivatives

"If I had a lever big enough I could move the world"

Archimedes

In this chapter we'll tackle a few situations where some special consideration is needed – leverage and derivatives.

Return on short positions

We'll begin with handling returns on short positions.

The first time I encountered a situation with shorts was in the late 1980s. I turned to an associate for his thoughts. The challenge with shorts is that the results can seem in reverse of what we expect. For example, let's say we decide to sell short 100 shares of a stock with a price of $20. That is, we are selling short a market value of $2,000. If, as we predict, the price drops, we will want to capture our return. Let's say it drops by 10%, to $18 a share. So our beginning market value was -$2,000 and our ending is -$1,800. If we apply our basic return formula

$$ROR = \frac{EMV - BMV}{BMV}$$

we have:

$$ROR = \frac{-1800 - (-2000)}{-2000} = \frac{200}{-2000} = -10\%$$

But this doesn't make sense, does it? We didn't lose 10 percent. So the suggestion was made to take the absolute value of the denominator:

$$ROR = \frac{EMV - BMV}{|BMV|}$$

Let's see how that affects our example:

$$ROR = \frac{-1800 - (-2000)}{|-2000|} = \frac{200}{2000} = 10\%$$

Which seems to work quite well. And so this is the way I would explain how to calculate returns on shorts. Until, that is, I read Jose Menchero's award-winning article on the subject.[1] While I'm aware that this other approach is still commonly used, Jose's method takes into consideration the full aspect of a short position, including interest.

We will now draw from Jose's article to explain the approach we should take. First, some background on short selling.

When we engage in short selling, we're borrowing the securities from somewhere else.[2] The investor has to pay interest on this loan and commits to repaying it (that is, to replace the securities) at some point in the future. The investor is betting that between the time they borrow and sell the securities that the price will drop, thus enabling them to acquire the asset at a reduced rate and making a profit on the spread (the difference between what they originally sold the securities for and the amount they later had to pay to acquire them, in order to repay them to the party who loaned them out).

When the investor sells the securities short, they don't get the proceeds; rather, they are held as collateral (in margin). The investor usually has to place additional funds in margin in case the security's price increases in value (*i.e.*, goes against the direction anticipated by the investor). For our purposes, we'll assume a margin amount of 50 percent. Note that the investor will get interest on both the proceeds from the sale as well as the funds that are on margin.

So, continuing with our earlier example, the proceeds from the short sale ($2,000) are retained by the broker, as well as a margin payment (50% of $2,000 = $1,000), for a total of $3,000. Let's assume that these funds will receive 3% interest.

As noted earlier, the price has dropped to $1,800.

Let's start by ignoring the interest that we receive and concentrate only on the fluctuation in the market value of the security. As Table 7-1 shows, we begin with a cash position of $1,000, which we use as our margin amount (50% of the proceeds of the short sale). Since the security is short, its value shows up as a negative amount on our books. The proceeds ($2,000) have joined the 50% margin payment (the $1,000) from cash. Thus, our total market value is as it began – $1,000. Now, a year later, the price of the asset has dropped by 20 percent.[3]

We can now calculate our return:

$$ROR = \frac{EMV - BMV}{BMV} = \frac{1200 - 1000}{1000} = \frac{200}{1000} = 20\%$$

	Starting Point	Initial Transaction	End of Period
Market Value of Security	--	($2,000)	($1,800)
Cash Position	$1,000	--	--
Margin Cash	--	$3,000	$3,000
Total	$1,000	$1,000	$1,200

Table 7-1: Short Sale Example, without Interest

We get the 20% return that we would have expected. Now, let's add in the interest we are entitled to because of the funds which are on margin (see Table 7-2).

	Starting Point	Initial Transaction	End of Period
Market Value of Security	---	($2,000)	($1,800)
Cash Position	$1,000	---	---
Margin Cash	---	$3,000	$3,000
Interest on Margin	---	---	(3% x $3,000) = $90
Total	$1,000	$1,000	$1,290

Table 7-2: Short Sale Example, with Interest

As you can see, our investor has not only benefitted because of her decision to short this security, but also because of the interest obtained during the period.

$$ROR = \frac{EMV - BMV}{BMV} = \frac{1290 - 1000}{1000} = \frac{290}{1000} = 29\%$$

	Starting Point	Initial Transaction	A year later (before purchase)	A year later (after purchase)
Market Value of Security	--	($2,000)	($1,800)	--
Cash Position	$1,000	--	--	$1,200
Margin Cash	--	$3,000	$3,000	--
Interest on Margin	--	--	(3% x $3,000) = $90	$90
Total	$1,000	$1,000	$1,290	$1,290

Table 7-3: Short Sale Data for Return Calculation

What if the investor decides to purchase the security in the open market and then replace it for the shares which were borrowed? As Table 7-3 shows, it's just a matter of accounting – where we account for our cash. We purchase the security for $1,800[4] and return the securities to the original owner (from where we borrowed them). We no longer have an obligation to maintain a margin position, so these funds are shifted to our cash position, which reflects the monies we began with ($1,000) and the difference in our original short sale price ($2,000) and our later purchase ($1,800). We have continued to isolate our interest received ($90), simply to highlight it. Our return would be identical to the one above, since our ending position has not changed.

While the simpler idea we discussed at the beginning of this chapter (using the absolute value of the denominator) may make intuitive sense, it fails to recognize the other accounting activities which are actually taking place in such a transaction. Through Jose Menchero's efforts, we can see that this more detailed approach yields the correct result and would be the preferred approach.

Return on derivatives

Perhaps we should begin with a definition of derivatives. In essence, they're securities which *derive* their value from another asset. Examples are options and futures. We'll briefly touch on both.

Return on futures

As with the short sale example, I recall asking a colleague the approach she used to derive returns on futures, since the "market value" of the portfolio could grow significantly because of the leverage which is employed when engaged in such an asset. She told me that she valued the portfolio at the total value of the future, thus showing a phenomenally large jump in value. This didn't make sense to me at the time. She suggested that when the future position was closed out, the value would return to a point where the math would all work out correctly. I didn't buy it and my intuition was correct.

In the very first issue of *The Journal of Performance Measurement*, John Stannard wrote his first of a two-part series on this topic.[5]

As John pointed out, "Investment return measures the relative change in market value. However, futures contracts are not like conventional assets such as stocks and bonds in which the market value is calculated as the number of hold-ings times the price. Futures have a 'price,' which is the basis for determining gains/losses on the futures position, but the investor is not required to pay this price on opening the contract."[6]

So how do we handle futures? John explained "futures have a *net realizable value* which represents the profit or loss arising from changes in price each day."[7]

With futures, we use what's called the "notional market value," which is the "equivalent amount of physical security that would cause the same change in net realizable value for a given change in the price of the underlying security."[8] We arrive at the futures contract's notional market value by multiplying the futures price by a constant value called the contract value multiplier or tick size.

Let's use the S&P futures contract as an example, with a price of 400. In this case, the contract value multiplier is $500. We can then calculate the notional mar-ket value, V_N, as follows:

$$V_{N_0} = 400 \times \$500 = \$200,000$$

We measure the "notional stock return" as the change in notional market value over time. If our S&P contract price increases by 5%, our notional value will change as follows:

$$V_{N_1} = 420 \times \$500 = \$210,000$$

We can now calculate our notional stock return as we do with market values:

$$ROR = \frac{EMV - BMV}{BMV} = \frac{V_{N_1} - V_{N_0}}{V_{N_0}} = \frac{210000 - 200000}{200000} = \frac{10000}{20000} = 5\%$$

Futures with stock position

The above method is the approach recommended by John Stannard to calcu-late returns of futures. And, as noted above, it's consistent with methods suggest-ed by others.

In 2003, the Leverage & Derivatives Subcommittee of the Investment Performance Council came up with proposed standards.[9]

As stated in this document, "In general, calculating returns for portfolios that use leverage and/or derivatives is the same as calculating returns for non-lever-aged portfolios. Returns are calculated by dividing the change in market value of the portfolio by the beginning market value of the portfolio."[10]

In an accompanying example, the document explains how this is done for futures. They show a case with stock plus long futures. While they don't go into the detail that Stannard does, the concept for the futures asset is essentially the same – the difference is in notional values.

They provide a simple example for a situation where we have stocks and futures: we have a $90 position in stocks, a futures position with a notional value of $60, and $10 on margin (for the futures position) (see Table 7-4). The market value for the starting point is $100. How was this arrived at? The $60 future isn't included in the market value.

At the end of the period, the stock position has gone to $96, while the notional value of the future is at $63. In addition, we've earned $0.02 in interest. The ending period market value doesn't include the futures value but the difference in notional values.

	Start	End
Stock Position	$90	$96
Margin Cash	$10	$10
Interest on Margin	--	$0.02
Difference in Notional Values	n/a	$63-$60=$3
Total Market Value	$100	$109.02

Table 7-4: Example from Leverage and Derivatives Subcommittee Proposed Standards

The return can be calculated using our standard method:

$$ROR = \frac{EMV - BMV}{EMV} = \frac{109.02 - 100}{100} = 9.02\%$$

In both this approach and the one Stannard suggests, we do not include the market value of the futures position in our portfolio market value; rather, we track the change in notional values.

Calculating a return for a portfolio investing on margin[11]

Here, we'll address the situation where the investor has a margin account which allows them to borrow in order to leverage their investment. Let's say that our investor puts $100 into their margin account. They are able to leverage two-to-one – that is, they have to have 50% of whatever the value is of what they're buying. Because they're borrowing the remaining amount, they're obligated to pay interest. Let's use an interest rate of 4 percent.

Table 7-5 provides us with an example where we have $100 to invest; meaning we can buy up to $200 in stock, which is what we do. At the end of the period, our investment has gone up by 5 percent. We owe $4.00 in interest. Our return is:

$$ROR = \frac{EMV - BMV}{EMV} = \frac{106 - 100}{100} = 6\%$$

	Start	Initial Purchase	End
Stock Position		$200	$210
Margin Cash	$100	---	
Loan Amount	---	$100	$100
Interest Owed	---	---	$100 ×. 04 = $4.00
Total Market Value		$200 - $100 = $100	$210 - $100 - $4 = 106

Table 7-5: Margin Example

The margin account allows us to leverage our investment. Thus, even though the stock only went up 5%, we were able to obtain an even greater return (6%), even after our interest payment.

Return on Currency Overlays[12]

Plan sponsors may turn to a currency overlay specialist to alter the portfolio's exposure to currency risk or to enhance the return via a currency strategy. Such strategies involve over-the-counter contracts – typically spot and forward foreign exchange contracts via futures or options. As is the case with the futures contracts noted above, these mandates do not involve the exchange of money – they're unfunded and are based on notional values.

When calculating the return on the overlay strategy, we use the notional value of the overlay:

$$ROR_{Overlay} = \frac{EndingNotionalValue - BeginningNotionalValue}{BeginningNotionalValue}$$

If the sponsor wishes to combine this strategy's performance with that of the entire portfolio, then we'd be looking again at a situation where we capture the change in notional value, as we did above.

Money-weighting impact

The astute observer will note that this chapter is essentially what appeared in the first edition (as Chapter 6). The new Chapter 6 contrasts time- and money-weighting and suggests that we employ money-weighting at the sub-portfolio level. What we have presented here is entirely from a time-weighted perspective. Additional research is needed to determine what, if any, changes are needed to incorporate the money-weighted approach.

Summary

Certain security or transaction types require their own rules for performance measurement. This chapter touched on a few of these. The concepts can no doubt carry over to other situations that may arise. The key is to be aware of what's taking place, and don't assume that because something seems intuitive that it's correct.

Exercises

1. A portfolio begins the year with $100 in cash and immediately shorts stock worth $200. At the end of the year, the stock is valued at $205. The interest earned on any cash in margin is 5 percent. What's the return?

2. An investor purchases an S&P futures contract with a price of 400. The contract value multiplier is $500. At the end of the month the contract is valued at 405. What's the notional stock return on this contract?

ENDNOTES

[1] Menchero (2002/2003), pages 39-50. Jose won the Dietz Award for this paper.

[2] You may be familiar with the concept of securities lending, where someone who owns securities makes them available to be lent. They receive compensation for this. Custodians and clearing brokers typically have securities lending departments that control these processes.

[3] We could possibly be entitled to reduce our margin commitment, given the drop in

price, but we're going to ignore these details in our example, as they don't enhance this presentation.

[4] For simplicity, we're not including the transaction cost in this example. It would obviously have a slight impact on our return, but such details aren't necessary to demonstrate what's taking place.

[5] Stannard (1996). We found that John's approach is consistent with other approaches; see for example, LIFFE (1992).

[6] Stannard (1996), pages 27-28.

[7] Ibid, page 28.

[8] Ibid, page 28.

[9] IPC (2003, 2). This proposal was met with a fair amount of opposition from the industry (this author was one who voiced concern), in part because of the mandate for firms using leverage to calculate Value at Risk and Tracking Error - such prescriptive requirements ran contrary to the way the standards had operated historically. At their Spring 2004 meeting in Brussels, the IPC decided to hold off on implementing such standards; however, they requested the subcommittee to carve-out the formulas from their draft and issue them as a guidance statement, which was introduced in late 2004 (see IPC (2004, 1)).

[10] IPC (2003, 2), page 10.

[11] This section benefits from Jose Menchero's presentation of his Dietz award-winning paper at The Spaulding Group's PMAR 2004 (Performance Measurement, Attribution and Risk Conference).

[12] Arun Muralidhar's talk at PMAR 2004 helped provide the basis for this presentation.

A return by itself provides little information.

At our local movie theater, they occasionally display various "factoids" before the movie begins. One day, the following appeared:

"Anthony Hopkins recorded his narration of
How the Grinch Stole Christmas
in a single day."

I didn't know if I was supposed to be *impressed* or *depressed* by this pronouncement, since I have no background in this industry. What's the normal amount of time for such work? Apparently a day wasn't. So, should it have taken more time or less? If the screen had stated "this should normally take two days or more," then I'd be impressed by Anthony's efficiency. However, if they had stated "this normally takes a couple hours," then I would have guessed that Anthony was wasting a lot of time.

The May 11, 2007 issue of *The Wall Street Journal* included the following: "A New Orleans report says two thirds of high school seniors failed graduation exams since the state's schools takeover following Katrina." Our conclusion? Without knowing what the rate was before Katrina we aren't able to draw one, are we?

A few years ago my wife and I went shopping for a gas grill. When viewing one model, the salesman explained "this unit puts out 15,000 BTUs," or something like that. Totally meaningless to me. While I recall from my college days that BTU stands for British Thermal Unit, I have no frame of reference to know whether 15,000 is a lot or a little; for us, it was a totally meaningless statistic.

In the same way, if a manager declares "our return last year was 5%," you cannot draw much of an inference without some additional information. If we knew that the market was up 4%, then we might be pleased with such a figure, but had we learned that the market was up 8%, then we'd wonder what the manager was bragging about.

Having a rate of return, by itself, does little as far as the evaluation process.

Purpose of a benchmark

In general, a benchmark gives us a perspective as to how well or bad we've performed. It helps us decide whether or not we did a good job. It can provide us with an insight into how well the manager performed.

As Bailey et al. put it, "We view an investment benchmark as a passive representation of a manager's investment process. In this sense, it represents the prominent financial characteristics that the manager's portfolio would exhibit in the *absence* of active investment judgements."[2]   A Sanford C. Bernstein paper explained: "The primary purpose of a benchmark is to set a realistic, attainable performance standard, so that, by closely replicating a manager's style and chosen risk level, any short- or long-run differences in performance that arise can be attributed to the manager's active decisions, and thus, eventually, to manager skill."[3] Bill Sharpe suggested the following regarding benchmark selection: "There are several desiderata[4] associated with the selection of a benchmark for performance measurement. A benchmark portfolio should be 1) a viable alternative, 2) not easily beaten, 3) low in cost, and 4) identifiable before the fact."[5]

While a benchmark alone may not fully answer this question, it is part of the process.

There are various types of benchmarks available. We'll discuss four:

- absolute
- market indexes
- peer groups
- custom.

You may find that you'll need to employ multiple benchmarks in order to adequately evaluate your success.

Evaluation criteria

In evaluating a benchmark's appropriateness we should employ some criteria. We've elected to use the criteria set out in Bailey (2007). A valid benchmark is:

1) Unambiguous: The identities and weights of securities constituting the benchmark are clearly defined.
2) Investable: It is possible to forgo active management and simply hold the benchmark.
3) Measurable: The benchmark's return is readily calculable on a reasonably frequent basis.

4) <u>Appropriate</u>: The benchmark is consistent with the manager's investment style or area of expertise.

5) <u>Reflective of current investment opinions</u>: The manager has current investment knowledge (be it positive, negative, or neutral) of the securities or factor exposures within the benchmark.

6) <u>Specified in advance</u>: The benchmark is specified prior to the start of an evaluation period and known to all interested parties.

7) <u>Owned</u>: The investment manager should be aware of and accept accountability for the constituents and performance of the benchmark. It is encouraged that the benchmark be embedded in and integral to the investment process and procedures of the investment manager.

Absolute benchmarks

"If risk is not defined as total risk and the purpose of risk management
is not to preserve wealth, then avoiding losses is not a paramount objective."
Alexander M. Ineichen[6]

An absolute benchmark is a fixed number that we're trying to equal or exceed. It also goes by other names, such as minimum acceptable return (MAR), minimum funding requirement (MFR),[7] actuarial rate, and liability-related return. We could simply call these our "target" return.

An absolute benchmark is usually tied to our needs – it's a *need-related* benchmark. For example, a 75-year-old widow invests $1 million, explaining that she needs $80,000 per year to live on. That is the equivalent of an 8% return. If the manager later explains "we beat the index by 200 basis points," but the index had a 4% return (meaning the manager's return was 6%), the widow will need to decide what expenses she'll have to forgo, because she won't get the $80,000 she requires.

It could be argued that the absolute approach adheres to Benjamin Graham's rule of investing: "The first rule of investment is don't lose. And the second rule of investment is don't forget the first rule. And that's all the rules there are."[8]

Pension funds and insurance companies often employ actuaries to evaluate their future funding needs. This can translate into a liability-related index.

In a down market, we often see investors shift to absolute indexes, as they are less impressed by their manager's skills in beating an index when both their portfolio and index returns are negative – while their portfolio didn't lose as much money as the index, it still lost money.

The Myners Report[9] championed the use of absolute benchmarks over others because of its sensitivity to the fund's needs. Ryan Labs[10] in New York is well known for its sensitivity to liability-related needs, and will create custom indexes which are tied to an institution's cash flow requirements.

Hedge funds, too, typically use absolute benchmarks. As Ineichen put it, "One of the major differences between mutual funds and hedge funds is how [they] measure performance. Mutual funds are measured on relative performance. Their performance is compared to a relevant benchmark index or to comparable peer mutual funds in their style group. Most hedge funds focus on absolute returns. The idea behind an absolute return approach is the attempt to make profits under all circumstances, even when markets fall."[11]

In spite of its apparent appeal and fairly common employment, how do absolute benchmarks stack up on our list of criteria?

1) Unambiguous: Yes!
2) Investable: No! We can't guarantee we'll be able to invest at the specified rate.
3) Measurable: Yes!
4) Appropriate: Yes!
5) Reflective of current investment opinions: No! The manager can't be expected to have investment decisions about an absolute return.
6) Specified in advance: Yes!
7) Owned: No! Chances are the manager may not be able to "take ownership" of the absolute benchmark.

Conclusion? Absolute benchmarks are deemed less than ideal given that we get poor marks for three of our seven criteria.

Market indexes

> "The market is the average result of what everybody is doing."
> Peter L. Bernstein

We're all familiar with market indexes. Perhaps the best known example is the

Dow Jones Industrial Average (DJIA). A market index is a collection of securities which attempts to represent a particular market. Usually it's a sample of the entire market that we're attempting to compare ourselves to in hopes that we can decide whether we did a good job or not.

When we talk about indexes, I'm reminded of another type of sampling: political polling. It's not unusual for the population to be polled about their opinions about candidates for office. If you pay close attention, you'll see that the actual size of the poll can be quite small – sometimes only 100-150 people. And yet, we believe that this subset can be used as a barometer of how the entire population feels.

In early 2004, during the U.S. presidential primary season, voters were polled just before the Democratic Iowa caucus. The hands-down favorite to win was Howard Dean. But, the day after this event, we learned that Dean finished a distant third, with only 18% of the votes. Perhaps the sample sizes weren't quite large or broad enough to accurately predict what would occur.

What would be the ideal sample size to most accurately predict the results? We'd say 100 percent. So, why don't we sample 100% of the voters? Because it would cost too much and take too long (and possibly not be achievable, anyway).[12] So, we rely on samples.

You've probably noticed that when the results of a poll are given, there's also a disclaimer that the results are accurate within a plus-or-minus x-percent. This means that the true figure is within the reported one, plus or minus this figure. But even then, there's a confidence level that's associated to say that the real number may still be something different.

Some market indexes, like political polls, rely upon sampling. The question that the index creator is faced with is *what do we include* and *how much do we include?* If we're trying to come up with an index for U.S. large cap stocks, how many stocks should we include? The DJIA has 30. Is this enough? For most people, the answer is "no." Thus, we rarely (if ever) see a portfolio compared with the Dow. Most investors feel that the S&P 500 (which represents approximately 75% of the capitalization of the entire U.S. stock market) or the Russell 1000 (which represents over 90% of the market cap) will serve as better measures.[13]

Intellectual property

When it comes to indexes, most investment firms rely on those that are created by independent third parties who make the decisions on how to construct them. By doing this, we've taken ourselves out of the index creation game and thus avoid suggestions that we've biased it in some way. It also allows managers to be compared to some common yardsticks.

These index providers don't do this effort for the good of the industry only. They do it to make money. They sell the index information. Therefore, these indexes represent intellectual property, and the issuers have certain rights, such as how the indexes are to be used. Some providers, for example, won't allow you to report an index, excluding something, without their approval or perhaps without them actually constructing it for you (for a fee, no doubt).

Index providers compete with one another, just as polling agencies compete. They can differentiate themselves in a variety of ways, including:

- market coverage – how much of the market is included in their index?
- turnover – how frequently are changes made (that is, securities removed and replaced)?
- security weighting – how is each security represented in the index?
- concentration – is any one or two securities or sectors dominant in the index?
- free-float – is the index sensitive to free float (see below for an explanation) and if yes, how is this done?
- other construction rules – what other rules are used?[14]

In an ideal world, the index will include 100% of the market. This won't happen. It's too costly and the marginal benefit above a certain level doesn't justify the added expense.[15] But how far into the market do we go? You get to decide. By looking at the *number* of issues in the index and their total *market value,* relative to the market value of the market, we get an idea of coverage.

If there's lots of turnover, then the investor needs to be sensitive to these changes, as they may affect their investment strategies.[16]

The weighting methods can vary from index to index. Here are a few of the options:

- price-weighted – here, the security's price is the basis for how the security's weight comprises the index. An example is the Dow Jones Industrial Average.[17]
- market-cap[18] weighted – the market cap of the security is the basis for the weighing.

- equal-weighted – each security is represented in the same way.
- float-weighted – here, we take into consideration free float (see below).

When we get into narrower indexes (e.g., country or sector indexes), we run a greater risk of finding a single or a few securities dominating the index. A good example of this is the MSCI Finland index, where we often see Nokia represent roughly 70% of the index. It is unlikely that a manager would allocate their funds in such a way.

John Dorfman pointed this out as a shortcoming with market-cap weighted indexes in a Bloomberg column, when commenting on both the S&P 500 and Nasdaq, during a period when both were down but not as far down as they might otherwise be, saying that the figures "soft-pedals the damage." He went on to say that "The indexes are holding up better than the average stock because a few large stocks are propping the indexes up. This is possible because both the S&P 500 and Nasdaq are market-cap weighted; that is, large stocks have greater weight."[19, 20]

Free-float takes into account the company's shares that are available for trading in the stock markets. It excludes those shares that aren't available (e.g., owned by governments, founders, employees, other firms unlikely to sell (cross-holdings)). Different index providers use different rules for deciding what to exclude. And, given the dynamics of the market, you can imagine how much of a challenge it must be to keep track of these figures. Free-float indexes are considered more replicable in that they better represent what's actually available for investing. It also eliminates the potential influence of a closely-held large cap stock on an index's movement. But not everyone is necessarily happy with this move, as it can lower a company's representation in an index and therefore reduce the market's interest. Fulman addressed the Standard & Poor's plan to shift three major indexes to float-adjusted weightings from all-share weightings and pointed out that "Big chunks of many companies in the index – such as Wal-Mart Stores Inc., with 38.9% held by insiders, and Coca-Cola Enterprises Inc., with 48.1% held by insiders – would not be included in the new weightings."[21] Wal-Mart, for example, would represent 1.46% of the S&P 500 after the change, down from 2.21% previously, according to estimates from brokerage firm Guzman & Co.[22]

The industry seems to be moving toward this approach to index construction.

Characteristics of an index

Indexes should have certain characteristics:

1. Objective – Indexes should be identified in advance.[23] In addition, we should understand the construction rules.
2. Replicable – That we can, if need be, mimic the index. That is, to move from a more active strategy to a more passive one.
3. Availability of holdings – That the index's holdings can be purchased; that the market is liquid. This allows the manager to analyze the benchmark's holdings and assess his investment decisions.
4. Relevant – That the index represents the strategy of the manager. That it does-n't reflect the manager's active decisions but rather allows us to reflect the effect of these decisions.

The relevancy issue is one we should touch on a bit more, as we have all seen cases where a portfolio is being measured against the wrong benchmark.

I recall a full-page advertisement that listed many of a fund family's offerings, showing how they had each outperformed the S&P 500's results for 1999. Upon further examination we discover that some of these funds were only present for part of the year; in one case, less than two months! Now, the fund company may say "well, we gave the S&P 500 a whole year, and we still beat them!" Sorry, but that's not the way it works – perhaps the short period the fund was open was the best time for the index, too. And, had you looked at the funds listed, you would have seen small cap, Japan, and other sectors for which the S&P 500 is hardly the appropriate index. And, without an appropriate index, investment skill is obscured, and any conclusions about performance can be erroneous.

We should, as the saying goes, be comparing *apples to apples.*

Blending of indexes

If the portfolio is one that crosses multiple indexes (e.g., a balanced index), then we may create an index from two or more market indexes, based on our allocation ratios. For example, if our portfolio is 55% equities and 45% bonds, we would multiply 0.55 times the stock index and add this to 0.45 times the bond index to come up with our custom index, which is also called a *blended* index.

Index shortcomings

While market indexes may have a lot of appeal, they have some shortcomings, too:

- Without income – often, the indexes won't include income until the end of the month. So, if we're measuring a portfolio between dates that aren't month-ends, we won't capture the income.[24]
- Without transaction cost – indexes don't reflect brokerage and other trading expenses. Thus, when an index has turnover (replacing securities with new ones), there is no cost to the index but quite an added expense to the fund.
- Unknown constituents – there are many cases (especially with fixed income indexes) where the underlying constituents (or securities comprising the index) aren't identified.[25] This can make comparisons and developing strategies a challenge.[26]

Evaluation

Taking into consideration our criteria, how do market indexes stack up?

1) Unambiguous: Yes!
2) Investable: Yes!
3) Measurable: Yes!
4) Appropriate: No! And why? This rejection is attributable to at least two short-comings of indexes: (1) there is no common definition of style (e.g., growth, value) and therefore the approach used by the manager may not match what the index uses and (2) there is also no common definition of market capitalization, that is what constitutes small, mid, large cap stocks; again, the manager's view may differ from the index's.
5) Reflective of current investment opinions: Yes!
6) Specified in advance: Yes!
7) Owned: Yes!

While clearly better than what we had under absolute, we still don't have a perfect match. Granted, there are no doubt many times when the index is appropriate, so this assessment is a rather broad one.

Peer groups

Peer groups provide a way for managers to compare themselves with other managers. We see peer group comparisons in many other disciplines. For example, when there are running races open to the public (e.g., 5-K, 10-K marathons), the organizers will often report results by age brackets (e.g., 30-39) and sex as a way to create peer rankings.

Various investment consulting firms provide peer group rankings, as do mutual fund analytic providers Lipper and Morningstar.

Advantages

Peer groups have active managers compared with other active managers. Thus, the participants are individuals who face the same challenges (e.g., client turnover, cash flows, client demands, market issues). And, unlike comparisons with indexes, the participants are also subject to transaction costs.

Disadvantages

One challenge with peer groups is the question as to whether the group is truly representative of peers. An example I like to use to demonstrate this point comes from the television program *Seinfeld*. There was an episode where one of the main characters, Kramer, was telling Jerry Seinfeld about his skill at karate: he said how he was the best student in his class. While we might initially be impressed by such a statement, we later came to learn that the other students were all children – hardly a fair comparison. Were these children truly Kramer's peers? (But knowing Kramer, that's probably an unfair question.)

Related to this is the degree of homogeneity of the index. Groupings in the U.S. tend to be much more homogeneous than in Europe, for example. One reason for this is that in Europe, in addition to addressing such factors as market capitalization and style, we also need to consider country allocations. However, if the peer groups were much more refined, their number would grow significantly. Consequently, the degree of dispersion between European peer groups is much greater than with those for the U.S.

While the industry peer groups may not be as extreme as this case, we are still concerned with the appropriateness of the groupings. Just because a manager claims to invest in a certain way, do they really? And, since many peer group organizers request returns from the manager, how do we know that the one provided is truly representative?

When a manager is competing against an index, they can study the index, identify the way the sectors are allocated and what securities are included, and then develop a strategy to try to beat it. The same can't be said for peer groups, as we don't know what the median manager will be (and this will often change over time) and therefore what its makeup is. Consequently, it's very difficult to create a strategy to beat it.

Bailey et. al. (1990) points out how a peer group violates many of the characteristics they feel are important for a benchmark. For example, we don't know who the median manager is in advance, and the median manager benchmark is not investable. The median manager benchmark is ambiguous in that its composition is unavailable for inspection, either before or after the evaluation period. The median manager's portfolio may contain securities that the manager being evaluated has no current investment opinion about.[27]

We also have the problem with *survivorship bias.* By this we mean that over time the poorer performing managers tend to drop off, and so we're left with the best of the best. It's more difficult to beat these managers, and the fact that we may still be in the race (compared with those that have dropped off) offers little solace – we're still compared only to the surviving few.[28]

Peer group construction

As mentioned above, there are some commercial peer groups available from a variety of sources. Some managers have decided to create their own peer groups. While this may have some attraction, there can be challenges here, too.

One firm we know will serve as our example. This particular firm is a manager of managers.[29] They created a peer group of only those companies that offered mutual funds in their country because these would likely be their competition. However, when selecting a manager, they weren't limited to this subset and could consider managers that hadn't marketed there. Consequently, they had a subset of the market but were using this subset as their tracking tool. A broader peer group would probably have served them better, especially given the fact that they weren't limited to this subset for replacement managers.

Evaluation

How do peer groups fair versus our criteria?

1) Unambiguous: No! We don't necessarily know how the peer group was creat-

ed and may argue about its suitability.

2) <u>Investable</u>: No! We don't know what our peers own and even if we did, we wouldn't know which one to copy.

3) <u>Measurable</u>: Yes!

4) <u>Appropriate</u>: No! We often question the appropriateness of a peer group, challenging the membership and possibly our assignment.

5) <u>Reflective of current investment opinions</u>: No! We don't know what's owned and, again, wouldn't be in a position to decide which issues to own of our peers.

6) <u>Specified in advance</u>: No! The median manager isn't known and, in fact, changes from period to period.

7) <u>Owned</u>: No! Given the shortcomings, not likely.

In spite of its fairly common use, peer groups don't do well with these criteria.

Custom Benchmarks

In spite of the fact that there are probably 100,000 indexes to choose from, an investment manager may still argue that there isn't a single index to compare his performance to. So, we may end up creating blended indexes.

Sometimes, these may be a market index, less something (for example, an Asian index, excluding [or "ex"] Japan; or, an index excluding certain sectors; or, we may create an index from scratch to represent our particular investment strategy.

Campisi offered an approach to creating custom bond indexes using familiar indexes and their component subindexes. He suggests that "As a rule, whenever indexes are used to create a benchmark, it is best to find ones that are distinct and therefore more representative of the systematic risk and style characteristics that make them unique. In practical terms, they should have no overlapping securities." He goes on to say "It is not advisable to use individual issues to form a bond benchmark, since this raises the costs significantly."[30]

More extensive custom indexes require some work to develop. Often the manager's investment criteria is employed against the market to identify her likely opportunity set, from which individual issues are drawn. In some cases the client's liabilities may also be taken into consideration.

There are benchmark providers who specialize in developing custom indexes as such an exercise isn't always a trivial undertaking.

And how do custom benchmarks compare to our criteria? Quite favorably:

1) <u>Unambiguous</u>: Yes!
2) <u>Investable</u>: Yes!
3) <u>Measurable</u>: Yes!
4) <u>Appropriate</u>: Yes!
5) <u>Reflective of current investment opinions</u>: Yes!
6) <u>Specified in advance</u>: Yes!
7) <u>Owned</u>: Yes!

Very good grades, yes? One criterion that's missing from Bailey's list is "manager comparability." That is, can we compare multiple managers against the selected benchmark? While we might say "yes" for absolute, market indexes, and peer groups, I'd suggest that the answer is "no" when it comes to custom benchmarks. What's the likelihood that multiple managers will employ identical custom benchmarks? This drawback isn't a trivial one, I believe.

Summary

If we're looking to gain insights into how well a manager is doing, the first logical step is to compare the manager's return with a benchmark. We've identified four possible ways to do this: absolute, indexes, peer groups, and custom.

	Criteria:	Benchmarks			
		Absolute	Market Indexes	Peer Groups	Custom
1	Unambiguous	Yes	Yes	No	Yes
2	Investable	No	Yes	No	Yes
3	Measurable	Yes	Yes	Yes	Yes
4	Appropriate	Yes	No	No	Yes
5	Reflective of opinions	No	Yes	No	Yes
6	Specified in advance	Yes	Yes	No	Yes
7	Owned	No	Yes	No	Yes

Table 8-1: Comparing Benchmarks with the Bailey Criteria

Each provides benefits. And each has shortcomings. And, when comparing them with our criteria, custom seems to be ideal but for a variety of reasons fails to be universally employed (see Table 8-1).

To know whether you did a good job or not, you need at least one benchmark. It should be representative of the investment approach so that it ideally serves as an indication of success. So choose wisely!

ENDNOTES

[1] Much of what I know about benchmarks I've learned from Neil Riddles, who I have often referred to as the "benchmark king." Therefore, much of what is contained here I gained from Neil.

[2] Bailey, et al., (1990), page 73.

[3] Sanford C. Bernstein & Co. (Date unknown)

[4] If you're like me, you may be reaching for your dictionary at this moment ! desiderata means something considered necessary or highly desirable.

[5] Sharpe (1992), page 16.

[6] Ineichen (2003), page 114.

[7] MAR and MFR are terms we credit to Frank Sortino.

[8] Ineichen (2003), pages 29-31.

[9] This was a U.K. government sponsored study of the U.K. pension fund industry. Paul Myners was the executive chairman of Gartmore Investment Management from 1987 to 2001. The report is accessible on the Internet.

[10] A new entry into this area is Ryan ALM, another New York City-based firm (Crawford (2004, 2)).

[11] Ineichen (2003), page 114.

[12] To give you some idea of how unrealistic this is, imagine you're trying to decide how a particular race is going to turn out. So, you start to ask all the people – but not everyone is registered, so you have to limit your search to registered voters. But, between the time you start the survey and you finish, some unregistered voters are now registered. You also have to realize that some registered voters won't bother to vote, so you now want to deal with those who are "most likely" to vote. But how do you decide this? By asking? And after you're done all of this work, some of the people will move, meaning they may

vote but not where you're interested in, some people will move in who weren't on your list to start with, and some of the most likely voters will die. It won't work. Can't work. So, sampling is the best we've got.

[13] Some indexes actually do include all of the securities within its market: the TOPIX (Tokyo Stock Price Index), which is commonly used as the benchmark for Japanese equity managers, includes all securities listed on the first section of the Tokyo Stock Exchange.

[14] Bond indexes are fraught with much greater challenges. Bond benchmarks are virtually impossible to replicate; they always have turnover from issues maturing or being called, and their construction rules are sometimes quite complex, addressing issues such as size and liquidity. These indexes are always stratified. That is, they represent various factors (duration, sector weightings, yield curve distribution, convexity, coupon distribution). Because of the virtual impossibility for a manager to "buy" a bond index (that is, to match the securities in the index because of liquidity constraints), the manager might identify the relevant strata and construct an index in a similar way, through different securities.

[15] As with the case we described above for voting samples, some of the stocks we'd include will go bankrupt, or may merge, or may drop out of our target market (because their market capitalization has changed), while new securities will come into play. Keeping up with these dynamics is a challenge enough with the sampling that's done.

[16] This is perhaps most impactful with index funds, where the manager is attempting to *replicate* the market. As securities are added or removed, the manager must buy and sell, incurring trading costs.

[17] For a sense of how this can be misleading, see Rosenberg (2001).

[18] Market capitalization (cap) is the value of the company, as viewed by the market place. It's the shares outstanding multiplied by the market price.

[19] Dorfman (2004).

[20] Others, too, have voiced concerns with market-cap weighting. Robert Arnott announced that he is creating a new stock index which is "based on fundamental factors" because his "belief that market-cap-weighted indexes are inefficient." "The key-insight: the cap-weighted index is inherently trend-following and tends to overweight the most overvalued stocks and underweight the ones that are the most undervalued." "That is, cap-weighted indexes tend to have their biggest exposures to stocks with the greatest momentum."

Arnott created a "1,000 stock index based on six fundamental factors, such as sales, dividends, and employment." The index weights these factors equally (Chernoff (2004), page 53).

[21] Fulman (2004), page 2.

[22] Zuckerman (2004).

[23] As opposed to waiting until the end of the period and searching for indexes we out-performed.

[24] Many index providers have total return indexes that capture income. A shortcoming of these is that many do not take into account non-reclaimable withholding tax.

[25] This is often done because of pricing details which the index provider doesn't want to provide without an additional fee. Bond prices are often difficult to come by, and the index provider guards these, too, as intellectual property.

[26] This can also be a problem with performance attribution when we are using a security-based approach, which requires details on both the portfolio's as well as the index's underlying securities.

[27] Bailey (1990), page 77.

[28] Ron Surz often uses the metaphor of a marathon, where 1,000 people begin the race but only 100 finish. If you come in 100th, are you in last place or the top decile?

[29] A manager-of-managers doesn't invest in securities themselves; rather, they select managers for various styles to do the investing. Their skill is surveying the marketplace to pick the best managers.

[30] Campisi (2002), page 19.

Chapter 9 –
Performance Attribution

"Managers with exceptional positive performance
will attribute the excess return to skill.
Those who perform exceptionally poorly are unlikely to blame
lack of skill but rather bad luck as the cause of their performance."[1]

Alexander M. Ineichen

In Chapter 1, we discussed the "3 Cs of investment performance." One of these is controversy. And perhaps more than any other area of investment performance, attribution is controversial.

In this chapter, we'll provide a relatively detailed overview of attribution,[2] which will give you a good grounding into this increasingly important area of investment performance.

What is it?

Attribution is another area that is taken from other disciplines. It generally refers to the act of identifying the cause(s) of some event. Certain professions devote quite a bit of time to this area. For example, police officers are trained in attribution: when there's a car accident, they are required to study the scene in order to determine what happened and who gets the blame. Fire officials typically inspect buildings after there has been a fire in order to identify the cause(s).

We also see attribution at work in sporting events. Prior to a game, teams typically study each other in order to develop a strategy. Once the event is over, it's not unusual for them to review the events of the game in order to determine *what went right* and *what went wrong* and to figure out the contributors to their victory (or what caused their loss).

Attribution is a technique to evaluate the cause(s) or source(s) of a manager's return. It basically answers the question "Where did the return come from?" In the case of investment performance measurement, it rests on the assumption that (a) we have a strategy and (b) the strategy was executed, so we employ attribution to (c) analyze the results.

It is, without a doubt, the hottest area of performance measurement today.

Performance attribution comes in many varieties

In this chapter, we'll provide an overview of much of what attribution is about. There are many approaches to doing attribution. One example is absolute versus relative attribution. In the case of absolute attribution (also referred to as "contribution"), we are attempting to reconcile to the portfolio's total return; that is, to be able to identify the securities or sectors[3] that contributed to the total return. In the case of relative attribution, we're trying to identify the factors that contributed to the relative return (portfolio return as compared with the benchmark return).

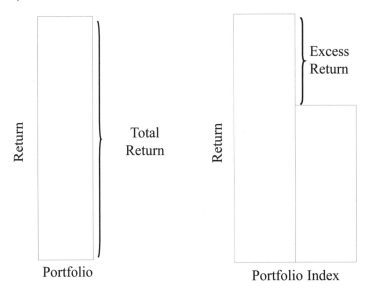

Figure 9-1: Absolute Attribution Reconciles to the Total Return

Figure 9-2: Relative Attribution Reconciles to the Excess Return

We also have options like geometric versus arithmetic attribution, holdings versus transaction-based attribution, and sector versus security-level attribution.

This is not only a "hot" area, it's quite a dynamic one, too.

Contribution – Absolute performance attribution

The first topic of controversy we'll touch on is whether or not contribution can be called "attribution." Without belaboring the point, suffice it to say that we've obtained enough evidence to justify the answer "yes." For example, we asked money managers, investment consultants, and plan sponsors if they considered contribution to be a form of attribution. Of those who responded, 77% of the money managers, 89% of the plan sponsors, and 100% of the consultants said "yes."[4]

Contribution is also called *absolute attribution*. Here, we assess how each security or sector contributed to the portfolio's overall return. The formula is quite simple:

$$Contribution = Weight \times Return$$

Weight is the portion of the portfolio that the security comprises. This is determined by its market value, relative to the overall portfolio's market value. So, an alternative formula for contribution is:

$$Contribution = \left(\frac{(BMV_i)}{\sum_{i=1}^{n}(BMV_i)} \right) \times R_i$$

where

    BMV = Beginning Market Value
    R = return
    i = individual component
    n = number of components

> **Contribution formula**
>
> $$Contribution = \left(\frac{(BMV_i)}{\sum_{i=1}^{n}(BMV_i)} \right) \times R_i$$

Let's look at Table 9-1.[5] Here, we list the securities and their respective returns and market values. We want to know how each contributed to the portfolio's overall return of 1.06 percent. Let's try the first security:

$$Contribution_A = \left(\frac{Wt_A}{\sum_{i=1}^{n}Wt_i} \right) \times R_A = \left(\frac{11}{100} \right) \times 0.015 = 0.11 \times 0.015 = 0.17\%$$

Ideally, the sum of the contribution effects should equal our portfolio's return. However, if there are any transactions (purchases and sales) during the period being measured, it's likely that this won't happen, since the formula uses the beginning-of-period values. By using the beginning market value only, when transactions occur, we are failing to properly attribute each security's contribution to the precision where we will account for 100% of the return. Thus, we will introduce a "residual."

This can be improved upon by taking into consideration the intra-period trans-actions. For example, we can use the same weighted flow concept which we discussed in Chapter 4:

$$Contribution = \left(\frac{\left(BMV_i + \sum_{j=0}^{m}\left(W_j \times C_j\right) \right)}{\sum_{i=1}^{n}\left(BMV_i + \sum_{j=0}^{m}\left(W_j \times C_j\right) \right)} \right) \times R_i$$

The necessity to move to a more precise method to calculate contribution effects will vary depending on the amount of activity. Like much of what we do in performance measurement, the decision should be based on a cost/benefit analysis.

In many cases, managers are only interested in looking at the top 5 or 10 and bottom 5 or 10 contributors. This means that the existence of a residual may therefore not be obvious. This doesn't mean that we shouldn't strive for accuracy, but

Security	ROR	Weight	Contribution Effects
A	1.50%	11.00	0.17%
B	1.80%	12.00	0.22%
C	2.00%	1.20	0.02%
D	0.50%	1.50	0.01%
E	0.70%	22.00	0.15%
F	-1.10%	1.30	- 0.01%
G	-0.30%	11.00	- 0.03%
H	1.00%	20.00	0.20%
I	0.20%	7.00	0.01%
J	2.50%	13.00	0.33%
Overall	1.06%	100	1.06%

Table 9-1: Individual Security Contributions

perhaps it should also be a factor in considering the approach to be taken.

If we're talking about monthly contribution, a basic approach may be adequate in many cases. However, as we lengthen our time period, to quarters and longer, we may find the need to improve the accuracy. This can be done by the method shown above, or by linking the subperiod figures, which is taken up later in this chapter.

The beauty of this concept is its simplicity. It's quite an intuitive way to identify how each security or sector contributed to the portfolio's return. For many, this is what they mean when they say "attribution."

Relative attribution

The more sophisticated way to deal with attribution is called *relative attribution*. Here, we look at the portfolio relative to the index. We're interested in how we got our excess return (also called active return and alpha).

In the world of equities, the most common method is the "Brinson formula." The problem is that there are actually two Brinson formulas: Brinson-Hood-Beebower (BHB)[6] and Brinson-Fachler (BF).[7] We'll look at both, simultaneously!

Let's begin by talking about what we generally try to do when we perform relative attribution. Here, we try to identify the *effects* that contributed to or detracted from our excess return. This is done via a model, which is a group of formulas. The goal is to identify the sources for the excess return; therefore, the sum of our effects should equal the excess return.[8]

In the world of equities, what can a manager typically do to outperform the index? She can make different allocation decisions or pick different securities. By allocation, we mean allocating more or less funds to a particular sector, subsector, or other subset of our portfolio; selection deals with the picking of individual securities. Thus, we have two effects we can look at: the effect from our allocation decision and the effect from our selection decision.

Selection decision

Both the BHB and BF models use the same formula to derive the effects from selection:

$$Selection = w_i \times \left(r_i - \bar{r}_i \right)$$

where

w_i = portfolio security or sector weight

r_i = portfolio return

$\bar{r}_i$ = benchmark sector or security return

The expression $r_i - \bar{r}_i$ represents our outperformance (or underperformance). We use the portfolio's weight to represent the overall impact of this performance, showing its impact on the overall return.

Let's look at an example:

Index return = 2%

Portfolio return = 3%

Portfolio weight = 5%

$$Selection = w_i \times \left(r_i - \bar{r}_i\right) = 0.05 \times (0.03 - 0.02) = 0.0005 = 0.05\%$$

Because we outperformed the index, we gained 5 basis points in our selection effect.

Allocation decision

The approach for allocation is where we find a difference between the BHB and BF methods. The BHB formula is:

$$Allocation_{BHB} = \bar{r}_i \times \left(w_i - \overline{w}_i\right)$$

where

w_i = portfolio security or sector weight

$\overline{W}_i$ = benchmark security or sector weight

$\bar{r}_i$ = benchmark sector or security return

While the BF formula is:

$$Allocation_{BF} = \left(\bar{r}_i - \overline{R}\right) \times \left(w_i - \overline{w}_i\right)$$

where

w_i = portfolio security or sector weight

$\overline{W}_i$ = benchmark security or sector weight

$\overline{R}$ = benchmark's overall rate of return

$\bar{r}_i$ = benchmark sector or security return

We can see that they both agree on the second factor, $w_i - \overline{w}_i$. This represents the over- or underweighting allocation decision of the portfolio relative to the benchmark. The difference in the two models is solely the first term.

In the BHB method, we multiply the weight difference by the benchmark's security or sector return. Thus, if we've overweighted a sector (i.e., if the portfolio weight is greater than the benchmark weight, yielding a positive result), then a positive return by that sector will yield a positive result (because a positive times a positive is a positive). If, however we underweighted (i.e., if the portfolio weight is less than the benchmark's weight, resulting in a negative term) a positively performing sector, we'll have a negative effect (because a positive times a negative is a negative).

Now, let's contrast this with what we find with the BF approach. Here, we have the sector's return in the benchmark minus the overall benchmark return. If we overweighted a sector that outperformed the overall benchmark (i.e., where the sector's return is greater than the benchmark's return), then we'll have a positive effect, regardless of whether the returns are positive or negative! But, if the sector underperformed the overall benchmark, then we'd have a negative effect.

If we underweighted a sector that underperforms the overall benchmark, we get a positive effect, but if the sector outperformed the benchmark return, then we'd have a negative effect.

Here's an example:

Overall benchmark return = 3%
Consumer goods return = 2%
Index weight for consumer goods = 5%
Portfolio weight for consumer goods = 7%

As you can see, our sector has a positive return (2%) but underperformed the overall index (3%). We chose to overweight this sector (7% vs. 5% in the index).

The BHB allocation formula yields the following effect for this scenario:

$$Allocation_{BHB} = \overline{r}_i \times \left(w_i - \overline{w}_i\right) = 0.02 \times \left(0.07 - 0.05\right) = 0.0004 = 0.04\%$$

Because we overweighted (7% vs. 5%) a positively performing sector (2%), we get a positive effect of 4 basis points for our allocation decision. This is saying that it was a good thing for us to overweight a positively performing sector.

The BF method yields a very different result:

$$Allocation_{BF} = \left(r_i - \overline{R}\right) \times \left(w_i - \overline{w}_i\right) = (0.02 - 0.03) \times (0.07 - 0.05) =$$

$$-0.0002 = -0.02\%$$

Because we overweighted a sector that underperformed the overall index (2% vs. 3%), we lose 2 basis points! This is a 6 basis point swing, which goes positive to negative. Here, we're saying that overweighting a sector that underperformed the overall benchmark, regardless of it having a positive return, was a bad thing.

Let's look at one other example:

Overall benchmark return = -3%
Technology return = -2%
Index weight for technology = 5%
Portfolio weight for technology = 7%

Now, we have a sector with a negative return (-2%), which outperformed our index (-3%). Once again, we've overweighted the sector. The BHB method yields:

$$Allocation_{BHB} = \overline{r}_i \times \left(w_i - \overline{w}_i\right) = -0.02 \times (0.07 - 0.05) = -0.0004 = -0.04\%$$

In this scenario, we have overweighted a sector with a negative return (-2%). This resulted in a negative 4 basis point effect, which essentially says that over-weighting a sector with a negative return is not a good thing to do.

The BF method, once again, tells a very different story:

$$Allocation_{BF} = \left(r_i - \overline{R}\right) \times \left(w_i - \overline{w}_i\right) = (-0.02 - (-0.03)) \times (0.07 - 0.05) =$$

$$0.0002 = 0.02\%$$

Because we overweighted a sector that outperformed the index, we are rewarded with 2 basis points, even though the sector's return was negative. The BF model doesn't look at the absolute value of the sector's return; rather, it looks at this return in comparison with the index's overall return, and, since, the sector outperformed the overall index, overweighting it is considered a good thing to do (overweighting those sectors that had higher returns than the overall index is a way to beat the index, regardless of whether the returns are positive or negative).

Table 9-2 shows an example of the application of these models with a 3-sector portfolio.

As you can see, our selection effects are identical; it's in the allocation effect where we see differences. And note that for the Chemicals sector, where the manager allocated in the same way as the index, our allocation effect is zero, as one

	Weights		Returns		BHB		BF	
	Portfolio	Index	Portfolio	Index	Alloc'n	Selection	Alloc'n	Selection
Banks	30%	20%	2.50%	3.00%	0.30%	-0.15%	0.07%	-0.15%
Tech	40%	50%	2.20%	2.00%	-0.20%	0.08%	0.04%	0.08%
Chem	30%	30%	2.80%	2.50%	0.00%	0.09%	0.00%	0.09%
Total	100%	100%	2.47%	2.35%	0.10%	0.02%	0.10%	0.02%
	Excess ROR = 0.12%				Sum of effects for each model = 0.12%			

Table 9-2: Application of BHB and BF Models to a Sample Portfolio

would expect (since no bet was taken). Also note that the totals for the allocation effects for both models are the same – it's at the sector level where we see differences. Hopefully, this makes sense.

The different approach to allocation is the sole difference between these two "Brinson" models. And, as we've seen, the difference isn't a slight one.

As we can see from Figure 9-3, BHB views the allocation decision relative to zero (overweight positively performing sectors / underweight negatively perform-

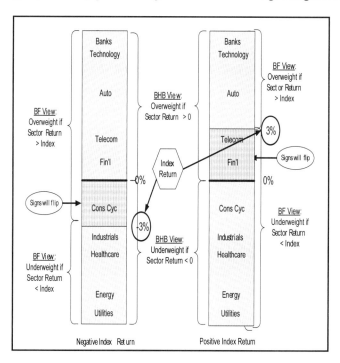

Figure 9-3: BF vs. BHB - Allocation Effect

ing ones; failure to do so results in a negative allocation effect). BF, on the other hand, views the decision relative to how the overall index performed (outperforming sectors (relative to the index) are to be overweighted; otherwise, underweight).

Interaction effect

There's one more effect that we should consider: the interaction effect. This is an effect which has yielded quite a bit of confusion.[9] While some may simply "plug" a number here,[10] we prefer to use an explicit formula. And, we believe that the formula is a key to understanding what interaction is:

$$Interaction = \left(w_i - \overline{w}_i\right) \times \left(r_i - \overline{r}_i\right)$$

It is essentially the product of allocation (weight differences) and selection (return differences), thus the term *interaction* (the interaction of two decisions).[11] Showing this effect is somewhat optional, however. The way we've defined selection and allocation above, there wouldn't be an interaction effect. This is because the selection effect, as noted above, uses the portfolio weight. And one could argue that this weight is the allocation choice. Alternatively, we could use the index weight:

$$Selection = \overline{w}_i \times \left(r_i - \overline{r}_i\right)$$

When this is done, regardless of whether we're employing the BHB or BF method, we'll need the interaction effect to account for the total excess return.

With the BHB and BF models, there is always an interaction effect. It's up to you whether or not you want to show it. If you use the benchmark weight in the selection effect, you'll isolate the interaction effect. If, however, you choose to use the portfolio weight, then the interaction effect won't appear, but this doesn't mean it's not there; it's essentially been combined with selection.

	Weights		Returns		BHB		BF		Inter-action
	Portfolio	Index	Portfolio	Index	Alloc'n	Selec'n	Alloc'n	Selec'n	
Banks	30%	20%	2.50%	3.00%	0.30%	-0.10%	0.07%	-0.10%	-0.05%
Tech	40%	50%	2.20%	2.00%	-0.20%	0.10%	0.04%	0.10%	-0.02%
Chem	30%	30%	2.80%	2.50%	0.00%	0.09%	0.00%	0.09%	0.00%
Total	100%	100%	2.47%	2.35%	0.10%	0.09%	0.10%	0.09%	-0.07%
	Excess ROR = 0.12%				Sum of effects for each model = 0.12%				

**Table 9-3: Application of BF and BHB Models to a
Sample Portfolio, with Interaction**

Table 9-3 shows our earlier example with the inclusion of an interaction effect. Note how the selection effects have changed as a result, demonstrating that the interaction effect was previously combined (Table 9-2).

Fixed income attribution[12]

Because fixed income managers don't typically rely solely on selection and allocation decisions, the models we've shown so far fail to meet their needs. Saying that, it's surprising how many firms use their equity model for fixed income.[13]

Although we don't actually state this, on the equity side we're trying to figure out the *sources of return*. And, in the approaches we discussed above we focused on selection and attribution. The same idea applies to the fixed income portfolio. Many approaches first evaluate the effect of sensitivity to interest rates and then apply an allocation/selection approach. Here, the sources of the return can vary, depending on the approach you wish to take. For example, Campisi cited the sources[14] as income and price change. Price change is further broken down into duration and change in yield. And change in yield comes from how the treasury curve moves from the start of the period to the end, as well as the change in spreads over the period. We could also include selection as another contributor to the portfolio return.[15] The effects we end up with are income,[16] treasury or duration, spread, and selection.

Like Campisi, many approaches to fixed income attribution first evaluate the change of the treasury curve on the returns. This is especially important because many fixed income managers make allocation decisions along the yield curve based on how they believe the curve will adjust over time, recognizing that this is a source of return. Changes in interest rates have a direct bearing on returns. And because interest rates vary across the yield curve, depending on the maturity of the bond, as these rates change the impact upon returns will vary as well. Duration is a measure of sensitivity to changes in interest rates and is therefore a major part of attribution for fixed income.

While fixed income managers may approach their investment decisions using various strategies, they typically consider things like:

• allocation along the yield curve (usually referred to as duration), to take advantage of anticipated changes in interest rates

- allocation across different types of bonds (e.g., corporates vs. municipals vs. governments), to take advantage of the risk premiums these bonds offer as well as to gain from changes in spreads (the measure of risk premium)
- allocation across different bond ratings (which reflect the "credit worthiness of the issuer"), again to take advantage of risk premiums and spread changes

The yield curve reflects the interest rate for different maturities (e.g., long-term bonds usually have a greater interest rate or yield than short-term bonds). These rates change and the bond manager may allocate differently than the bench-mark, based on her expectations of future rates. We would want an effect to take this into consideration. This is typically called the "duration effect" or "treasury effect."[17]

Anytime you invest in a bond other than a "risk-free bond,"[18] such as a U.S. Treasury, you're entitled to additional compensation for taking on this added risk: the risk premium. This risk may be the risk of default, the risk of prepayment (in the case of a mortgage-backed security, for example), the risk of the bond being called early, and other risks. This additional premium is called "spread." These spreads may vary over time, depending on the market's appetite for the bonds and the associated risks. And these premiums will vary, based on the *type* of bond and the *bond ratings*. Consequently, these allocations need to be measured, too, and this is often done through the "spread effect."

While we generally find that "selection" has little meaning in bond investing,[19] some models will isolate this effect as well. And some include an interaction effect, as we saw with the equity models.

This is a growing and dynamic area within investment performance, and we've seen the development of numerous fixed income models in the recent past, with more coming.

We have come to realize that there are often two audiences for attribution: the individual clients and the portfolio managers. While for equity attribution, both groups are usually satisfied with the same model;[20] this isn't always the case with fixed income. Bond managers employ rather complex strategies and may want to understand the "barbell effect," the "twist effect," the "parallel effect," the "non-parallel effect," and other rather complex characterizations of how the curve's shape may change. Their clients, however, may get easily confused with this level of detail. Therefore, we're beginning to see multiple models being employed with-in investment firms to satisfy the needs of each group: one that addresses the much more complex analysis that the manager may want to see, and a second, less complex and perhaps more intuitive approach for the individual clients. By no means is this universal, and some clients want to also see the more complex analysis while some managers are satisfied with the less complex models.

In a note to the author, Corné Reniers saw the distinction between these two approaches in a different way: "The distinction I see is this one: one way or another a bond manager starts by creating expectations, which for a fixed income manager means he is going to think about how the yield curve is going to change. Somewhere in the process he is going to decide which bonds to buy and sell. In other words, he has translated his expectations about yield curve changes into exposures/positions/weights he wants in his portfolio. The difference between the two approaches is that one approach simply starts after the portfolio manager translated his expected yield curve changes in weights for yield curve buckets, weights per credit rating, etc., where the other approach puts all the complexity of the translation from yield curve changes into weights in the model. It is therefore a matter of a different starting point in the investment process; not a difference in audience."[21]

For equities, we've had the "Brinson" models around for some time; however, we haven't had a "Brinson-type" model on the fixed income side that has gained the same level of interest; that is, a model that has been widely adopted by both software vendors and money management firms. However, in the past few years we've seen many new models developed and published.[22] And while it's also true that many software vendors have created new models as part of their development effort, we're starting to see vendors take advantage of some of these already published articles.

Regardless of the model, they tend to be more complex than the equity models we discussed previously. We will briefly touch on the Campisi model to give you a sense of how these models work.

The article from which this model is drawn was a primer and addressed attribution at a total portfolio level. The methodology can be applied to each sector in the portfolio, thereby providing a simple, consistent way to evaluate not only average duration but yield curve exposure. In this case, the yield curve exposures or key rate durations are simply the weights to the durations of each sector. This has the advantage of being a non-arbitrary selection of the key rates (as opposed to methods that select them according to how easy it is to find a treasury rate ... one year, two years, three years, five years, etc.). This method links the selection of which Treasury rates you evaluate by the durations and weights the manager deliberately caused in each sector. This also has the advantage of providing a linear average treasury change, which combines with the portfolio's average duration to provide a total treasury curve effect (including parallel, nonparallel and reshape effects). The parallel effect is calculated by applying the portfolio's average duration to the treasury change at that average duration (different from the prior effect's treasury change). The difference between the overall treasury effect and the parallel effect is the sum of the two nonparallel effects: shift and reshape. It's not as complex or difficult to understand as some other methods. You can simply subtract attribution effects because the effects are 100% of each component of total return.[23]

For our analysis, we'll use the scenario shown in Table 9-4.[24]

	Benchmark Return	Portfolio Return	Benchmark Weight	Portfolio Weight
Treasury/Agencies	0.93%	1.23%	35.18%	5.50%
Mortgage-Backed Securities (MBS)	0.90%	0.81%	35.79%	22.80%
Asset-Backed Securities (ABS)	0.66%	0.64%	1.64%	8.70%
Commercial Mortgage-Backed Securities (CMBS)	1.02%	1.14%	2.81%	9.20%
Corporates	1.23%	1.40%	24.58%	45.40%
High Yield	1.37%	1.59%	0.00%	4.70%
Emerging Markets	3.20%	2.65%	0.00%	3.70%
Total	0.99%	1.22%	100%	100%
Duration	4.77	5.22		

Table 9-4: Portfolio and Benchmark Basic Data for Attribution Example

Table 9-5 summarizes the calculations we'll employ to derive our returns. The way we weight the effects to arrive at the total is different than how we handle it on the equity side, as you can see in Table 9-6.

A key strategy of virtually every fixed income system is to calculate a treasury or duration effect, which ties into how the yield curve moved from the beginning to the end of the measurement period. Table 9-7 provides U.S. treasury curve rates for certain maturities for June and July, 2004. We've graphed the curves in Figure 9-4. Figure 9-5 shows the changes which occurred from June to July.

Attribution Factor	Formula
Income	Coupon ÷ Beginning Price
Treasury Change Return	- Duration × Treasury Change (for a sector)
Yield Curve Exposure	Weighted average of Sector Treasury Effects (For the portfolio
Spread Return	- Duration × Index Spread Change (For each sector
Selection (Active residual)	Excess return - Income - Treasury Change - Spread

Table 9-5: Campisi Model Attribution Formulas

Attribution Factor	Weighting Factor
Return Effects	Market
Duration	Market
Coupon	Par
Price	Par
Unit spread change	Dollar duration
Yield change	Dollar duration

Table 9-6: Weighting Factors

We'll begin by calculating the contributions[25] for the benchmark, using the following formulas:

$$IncomeContribution = \frac{Coupon}{Beginning\ Pr\,ice}$$

$$TreasuryContribution = TreasuryChange \times (-Duration)$$

$$SpreadContribution = \operatorname{Re}turn - \left(IncomeContribution + TreasuryContribution\right)$$

As you can see, we *back into* the spread contribution, since for the benchmark we only show three contributions. And, knowing what the return is, and having calculated the effects for income and treasury, what's left is the contribution from spread.

We also calculate the Spread Change:

$$SpreadChange = \frac{SpreadContribution}{-Duration}$$

You'll note that the benchmark doesn't have a selection contribution since there is no selection going on in the benchmark. However, as you'll see shortly, there is one for the portfolio.

Table 9-8 shows the input data for the benchmark, as well as the effects using the above formulas.

We're now ready to tackle the portfolio contributions. We use the same formulas, as above, for the income and treasury effects. However, for the spread effect we use the following:

$$PortfolioSpreadContribution = -Duration \times BenchmarkSectorSpreadChange$$

As Steve explained in an e-mail message to me, to break out the selection contribution, you need to account for the difference in sector allocation – that's what the spread effect is, an allocation difference. You earn index returns (i.e., spread changes) in each sector, but you hold different sector weights than the benchmark. The spread effect is an allocation effect. Sector weighting is the result of both money and duration.

The selection contribution is then arrived at by finding what's left over:

$$PortfolioSelectionContribution =$$
$$Portfolio\ Re\ turn - (IncomeContribution + TreasuryContribution +$$
$$SpreadContribution)$$

Table 9-9 provides the details for the portfolio using these formulas.
The attribution effects are calculated as follows:[26]

$$SpreadEffect = -PortfolioDuration \times$$
$$\left(BenchmarkSpreadContribution \div \left(-Duration\right)\right)$$

$$Allocation = \left(PortfolioWeight - BenchmarkWeight\right) \times IndexSpreadAdvantage +$$
$$PortfolioWeight \times \left(PortfolioSpreadEffect - BenchmarkSpreadEffect\right)$$

$$SelectionEffect = PortfolioWeight \times SelectionContribution$$

Maturity	June	July	Change
1.00	1.98	2.06	0.076
2.00	2.68	2.68	0.000
2.50	2.88	2.84	- 0.032
3.00	3.07	3.01	- 0.063
3.50	3.25	3.18	- 0.065
4.00	3.42	3.35	- 0.068
4.25	3.51	3.44	- 0.069
4.38	3.55	3.48	- 0.069
4.50	3.59	3.52	- 0.070
4.75	3.68	3.61	- 0.071
5.00	3.77	3.69	- 0.072
5.25	3.81	3.73	- 0.074
5.38	3.83	3.75	- 0.075
5.50	3.85	3.77	- 0.075
5.75	3.89	3.81	- 0.077
6.00	3.98	3.85	- 0.079
6.50	4.01	3.93	- 0.082
7.00	4.09	4.01	- 0.086
7.50	4.17	4.08	- 0.089
8.00	4.26	4.16	- 0.092
9.00	4.42	4.32	- 0.099
10.00	4.58	4.48	- 0.106
30.00	5.29	5.20	- 0.091

Table 9-7: Yield Curve Changes: June and July 2004

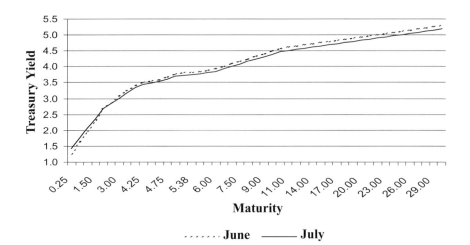

Figure 9-4: U.S. Treasury Yield Curves - June and July 2004

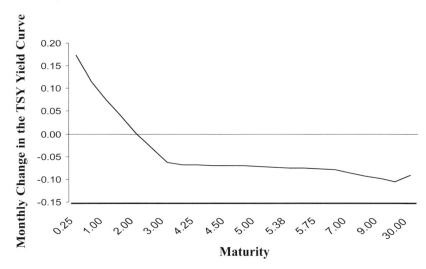

Figure 9-5: U.S. Treasury Yield Curve Changes (June - July)

	Coupon	Price	Duration	Treasury Change	Return	Income	Treasury Effect	Spread Effect	Spread Change
Treasury/Agencies	0.38	104.38	4.93	0.07	0.93%	0.37	0.35	0.21	0.04
Mortgage-Backed Securities (MBS)	0.46	100.39	4.13	0.07	0.90%	0.45	0.28	0.16	0.04
Asset-Backed Securities (ABS)	0.38	101.49	2.63	0.04	0.66%	0.37	0.10	0.18	0.07
Commercial Mortgage-Backed Securities (CMBS)	0.49	104.24	4.62	0.07	1.02%	0.47	0.32	0.23	0.05
Corporates	0.51	104.76	5.62	0.08	1.23%	0.49	0.43	0.31	0.06
High Yield	0.72	100.35	4.63	0.07	1.37%	0.72	0.33	0.33	0.07
Emerging Markets	0.69	97.71	5.38	0.07	3.20%	0.71	0.40	2.09	0.39
Total	0.44	102.95	4.77	0.07	0.99%	0.43	0.34	0.22	0.05

Table 9-8: Benchmark Data

	Coupon	Price	Duration	Treasury Change	Return	Income Effect	Treasury Effect	Spread Effect	Selection Effect
Treasury/Agencies	0.46	109.45	7.09	−0.09	1.23	0.42	0.61	0.30	−0.10
Mortgage-Backed Securities (MBS)	0.50	101.81	3.90	−0.07	0.81	0.49	0.26	0.16	−0.10
Asset-Backed Securities (ABS)	0.37	101.61	2.54	−0.03	0.64	0.36	0.08	0.18	0.02
Commercial Mortgage-Backed Securities (CMBS)	0.57	103.85	5.11	−0.07	1.14	0.55	0.37	0.25	−0.03
Corporates	0.58	106.08	6.12	−0.08	1.40	0.54	0.49	0.34	0.03
High Yield	0.68	103.11	5.57	−0.08	1.59	0.66	0.42	0.40	0.12
Emerging Markets	0.57	96.45	5.62	−0.08	2.65	0.59	0.43	2.19	−0.56
Total	0.54	104.13	5.62	−0.08	1.22	0.52	0.39	0.34	−0.03

Table 9-9: Portfolio Data 0.43

	Income	Treasury	Allocation	Selection	Total
Treasury/Agencies	0.02	0.01	0.01	−0.01	0.03
Mortgage-Backed Securities (MBS)	0.00	0.00	0.00	−0.02	−0.01
Asset-Backed Securities (ABS)	−0.01	−0.02	0.00	0.00	−0.03
Commercial Mortgage-Backed Securities (CMBS)	0.01	0.00	0.00	0.00	0.01
Corporates	0.04	0.04	0.03	0.01	0.13
High Yield	0.01	0.00	0.01	0.01	0.03
Emerging Markets	0.01	0.00	0.07	−0.02	0.06
Total	0.08	0.00	0.13	−0.03	0.23

Table 9-10: Attribution Effects

Table 9-10 provides the results of this analysis.

Multicurrency Attribution

Whenever a portfolio is invested in different currencies, there's an additional source of potential return: the currency fluctuations. Let's say, for example, that we have a U.S. client for whom we buy BMW stock. Since BMW's country of origin is Germany where the currency is the Euro, we need to convert our dollars into Euros in order to execute this trade. Some time goes by, and we decide to sell our stock. If our stock price went up, we'll probably be happy. However, if the dollar strengthened against the Euro during this period, we won't get back as many dollars as we might have wanted, and so our overall return may have suffered. Therefore, understanding and capturing the currency effect is important for international portfolios.

We'll discuss a rather simple way to arrive at this effect. But first, let's get some terminology down: base return refers to the return expressed in the currency of the investor, while local return is for the security. So, if our investor is U.S.

based and invests in Germany, the base return will be for dollars, while the local will be for Euros.

The formula is:

$$CurrencyEffect = \left[w_i \times \left(r_{B_i} - r_{L_i} \right) \right] - \left[\overline{w}_i \times \left(\overline{r}_{B_i} - \overline{r}_{L_i} \right) \right]$$

where

w = weights

r = returns

B = basc

L = local

overbar ($^-$) is for the index

without the overbar is for the portfolio

Let's say, for example, that our U.S. investor's portfolio holdings in Germany are as depicted in Table 9-11, relative to the index.

	Weight	Local ROR	Base ROR
Portfolio	15%	5.00%	6.00%
Benchmark	10%	4.80%	5.85%

Table 9-11: Weights and Returns

As we can see, our manager decided to overweight this particular country by 5 percent.

We first need to calculate the contribution for both the portfolio and index. This is done by multiplying the base return by the weight:

$$Contribution_P = 15\% \times 6.00\% = 0.90\%$$

$$Contribution_B = 10\% \times 5.85\% = 0.59\%$$

We can now find the excess return for this country: 0.90 - 0.59 = 0.32 percent.[27] This is the value we will attempt to account for.

Let's calculate our other effects before we move onto the contribution effect. We'll use the BHB model. These effects are referred to collectively as the *market effects*. These are the effects from the local market – the market of the issue – in our case, Germany. So, we use the local returns in our formulas.

First, let's calculate the allocation effect:

$$Alloc'nEffect_{BHB} = \overline{R}_{L_i} \times \left(w_i - \overline{w}_i \right) = 4.80\% \times \left(15\% - 10\% \right) = 0.24\%$$

Next, the selection effect:

$$SelectionEffect = \overline{w}_i \times \left(r_{L_i} - \overline{r}_{L_i} \right) = 10\% \times (5.00\% - 4.80\%) = 0.02\%$$

And now, the interaction effect:

$$InteractionEffect = \left(w_i - \overline{w}_i \right) \times \left(r_{L_i} - \overline{r}_{L_i} \right)$$

$$= (15\% - 10\%) \times (5.00\% - 4.80\%) = 0.01\%$$

Now that we have the three market effects, we can calculate the effect from currency:

$$CurrencyEffect = \left[w_i \times \left(r_{B_i} - r_{L_i} \right) \right] - \left[\overline{w}_i \times \left(r_{B_i} - \overline{r}_{L_i} \right) \right]$$

$$= \left[15\% \times (6.00\% - 5.00\%) \right] - \left[10\% \times (5.85\% - 4.80\%) \right] = 0.32\%$$

Table 9-12 summarizes the effects we calculated. As you can see, we have fully accounted for our excess return.

	Market Effects				
Excess Return	Allocation Effect	Selection Effect	Interaction Effect	Currency Effect	Sum of Effects
0.32%	0.24%	0.02%	0.01%	0.04%	0.32%

Table 9-12: Our Global Portfolio's Attribution Effects

While 28 basis points of our 32 basis point excess return came from the market (allocation, selection, and interaction), currency contributed the remaining 4 basis points.

This approach to multicurrency attribution works fine, unless you're engaged in a separate currency strategy, involving hedging and cross-hedging, resulting in currency weights that don't match the market weight. In that case, you would probably want to use a more advanced method, such as the Karnosky-Singer model. This model's complexity is beyond the scope of this book.[28]

Multi-period attribution

So far, we've addressed calculating attribution for a single period, be it a day or a month.[29] But what if we want to calculate attribution for longer periods; for example, a year?

In Chapter 5 we addressed multi-period rates of return and showed how we can use geometric linking to *link* the returns across time. Geometric linking *com-*

pounds the returns. Can we do the same thing here?

While there are some who argue that attribution effects are not supposed to compound, most people believe they should. As we noted above, when we calculate our attribution effects, we want to account for the entire excess return. We want the same thing to occur when we measure attribution across time – to account for the entire period's excess return.

We have come to find that geometric linking does not work with attribution. We'll use the two months of returns and effects as shown in Tables 9-13 and 9-14 to demonstrate this.

	Portfolio ROR	Portfolio Wt	Index ROR	Index Wt	Selection	Allocation	Interaction
Tech	2.00%	40%	1.80%	50%	0.100%	-0.180%	-0.020%
Banks	2.50%	60%	2.45%	50%	0.025%	0.245%	0.005%
Total	2.30%	100%	2.125%	100%	0.125%	0.065%	-0.015%
Excess ROR =	0.175%				Total of effects =		0.175%

Table 9-13: Attribution Effects, Using BF Model, for Month 1

	Portfolio ROR	Portfolio Wt	Index ROR	Index Wt	Selection	Allocation	Interaction
Tech	1.75%	40%	1.70%	50%	0.025%	-0.170%	-0.005%
Banks	1.85%	60%	1.90%	50%	-0.025%	0.190%	-0.005%
Total	1.810%	100%	1.800%	100%	0.000%	0.020%	-0.010%
Excess ROR =	0.010%				Total of effects =		0.010%

Table 9-14: Attribution Effects, Using BF Model, for Month 2

If we link our monthly portfolio and index returns, and also link our monthly attribution effects, using geometric linking, we get the results as shown in Table 9-15.

Portfolio ROR	4.152%	Selection	0.125%
Index ROR	3.963%	Allocation	0.085%
Excess ROR	0.188%	Interaction	-0.025%
		Total	0.185%

Table 9-15: Geometrically Linked Returns and Attribution Effects

As you can see, we have a three basis point difference between the excess return for this two-month period and the sum of the linked attribution effects, meaning that we're not fully accounting for the differences. This difference is the multi-period residual.

There's a rather simple way to eliminate this residual.[30]

- Step 1: Calculate the ratio of the total of the linked excess return / linked effects:

$$RatioOfActualToCalculated = \frac{0.188\%}{0.185\%} = 1.01819$$

- Step 2: Adjust the linked selection effect by multiplying it by this ratio:

$$AdjustedLinkedSelection = 1.01819 \times 0.125\% = 0.127\%$$

- Step 3: Adjust the linked allocation effect in a similar manner:

$$AdjustedLinkedAllocation = 1.01819 \times 0.085\% = 0.087\%$$

- Step 4: Adjust the linked interaction effect in the same way:

$$AdjustedLinkedInteraction = 1.01819 \times \left(-0.025\%\right) = -0.025\%$$

If we sum these effects, we get 0.188%, which is our excess return. Thus, we've managed to account for 100% of the excess return.

This method is quite easy to apply and is relatively intuitive. During the past few years, much research and analysis has gone into this area of attribution, with some excellent models being introduced (see Appendix 9-A). These more complex models are beyond the scope of this book. It's worth pointing out that this is an area where much discussion and controversy takes place. If you're involved with attribution, it's important to understand the method that's being employed to achieve multi-period attribution to ensure you're comfortable with how it works.

One point that's worth mentioning regarding these linking methods that have been developed: they aren't "attribution models" like the Brinson-Fachler, Brinson-Hood-Beebower, or Karnosky-Singer models. Rather, they are tools to take these single-period models and extend them across multiple time periods.

Suffice it to say, we can accomplish multi-period attribution – we just need a little help.

Geometric attribution[31]

The models we provided earlier fall into the category of arithmetic (also referred to as additive). There is an entirely different view, however, which is called "geometric" (also referred to as "multiplicative"). Geometric attribution should not be confused (although it often is) with geometric linking. The starting point for the difference is how excess return is defined. As we have defined it so far, it is:

$$ER_A = R - \overline{R}$$

which is simply the arithmetic difference between the portfolio and index returns.

The geometric view is quite different:

$$ER_G = \frac{R+1}{\overline{R}+1} - 1$$

The arithmetic calculates the portfolio's excess return relative to how the benchmark did, while the geometric approach calculates the excess return relative to how we would have done had we been invested in the benchmark. A simple example may help.

Our portfolio begins with ¥100,000, and has a 10% return. It therefore ends the period with ¥110,000. The index had a return of 6 percent, meaning that had the portfolio been invested in the benchmark, its ending value would have been ¥106,000. The arithmetic excess return can be calculated in two ways. The first, using our formula:

$$ER_A = R - \overline{R} = 10\% - 6\% = 4\%$$

And for the second, we take our gain (¥10,000) relative to what we would have gotten in the benchmark (¥6,000), divided by our starting value:

$$ER_A = \frac{10,000 - 6,000}{100,000} = \frac{4,000}{100,000} = 4\%$$

Likewise, we have two ways to derive our geometric excess return; first, using the formula we just introduced:

$$ER_G = \frac{R+1}{\overline{R}+1} - 1 = \frac{0.10+1}{0.06+1} - 1 = \frac{1.10}{1.06} - 1 = 3.77\%$$

And the second, by taking our gain, relative to where we would have been had we been in the benchmark:

$$ER_G = \frac{10,000 - 6,000}{106,000} = \frac{4,000}{106,000} = 3.77\%$$

The formulas with the amounts we earned are probably better in distinguishing how these methods differ. For arithmetic, we're comparing our gain relative to our starting point; for geometric, it's relative to where we would have been had we been in the benchmark. We have two very different views and therefore two very different results.

As we noted at the beginning of this chapter, with relative attribution we strive to account for or reconcile to the portfolio's excess return. Thus, with an arithmetic model, we are reconciling to an arithmetic excess return, while with a geometric model we are reconciling to a geometric excess return.

With geometric attribution we show the excess return as a ratio. And, as you might expect, we can get some very big differences. Menchero used the following example to demonstrate how different they can be:[32]

Portfolio Manager A's return = 30%; his index's return = 20%
Portfolio Manager B's return = 9%; her index's return = 0%

Using the arithmetic excess return, Manager A outperforms Manager B:

$$ER_A^A = 0.30 - 0.20 = 0.10 = 10\%$$

$$ER_A^B = 0.09 - 0.00 = 0.09 = 9\%$$

Using the geometric excess return, Manager B outperforms Manager A:

$$ER_G^A = \frac{1.30}{1.20} - 1 = 8.33\%$$

$$ER_G^B = \frac{1.09}{1.00} - 1 = 9\%$$

Geometric attribution, like arithmetic attribution, isn't a model, *per se,* but rather an approach to modeling. The Brinson-Fachler model we introduced earlier can be represented in a geometric framework. We just need to introduce a new concept called the "semi-notional" return:

$$R_S = \sum_{i=1}^{n} w_i \times \overline{r}_i$$

which is the sum of the individual security or sector products of the portfolio weights and respective index returns. We can then construct a geometric view of the BF as follows:

$$Selection = w_i \times \left(\frac{(1 + r_i)}{(1 + \overline{r}_i)} - 1 \right) \times \left(\frac{1 + \overline{r}_i}{1 + R_S} \right)$$

$$Allocation = \left(w_i - \overline{w}_i \right) \times \left(\frac{1 + r_i}{1 + \overline{r}_i} - 1 \right)$$

You will hopefully be able to see how these equations are quite similar to what we introduced above, just in a geometric style.[33] The selection effect has the portfolio weight times the difference in returns, just as we did in the arithmetic model, while the allocation effect has the difference in weights times the relative difference between the sector's return and the overall index return.

As we stated earlier, we can have an interaction effect by replacing the portfolio weight with the index weight in the selection effect:

$$Selection = \overline{w}_i \times \left(\frac{(1+r_i)}{(1+\overline{r}_i)} - 1 \right) \times \left(\frac{1+\overline{r}_i}{1+R_S} \right)$$

Our interaction effect is then quite similar to what we saw previously, using the arithmetic approach:

$$Interaction = \left(w_i - \overline{w}_i \right) \times \left(\frac{(1+r_i)}{(1+\overline{r}_i)} - 1 \right) \times \left(\frac{1+\overline{r}_i}{1+R_S} \right)$$

Geometric has several advantages over arithmetic. For example, it's proportionate. Let's say that you have two managers: Manager A outperforms her benchmark 11% to 10%, while Manager B outperforms his 41% to 40%. From an arithmetic excess return perspective, they both achieved a 1% alpha. However, from geometric, the results are quite different:

$$ER_{G_A} = \frac{0.11+1}{0.10+1} - 1 = \frac{1.11}{1.10} - 1 = 0.91\%$$

$$ER_{G_B} = \frac{0.41+1}{0.40+1} - 1 = \frac{1.41}{1.40} - 1 = 0.71\%$$

The geometric approach distinguishes between these two managers, suggesting that what Manager A did was more difficult than what Manager B accomplished. This sensitivity to proportionality is missed with the arithmetic approach.

Another advantage is that the geometric approach naturally compounds when extending attribution effects across periods. You should hopefully see this when you consider how the ratio has the returns configured in the same way as we use when we do geometric linking. This means that there won't be a residual as there is with arithmetic attribution; thus, we don't require a multi-period model as we discussed in the prior section. Another benefit is that we can add on new periods quite easily (e.g., to extend a 12-month multi-period result to 13 months). This isn't always the case with arithmetic linking models.

You will see differences in your results if you choose to use a geometric model. While arithmetic tends to be a more common approach, there are many that prefer the geometric way. There are advantages and disadvantages to both. Again, the intent of this chapter was simply introductory, and so we have chosen not to go into more detail here on this approach.[34]

Holdings- vs. transaction-based attribution

To put it simply, a holdings-based approach uses the sector's weights at the beginning of the period and does not account for intra-period activity, while the transaction-based method uses the intra-period transactions and adjusts the weights accordingly.

Early on, we mentioned that our goal with relative attribution is to account completely for the excess return. If we employ a holdings-based model however, which as we said assumes that the sector (or security) weight at the start of the period remains constant, and that there are no intra-period transactions, we may not be able to do this, especially if there's a lot of trading during the period.

Consequently, we can utilize a transaction-based model, which accounts for the intra-period activity. While the models we discussed above will work in either a holdings- or transaction-based approach, the key is that the weights must reflect additional purchases and sales (as well as corporate actions), and the returns must reflect the results of any intra-period activity. In addition, we don't just look at what is in the portfolio at the start; we also include the trades that take place and introduce new securities during the period.

There are various approaches to doing transaction-based attribution. The approach we suggested earlier, for absolute attribution (taking into consideration the weighted cash flows) is one method to improve our accuracy.

Other approaches to the transaction-based model require more data to work properly; we may take into consideration all of the trades, income, and corporate actions, and ensure our portfolio is properly valued when these events occur.

When trying to decide which approach to use, you should look at your firm's approach to trading. If you tend to be a buy-and-hold manager, with minimal intra-month activity, then a holdings-based model will probably suffice. However, if there's a lot of turnover during the month and/or day trading taking place, then a holdings-based model will not properly account for everything and we'll end up with a *residual,* which reflects our shortcomings. In addition, the effects may not be accurate as well. While some argue strongly on one side or the other,[35] my view is that *it depends*. And, since we can do holdings-based on a daily basis, you might find this of sufficient accuracy.[36]

As with many things, it's a matter of trade-offs: the trade-off of the additional cost and time, for the incremental benefit in accuracy. And, unless corporate actions are properly processed, etc., it may not be more accurate.

Sector- vs. security-level attribution

Many feel that to achieve the greatest accuracy we need to employ a security-level attribution model. But our concern is whether or not attribution makes sense at this level. For example, does the manager actually make *allocation* decisions at the security level? We suspect that in most cases the answer is "no." That these are *sector level* decisions.

At the security level, there are three possible scenarios:

- #1: the portfolio has a security that isn't in the index
- #2: the index has a security that isn't in the portfolio
- #3: the portfolio and index have the same security

For cases #1 and #2, are these allocation or selection decisions? How will the models handle them? I would suggest that these are selection decisions.

And for case #3, what would you call this? We're in the same security, but our allocation may be different. So, is this an allocation decision?

The results you get using the above models at the security level may not be as you would expect. While vendors may apply overrides or allow you to say how you want these situations handled, we think that the results can often be other than you would like.

Therefore, we believe that contribution (absolute attribution) is more useful and meaningful at the security level, while relative attribution makes clear sense at the sector level. Suffice it to say that this is yet another area of controversy.

What do we do with attribution?

Now that we've spent some time talking about attribution and its different facets, what do we do with it?

Attribution is a critically important diagnostic and analysis tool in that it provides insights into what is taking place in the portfolio. If properly employed, it can show *where* the return actually came from; what the contributors and detractors were.

It can be used by the investment firm's internal management to identify *what is working* and *what isn't working*. It can be used as part of the firm's compensation system. And, it can be used to demonstrate skill to prospects and validate claims to clients. And, when returns haven't worked out as expected, it can be used to demonstrate to a client that you know what took place and that you're working to correct the situation. Thus, it can be part of the firm's control system, too.

Plan sponsors can use attribution to monitor their managers and confirm that they're performing as they expected.

Attribution has been a great force in moving the performance measurement team closer to the front office by allowing them to help with the investment process by showing where the returns are coming from.

Attribution is an important part of a firm's tool set.

Properly employing attribution

If you read carefully above, you'll see that it reads "If properly employed, it can show..." What do we mean by "properly employed"?

First, that you have the right attribution model; that the model makes sense for the way you invest; that it is analyzing the results of your decisions. As we saw above, different models can yield different results.

Second, that the implementation of the model is correct. For example, that you've weighted the pros and cons of the holdings- versus transaction-based options and selected the one that makes the most sense for your firm.

Third, that you're using the right index. If you're not, the results will likely be meaningless.

In Chapter 6 we briefly touched on the suggestion that money-weighting replace time-weighting in attribution. This is still a relatively new idea and little has yet been done; perhaps we'll have more to say in the third edition!

Attribution is very complex. Employing it is a great idea, but getting it right requires a lot of thought.[37]

Summary

Attribution is the hottest area of investment performance measurement today.

It is extremely dynamic and controversial. While we didn't explicitly touch on all of the areas of controversy, here is a summary of many of them:

- is contribution attribution?
- which is better, geometric or arithmetic?
- which is better, holdings- or transaction-based attribution?
- is daily attribution better than monthly?
- which is better, sector or security-level attribution?
- which linking method is better?

Attribution is fun and challenging. It is playing an ever-important role within the investment industry, as it provides great insights into what is occurring and where the returns came from.

If you're going to start to use attribution, a lot of time and thought is needed, as the options for employing it are quite varied and can be very complex.

Exercises

1. Calculate the contribution effects for the portfolio in Table 9-E-1.

Security	ROR	Weight
A	2.00%	10%
B	1.11%	12%
C	1.45%	11%
D	0.18%	8%
E	1.55%	13%
F	-2.33%	10%
G	-1.40%	9%
H	1.00%	8%
I	1.02%	7%
J	2.22%	12%
	0.77%	100%

Table 9-E-1: Sample Portfolio

2. Calculate the attribution effects for the following scenario, using the BF model, with the interaction effect:

	Portfolio ROR	Portfolio Weight	Index ROR	Index Weight
Tech	2%	55%	1%	50%
Banks	3%	45%	2%	50%
Total	2.60%	100%	1.50%	100%

Table 9-E-2: Sample Portfolio

3. Using Table 9-E-2, calculate the attribution effects, using the BF model, without the interaction effect.

4. Using Table 9-E-2, calculate the attribution effects, using the BHB model, showing the interaction effect.

Appendix 9-A – Attribution References

Attribution references you might find of interest (note: this is hardly a complete list):

Attribution, in general

Mirabelli, Andre. "The Structure and Visualization of Performance Attribution." *JPM*[8]: Vol 5, #2.

Singer, Brian. "Evaluation of Portfolio Performance: Attribution Analysis." *JPM*: Vol 1, #2.

Books:

Bacon, Carl. *Practical Portfolio Measurement and Attribution*. Second Edition. John Wiley: 2008.

Bacon, Carl, ed. *Advanced Portfolio Attribution Analysis*. Risk Books: 2007.

Colin, Andrew. *Fixed Income Attribution*. John Wiley: 2005.

Feibel, Bruce. *Investment Performance Measurement*. John Wiley: 2003.

Spaulding, David. *Investment Performance Attribution*. McGraw-Hill: 2003.

Spaulding, David & Stephen Campisi. *Readings in Fixed Income Attribution*. TSG Publishing: 2007.

Equity Attribution

Brinson, Gary P. and Nimrod Fachler. "Measuring Non-U.S. Equity Portfolio Performance." Classics in Investment Performance Measurement. TSG Publishing, 2009.

Brinson, Gary P., L. Randolph Hood, and Gilbert L. Beebower. "Determinants of Portfolio Performance." *Financial Analysts Journal*: August 1986.

Brinson, Gary P., Brian D. Singer, and Gilbert L. Beebower. "Determinants of Portfolio Performance II: An Update." *Financial Analysts Journal:* May/June 1991.

Surz, Ronald J. "Attribution with Style." *JPM*: Vol. 3, #4.

Fixed Income Attribution

Lord, Timothy J. "The Attribution of Portfolio and Index Returns in Fixed Income." *JPM*: Vol. 2, #1.

van Breukelen, Gerard. "Fixed Income Attribution." *JPM*: Vol. 4, #4.

Campisi, Stephen. "Primer on Fixed Income Attribution." *JPM*: Vol. 4, #4.

Ramaswamy, Srichander. Fixed Income Portfolio Management: Risk Modeling, Portfolio Construction and Performance Attribution." *JPM*: Vol. 5, #4.

McLaren, Andrew. "A Framework for Multiple Currency Fixed Income Attribution." *JPM*: Vol. 6, #4.

Esseghaier, Zoubair, Tilak Lal, Peter Cai, and Phil Hannay. "Yield Curve

Decomposition and Fixed Income Attribution." *JPM:* Vol 8, #4.

Multi-period attribution

Singer, Brian D., Miguel Gonzalo, and Marc Lederman. "Multi-Period Attribution: Residual and Compounding." *JPM*: Vol. 3, #1.

Cariño. David. "Combining Attribution Effects Over Time." *JPM*: Vol. 3, #4.

Kirvievsky, Leonid. "Attribution Analysis: Combining Attribution Effects Over Time Made Easy." *JPM*: Vol. 4, #4.

Menchero, Jose G. "An Optimized Approach to Linking Attribution Over Time." *JPM*: Vol. 5, #1.

Davies, Owen. "Multiple-period Performance Attribution Using the Brinson Model." *JPM*: Vol. 6, #1.

Frongello, Andrew Scott Bay. "Linking Single-period Attribution Results." *JPM*. Vol. 6, #3.

Spaulding, David. "Is Linking Attribution Effects as Hard as it Looks?" *JPM*: Vol. 6, #3.

Laker, Damien. "A View from Down Under." *JPM*: Vol. 6, #4.

Spaulding, David. "Attribution Linking From a Religious Perspective." *JPM*: Vol. 7, #1.

Bonafede, Julia K. "A Multi-period Linking Algorithm That Has Stood the Test of Time." *JPM*: Vol. 7, #1.

Campisi, Stephen. "Long-term Risk-adjusted Attribution." *JPM*: Vol. 7, #1.

Cariño, David. "Refinements in Multi-period Attribution. *JPM:* Vol 7, #1.

Frongello, Andrew Scott Bay. "Attribution Linking: Proofed and Clarified." *JPM*:

Vol. 7, #1.

Menchero, Jose. "Linking Differences Do Matter." *JPM*: Vol. 7, #3.

Geometric attribution

Menchero, Jose G. "A Fully Geometric Approach to Performance Attribution." *JPM:* Vol. 5, #2.

McLaren, Andrew. "A Geometric Methodology for Performance Attribution." *JPM:* Vol. 5, #4.

Bacon, Carl. "Excess Returns – Arithmetic or Geometric?" *JPM:* Vol. 6, #3.

ENDNOTES

[1] Ineichen (2003), page 19.

[2] For a more in-depth look at this topic, we suggest you begin with Spaulding (2003).

[3] We're using the term "sector" to refer to sub-portfolio groups, such as industry or country.

[4] TSG (2002, 2), pages 21, 45, 54.

[5] This example is taken from Spaulding (2003, 2), page 17.

[6] See Brinson, *et al.* (1986).

[7] See Brinson and Fachler (1985).

[8] We'll discuss why this may not occur below.

[9] To learn more about interaction, we suggest Laker (2000), Spaulding (2003/2004), Campisi (2004, 2), Spaulding (2008, 2).

[10] If we simply have interaction equal whatever is left over (after we subtract the selection and allocation effects from our excess return), then we're also including residual, which isn't correct.

[11] In the BHB paper (Brinson, *et al.* (1986)), this term is referred to as "other." I have also seen it referred to as "cross-product."

[12] Because of the complexity of this subject matter, we're providing a high-level summary of this topic. For further discussion, we suggest you consider Spaulding (2003, 2), as well as the numerous articles which have been published on fixed income attribution (a list is included in Appendix 9-A).

[13] The Spaulding Group's 2004 survey reported that 34% of the money managers participating use their equity model for fixed income attribution. (See TSG (2005), page 4.)

[14] Campisi (2000), page 16.

[15] Campisi, as well as others, do not include a selection effect for the index, arguing that the index has no selection.

[16] It's interesting to note that many fixed income models don't include an income effect, which can be viewed as controversial by some, given the role that income plays in the portfolio's return. Some might suggest that without an income effect, the model fails the test of being a "true, fixed income model." The author will let others debate this subject, however.

[17] It's called "Treasury effect" because the yield curve in the States is typically built from U.S. Treasury rates. We understand that some firms distinguish between duration effect (absolute basis relative to the benchmark duration) and the yield curve effect (overweighting/underweighting certain points of the yield curve). You can have the same duration using different approaches (e.g., bullet vs. barbell), but each has a unique yield curve structure. We mention this here to indicate that there are various approaches, not to initiate further discussion at this time because it goes beyond the scope of this text.

[18] The reality is that all bonds, even U.S. Treasuries, have risks. But we typically refer to these bonds, because of their extremely high credit status, as "risk-free."

[19] Except, perhaps, with high-yield and emerging market debt.

[20] In actuality, on the equity side some portfolio managers want multi-factor models which go beyond what we've introduced here, as well.

[21] Reniers (2004), page 2.

[22] See Appendix 9-A.

[23] This was taken from comments shared with the author via an e-mail from Steve Campisi following a review of this section.

[24] This example is taken from a presentation Steve Campisi gave at the 2004 Fixed Income Attribution (FIA) Symposium. We thank Steve for allowing us to use it here.

[25] Campisi uses the term "effects" at this point, but we're going to use the term "con-

tributions," to differentiate what we do at the benchmark and portfolio levels, and what we do when we combine them.

[26] The "Index Spread Advantage" referenced in the Allocation formula is analogous to the way the Brinson-Fachler model handles allocation. It's the difference in spread change, between the sector and the index.

[27] There's some rounding going on here.

[28] For further information on the K-S model, we suggest Karnosky and Singer (1994), Spaulding (2003, 2), and Bacon (2008).

[29] This is usually the periods over which we'd calculate attribution, although we could see it done for as long as a quarter or over a multi-day period, too.

[30] We thank Steve Campisi for showing us this approach.

[31] Much gratitude is offered to Carl Bacon for his work in this area. (See Bacon (2002)).

[32] Menchero (2004), page 77.

[33] The only part of this system which is a bit of a challenge to explain is the third factor in the selection effect where we see the semi-notional return being employed. As it was explained to the author, this factor was needed to get the formulas to achieve their proper result.

[34] For further discussion, we suggest Spaulding (2003, 2) and the articles in the Appendix 9-A.

[35] The Fall 2003 issue of *The Journal of Performance Measurement* was entirely devoted to this topic. You may find these discussions of interest.

[36] There are some systems where you input the correct return and any residual is classified as the "trading effect." While this, too, is debatable, it is done.

[37] One additional point: the Performance Measurement Forum developed standards for attribution (see Spaulding (2002/2003), pages 13-21). They are on our company's Web site (www.SpauldingGrp.com).

[38] Shorthand notation: *JPM = The Journal of Performance Measurement.*

Chapter 10 –
The 3 Ms of Risk[1]

"Quantitative measures of risk
for individual portfolios
leave much to be desired."
David F. Swensen[2]

This quote is hardly a ringing endorsement for the notion of measuring risk, is it? And yet, I haven't found anyone who has disagreed with it, which perhaps makes it even more of a challenge. And, when we consider the following quotes:

"Risk is at the center of all investment decisions."
Peter L. Bernstein

"The essence of investment management is the
management of risks, not the management of returns."
Benjamin Graham

"Risk is the source of the returns."
Jacob Rosengarten[3]

we quickly realize that we've got to do something to measure this very important element of our investment process. And why? Because if we look at two portfolios with the same return, we might be tempted to think they're the same. However, we should ask the question "How much risk did each manager take to achieve their return?" Risk measurement provides us with a perspective on this matter. And, in addition to finding out how much risk was taken, we might also want to know whether we were compensated properly for this degree of risk.

"In a world that is changing faster than we can grasp, risk seems more difficult to understand and control."[4] Risk measurement, like many of the other areas of investment performance, isn't unique to our industry. We are faced with many other areas of risk, many of which are measured and some of which are highlighted. For example, the number of airline crashes are captured, as are the incidents of various diseases. And cigarette packages have warnings highlighting the risks cigarettes pose.

The challenge is that there's an emotional side to risk which is difficult (if not impossible) to quantify. Table 10-1 provides some thoughts on risk.

We're sure you know of some people who love to engage in "extreme sports," be it skydiving, rock climbing, or extreme skiing. Why is it that some people enjoy, actually live for, these risky events while others wouldn't dream of trying them?

Or, go to an amusement park. You'll no doubt see lines of people waiting for the most dangerous-looking rides. My younger son, Doug, would be among them as he loves these rides. But not me – I have no interest in them.

The reality is that some people are *risk averse*, while others are *prone* to engage in risky activities. And, some avoid one type of risk while feeling quite comfortable taking on other types of risk.

But What is Risk?

If you look up the definition in just about any dictionary, you'll likely see a reference to the chance or potential for loss – the possibility of losing something. But if you ask others, you may get different definitions, such as volatility,[6] uncertainty, or failure to achieve an objective. We believe that one of the first things you need to do when trying to figure out *how to measure risk* is to decide *what does risk mean to us?* Then, you can choose a measure that best meets these objectives – better yet, a few such measures.

What some have said about risk	
"Courage is not simply one of the virtues but the form of every virtue at the testing point." – C.S. Lewis	"A man who carries a cat by the tail learns something he can learn in no other way." – Mark Twain
"The credit belongs to the man who is actually in the arena, whose face is marred by dust and sweat and blood, who knows the great enthusiasms, the great devotions, and spends himself in a worthy cause; who at best, if he wins, knows the thrills of high achievement, and, if he fails, at least fails daring greatly, so that his place shall never be with those cold and timid souls who know neither victory nor defeat." – Theodore Roosevelt	"If the creator had a purpose in equipping us with a neck, he surely meant us to stick it out." – Arthur Koestler "It is better to die on your feet than to live on your knees." – Dolores Ibarruri "Life is a fatal adventure. It can only have one end. So why not make it as far-ranging and free as possible?" – Alexander Eliot

Table 10-1: Some Thoughts on Risk[5]

Is risk bad?

Most people, I think, recognize that risk is a necessary ingredient in the investment process – without risks, there are no rewards.

> "Risk is not bad. What is bad is risk that is
> mis-priced, misunderstood, or unintended."
> Leslie Rahl[7]

We know that it tends to be the risk takers who gain the success. Likewise in investing, we need to take on risks in order to get a return. But knowing how much risk we're taking and having some confidence that it's reasonable are critically important.

The benchmark's role in risk

Risk should, in many cases, be related to the benchmark. Why? Because the benchmark is our starting point – it represents the risk that we're comfortable with. Now, we want to see how much more or less risk the manager took, in order to achieve their results, in order to decide if (a) the manager got the return he deserved for the added (or reduced) risk, and (b) if we're comfortable with this level of risk.

As you'll shortly see, not all risk measures use an index. However, there's usually a way to bring the index into play, just as we compare the portfolio's return with the index's return.

Risk measures

There are many ways to measure risk.[8] But, as Swensen suggests, these are lacking a bit. Never the less, they're all we've got, although we're working on more. We will discuss some of the more common measures.

Standard deviation

> "If your broker [or investment advisor] is not familiar with the concept
> of standard deviation, get a new one."
> William Bernstein, *The Intelligent Asset Allocator*

While standard deviation is the most common risk measure,[9] it is also probably the most criticized.[10]

Let's begin with talking about *what it is*. Standard deviation is a measure of dispersion or volatility. It reflects how disparate or spread out the elements are within a group or sample. It tells us how tight a set of values are clustered around the average of the distribution. It's a measure of dispersion or variation in a group of numbers. We typically associate it with the "bell-shaped curve," also called a "normal distribution." Figure 10-1 shows an example of a normal distribution.

The larger the value of the standard deviation, relative to the average of the distribution, the more spread out the elements are; likewise, the smaller the standard deviation, the tighter the distribution.

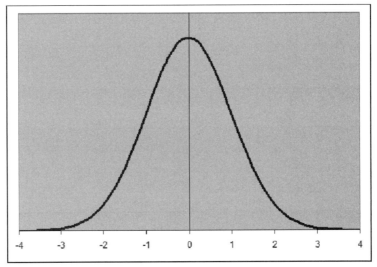

Figure 10-1: Bell-shaped Curve / Normal Distribution

One standard deviation represents roughly two-thirds of the population, meaning that the average, plus-and-minus one standard deviation, will include approximately two-thirds of all the elements in the group. If we were to extend our measure to two standard deviations (i.e., our average plus-and-minus two standard deviations), we will pick up approximately 95% of the distribution. For our purposes, we usually only deal with one standard deviation.

Why is it the most common method?

We encounter standard deviation in many other disciplines, including basic statistics classes and social sciences. For many of us, we were introduced to the "bell-shaped curve" in our earliest years of school. So, it's not a foreign concept to us.

It's also fairly intuitive. We can visualize a distribution being grouped together, calculating an average, and then identifying how the other elements fall within the distribution.

Why is it criticized?

> "It is unsound in general to equate variability of return to investment risk."[11]
>
> R.S. Clarkson

The first reason standard deviation is often not thought very well of is that it can be argued that it isn't a risk measure; rather, it's a measure of volatility. And many believe that volatility or variability isn't risk.

But, as we've said, this stuff is controversial. So, if your definition of risk is "volatility," then by all means, it would make sense to use this measure for this is what it measures. But, if you categorize risk as a "measure of potential loss" or "failure to reach an objective," then you would be hard pressed to explain how standard deviation accomplishes this.

> "Perhaps the greatest disservice done to standard deviation...
> has been to call it *the* measure of investment risk."[12]
>
> Leslie A. Balzer

Saying this, standard deviation has been recognized as a risk measure for quite a while. Even Dietz cited it: "A more appropriate measure of risk is the standard deviation from the average return; that is, a measure of the fluctuation around the average return."[13] He even cited Nobel Prize winner Harry Markowitz as being a champion of standard deviation: "of the six possible measures of risk Markowitz discusses in his book, *Portfolio Selection,* he chooses the standard deviation as the most suitable."[14] If we look at Dietz's definition of risk, we can see why: "Risk is the degree of probability of realizing the expected return."[15]

Another criticism of standard deviation is its assumption of a normal distribution. This is often not the case. Taleb (2007) discussed the failings of this assumption quite extensively.

If we were to study various distributions, we'd find that some are skewed (see Figure 10-2) one way or the other, or they may have "fat tails"[16] or other abnormalities which causes them to fail the normal distribution assumption.

But this assumption of a normal distribution will be reflected in the statistics which are produced, which will therefore give a misleading representation of what is really present. Taleb (2007) is especially critical of the assumption of normality.[17]

Another problem with standard deviation is that it treats the plus-side of the mean the same as the negative-side. The reality is that few people mind being "above average,"[18] while most would want to avoid being labeled "below average." Thus, we don't mind above-average returns – it's the below-average returns we wish to avoid. But standard deviation does not draw a distinction between them.

In order to have any meaningful information with standard deviation, we need a relatively large sample size. How large? It's hard to say. While we've seen people measure standard deviation with distributions of under 10 elements (even as low as one![19]), we can't draw much information from such small groups. A minimum of ten should be used.[20]

How do we calculate it?

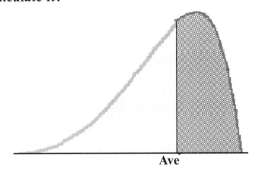

Ave

Figure 10-2: Skewed Distribution

The method for deriving standard deviation is quite simple. We begin by calculating the average for the distribution. Next, we compare each individual element in the distribution with the average (i.e., we subtract one from the other – it doesn't matter which way you do this). Next, we square each of these differences and then sum them up (commonly referred to as the "sum of the squares").

We next divide this sum by the number of elements in our distribution and finally take the square root of this number.

Table 10-2 gives an example of this. Our portfolio's average return for the period is 1.57%, while its standard deviation is found to be 1.34 percent.

Monthly Returns	x_i	$x_i - x$	$(x_i - x)^2$
1	3.00%	1.44%	0.0206%
2	3.10%	1.54%	0.0236%
3	2.80%	1.24%	0.0153%
4	1.75%	0.19%	0.0003%
5	-0.14%	-1.71%	0.0291%
6	0.28%	-1.29%	0.0165%
7	1.76%	0.20%	0.0004%
8	3.31%	1.75%	0.0305%
9	1.75%	0.19%	0.0003%
10	1.21%	-0.36%	0.0013%
11	1.14%	-0.43%	0.0018%
12	-1.18%	-2.75%	0.0754%
Average (x) =1.57%		Sum= 0.2149%	
		Sum ÷12 = 0.0179%	
		Square Root =1.34% Standard Deviation = 1.34%	
Average, +/- 1 Standard Deviation =		Low: 0.23%; Average = 1.57%; High = 2.90%	

Table 10-2: Portfolio Returns and Standard Deviation

Standard deviation adds value when we compare it with our index and/or other similar portfolios. Table 10-3 provides the equivalent statistics for our benchmark.

As you can see, the index's average was one basis point less than the portfolio; thus, the portfolio's excess return was 0.01 percent. But, the index had a much lower standard deviation (1.21% vs. 1.34% for the portfolio), suggesting that the portfolio took on more risk than the index did, to achieve only a one-basis-point advantage.

Monthly Returns	x_i	$x_i - x$	$(x_i - x)^2$
1	2.89%	1.33%	0.0176%
2	2.99%	1.43%	0.204%
3	2.70%	1.14%	0.0129%
4	1.77%	0.21%	0.0004%
5	-0.10%	-1.66%	0.0277%
6	0.90%	-0.66%	0.0044%
7	1.80%	0.24%	0.0006%
8	2.80%	1.24%	0.0153%
9	1.77%	0.21%	0.0004%
10	1.23%	-0.33%	0.0011%
11	1.16%	-0.40%	0.0016%
12	-1.15%	-2.71%	0.0736%
Average (x) = 1.56%		Sum = 0.1760%	
		Sum ÷12 = 0.0147%	
		Square Root =1.21% Standard Deviation = 1.21%	
Average, +/- 1 Standard Deviation =	Low: 0.35%; Average = 1.56%; High = 2.77%		

Table 10-3: Benchmark Returns and Standard Deviation

Sharpe Ratio

While the standard deviation by itself can provide some insight into volatility, another approach is to use the Sharpe Ratio, named for Nobel Prize winner Bill Sharpe, who created it (see Sharpe (1966)).

The Sharpe Ratio is actually not a risk measure, *per se*. Rather, it's a *risk-adjusted* measure. And like a few risk-adjusted measures we'll be looking at, it is a ratio, where a representation of the return is in the numerator and the risk statistic is in the denominator. These measures *adjust the return for the risk that's taken.*

In the case of the Sharpe Ratio, the risk measure that's used is the standard deviation. And the return is represented by the equity risk premium, which is the additional compensation that an investor is entitled to receive for taking added risk. It's simply the portfolio return minus the risk-free return. The formula is:

$$SharpeRatio = \frac{\overline{r_p} - \overline{r_f}}{\sigma_p}$$

where

r_p = average (over bar) portfolio return

r_f = average (over bar) risk free return

σ_p = standard deviation

Actually, there are alternative formulas for the Sharpe Ratio, including one that Sharpe later derived (see Sharpe (1994)):

$$SharpeRatio = \frac{\overline{r_p} - \overline{r_f}}{\sigma\left(r_{p_i} - r_{f_i}\right)}$$

At this time it is difficult to say which is more common, but we will use the original formula for our examples.

As we look at the formula, you can probably guess whether or not we want the number to be large or not. The numerator represents our return, adjusted for the risk-free rate; we'd want this to be as large as possible. And the denominator is our risk measure, the standard deviation. And, as we discussed above, the larger the standard deviation, the greater the volatility, so we'd want this to be small. A large numerator and a small denominator should yield a large number – thus, the larger the Sharpe Ratio, the better; the more return we're getting per unit of risk taken.

Using our above example, and assuming our risk-free rate to be 0.17%, we find our Sharpe Ratio to be:

$$SharpeRatio = \frac{\overline{r_p} - \overline{r_f}}{\sigma_p} = \frac{1.57\% - 0.17\%}{1.34\%} = 1.04$$

The Sharpe Ratio for the index is found in a similar manner:

$$SharpeRatio = \frac{\overline{r_p} - \overline{r_f}}{\sigma_p} = \frac{1.56\% - 0.17\%}{1.21\%} = 1.15$$

Since the portfolio's Sharpe Ratio (1.04) is lower than the index's (1.15), it has a lower return per unit of risk taken; it was less efficient in its use of risk than the index was.

Interestingly, when the returns are negative, the results aren't necessarily as intuitive as one might expect. Please refer to Table 10-4.

	Excess Return	Risk	Sharpe Ratio
Fund A	9%	5%	1.80
Fund B	9%	10%	0.90

Table 10-4

The goal with Sharpe Ratios is to have a high number, yes? So, when we compare these two funds we conclude that Fund A did a better job in managing risk, as it achieved the same return as Fund B but took on less risk.

Now, let's look at Table 10-5.

	Excess Return	Risk	Sharpe Ratio
Fund A	-9%	5%	-1.80
Fund B	-9%	10%	-0.90

Table 10-5

In this case Fund B again took on more risk; however, we get what some might argue are counterintuitive results, as the Sharpe Ratio for Fund B is lower than Fund A's.

As with much of what we deal with in performance measurement, there are differing views as to whether this actually is a problem or not. Much has been written on this subject, and I plan to offer a piece at a later date that will go into much greater detail on this topic. But for now I'll simply provide one of the suggested alternatives should you feel that the results are incorrect.

Israelsen[21] proposed a modification to the Sharpe Ratio when excess returns are negative: we simply raise the denominator to the negative one power, which is equivalent to multiplying it by the numerator. This adjusts our earlier formulas as follows:

$$SR_{1'} = \left(\overline{r}_p - \overline{r}_f \right) \times \sigma_r \qquad SR_{2'} = \left(\overline{r}_p - \overline{r}_f \right) \times \sigma \left(r_p - r_f \right)$$

Table 10-6 provides the results if we employ this variation. Here we find that Fund A gets a higher ratio. Note that the same challenges with negatives to the Sharpe Ratio apply to the Information ratio, so if you modify one you may want to modify the other. Sharpe is aware of this situation and feels that the formula behaves properly and that no adjustments are needed. If you do make an adjustment, you should indicate this.

	Excess Return	Risk	Sharpe Ratio
Fund A	-9%	5%	-0.0045
Fund B	-9%	10%	-0.0090

Table 10-6

A criticism of the Sharpe Ratio is that the number alone doesn't say a whole lot – it's really best when compared with the Sharpe Ratios of other portfolios or the benchmark.

Other problems with the Sharpe Ratio have been noted. For example, Bill Sharpe himself said, "The Sharpe Ratio is oversold." Guy Miller from BARRA said, "You want to know if a number is very fuzzy or just has a little peach fuzz on it. Sharpe Ratios tend to be buried in hair." How's that for a visual image! And Jack Bogle, founder of the Vanguard Group, said, "In terms of how the Sharpe Ratio has done in evaluating mutual funds, I would say the answer is poorly."[22] Often the criticism is based on the use of standard deviation and therefore the assumption of normality; however Eling & Schuhmacher (2007) determined that this really isn't a problem.

In spite of this criticism, the Sharpe Ratio remains a very commonly used risk statistic.

Downside risk

"Loss aversion – the greater impact of the downside than the upside – is a fundamental characteristic of the human pleasure machine."

Amos Tversky

As noted above, standard deviation looks equally at the above- and below-average sides of the average. Some feel that this is inappropriate. Consequently, we can look at just the below-average side, which is also called the "downside." Here, we employ the downside risk (also referred to as "downside deviation"[23]).

Rom and Ferguson explain that "Downside risk is measured by target semi-deviation (the square root of target semi-variance) and is termed downside deviation." They go on to say "A familiar way to view downside risk is the annualized standard deviation of returns."[24] This is the "discrete" form and can be calculated as follows:

$$DownsideRisk = \sqrt{\frac{\sum_{i=1}^{n}\left(r_i - Mean(R)\right)^2}{n}}$$

or against a target

$$DownsideRisk = \sqrt{\frac{\sum_{i=1}^{n}\left(r_i - T\right)^2}{n}}$$

which are offered by Feibel (2003).[25]

We would annualize these results by multiplying by the square root of 12.

Rom explains that the continuous form is preferred and offers two reasons:

1. The continuous form permits all calculations to be made using *annual* returns, the natural way for investors to specify their investment goals. The discrete form requires monthly returns for there to be sufficient data points to make a meaningful calculation, which in turn requires converting the annual target into a monthly target. This significantly affects the amount of risk that is identified.

2. A second reason for preferring the continuous form to the discrete form has been proposed by Sortino and Forsey (1996): "Because we make an investment, we don't know what the outcome will be... After the investment is made, and we want to measure its performance, all we know is what the outcome was, not what it could have been. To cope with this uncertainty, we assume that a reasonable estimate of the range of possible returns, as well as the probabilities associated with those returns, can be estimated... In statistical terms, the shape of [this] uncertainty is called a probability distribution. "In other words, looking at just the discrete monthly values does not tell the whole story. Instead, these values need to be used to help identify a distribution of all the values that could have been earned."[26] The formula is:

$$DownsideRisk_{Continuous} = \sqrt{\int_{\infty}(t-r)^2 f(r)dr}$$

where

t is the annual target return

r is the random variable representing the return for the distribution of annual returns, f(r)

f(r) is a normal or three-parameter lognormal distribution.

If you'd like more information on these last formulas, we suggest Rom and Ferguson (1997/1998). For our presentation, we have opted to go with the discrete form, as it's much easier to calculate and more straightforward.

Tables 10-7 and 10-8 show our portfolio's and index's downside deviation, respectively. As you can see, we only consider those months that had a return below the average, but still divide by the total number of elements.

Once again, the index has a lower number, which indicates less volatility, which translates into less risk.

Two alternatives to using the average for this calculation are (1) to use zero as the demarcation line (i.e., to calculate the downside relative to zero – using only those occurrences with returns below zero, or (2) to use the absolute return (the liability-related return, the minimum funding requirement, the minimum acceptable return, or just target [T]).[27]

Monthly Returns	x_i	$x_i - x$	$(x_i - x)^2$
1	3.00%		
2	3.10%		
3	2.80%		
4	1.75%		
5	-0.14%	-1.71%	0.0291%
6	0.28%	-1.29%	0.0165%
7	1.76%		
8	3.31%		
9	1.75%		
10	1.21%	-0.36%	0.0013%
11	1.14%	-0.43%	0.0018%
12	-1.18%	-2.75%	0.0754%
Average (x) = 1.57%		Sum = 0.2140%	
		Sum ÷12 = 0.0103%	
		Square Root =1.02% Downside Deviation = 1.02%	

Table 10-7: Portfolio Returns and Downside Deviation

This second approach is a way to have this statistic provide more relevance when an absolute return exits for the portfolio. It gives you an idea of the frequency of below-the-absolute-value occurrences there are.

Monthly Returns	x_i	$x_i - x$	$(x_i - x)^2$
1	2.89%		
2	2.99%		
3	2.70%		
4	1.77%		
5	-0.10%	-1.66%	0.0277%
6	0.90%	-0.66%	0.0044%
7	1.80%		
8	2.80%		
9	1.77%		
10	1.23%	-0.33%	0.0011%
11	1.16%	-0.40%	0.0016%
12	-1.15%	-2.71%	0.0736%
Average (x) = 1.56%		Sum = 0.1084%	
		Sum ÷12 = 0.0090%	
		Square Root = 0.95% Downside Deviation = 0.95%	

Table 10-8: Index Returns and Downside Deviation

Sortino Ratio

Since we're talking about the downside of the distribution, we may as well touch on another way to evaluate this information, and that's the Sortino Ratio, named for its creator, Frank Sortino.[28] As you will see, it bears a strong resemblance to the Sharpe Ratio:

$$SortinoRatio = \frac{R_p - R_T}{\sigma_{Downside}}$$

The differences are that in the numerator, instead of the risk-free rate being subtracted from the portfolio return, we use the absolute return (in this case, we show it as the target, T). And, for our risk statistic, we use downside deviation in the denominator rather than standard deviation.

If we use the downside deviation information from above, but define our target as 1.40%, then we can calculate our Sortino Ratio as follows:

$$SortinoRatio = \frac{R_p - R_T}{\sigma_{Downside}} = \frac{1.57\% - 1.40\%}{1.02\%} = 0.1667$$

We can calculate the index's Sortino Ratio in a similar manner:

$$SortinoRatio = \frac{R_p - R_T}{\sigma_{Downside}} = \frac{1.56\% - 1.40\%}{0.95\%} = 0.1684$$

With a higher Sortino Ratio, we can once again see that the index is doing a better job of managing risk.

Another formula to consider is the "Active Sortino." Here, the excess (or active) return is divided by the downside risk. The MAR is set to zero. This is a way to calculate the downside risk relative to an index.

$$ActiveSortino = \frac{R - \overline{R}}{\sigma_{Downside}}$$

Beta

Beta, like standard deviation, is a measure of volatility. It is the market-weighted average of the individual stock betas and can vary, depending on what benchmark is used. It measures the systematic risk of a security or the entire portfolio. It describes the sensitivity of a portfolio (or the security) to the market. This statistic measures the tendency of a portfolio (or security) to move relative to the market. The numerator shows the covariance of the portfolio (or security) with the market; the denominator has the variance of the market.[29]

$$\beta = \frac{Cov(R,\overline{R})}{Var(\overline{R})}$$

This formula can be broken down further:

$$\beta = \frac{Cov(R,\overline{R})}{Var(\overline{R})} = (\rho) + \left(\frac{\sigma_P}{\sigma_M}\right)$$

Correlation   Relative Volatility

You wouldn't normally be expected to calculate Beta – pricing services typically have this information available.

The market's beta is defined as 1.00. Therefore, a portfolio or security with a greater beta is taking on greater volatility relative to the market and therefore more risk. It's also expected to get a greater return for this added risk. In contrast, a portfolio with a beta below 1.00 would have less volatility, less risk, and therefore would be expected to have a lower return. "In the classical CAPM [Capital Asset Pricing Model] framework, the expected return on an asset is related to the beta of the asset with the respect to market portfolio. For instance, an asset with the beta of 2 is expected to have a risk premium that is twice as high as the market portfolio's risk premium."[30]

Treynor Ratio

Jack Treynor developed a risk statistic which is quite similar to the Sharpe Ratio:[31] It actually preceded Sharpe's approach and arguably served as the basis for what Sharpe developed.

$$Treynor = \frac{R_p - R_F}{\beta}$$

As you can see, the numerator is identical to the Sharpe Ratio – the difference lies in the risk statistic which is used; rather than standard deviation Treynor used Beta. The Sharpe Ratio is for a concentrated portfolio containing significant idiosyncratic risk, while the Treynor Ratio is for a fully diversified portfolio.[32]

Alpha & Jensen's Alpha

One thing that's common in performance measurement is the use of multiple terms to mean the same thing, and the same term to mean multiple things. An example is the term "alpha." In general, alpha is equivalent to excess return and active return. It's simply the portfolio return minus the benchmark return.

$$Alpha = R - \overline{R}$$

Jensen's alpha[33] takes into consideration the portfolio's beta. It's therefore a risk-adjusted performance measure that is the average return on a portfolio over and above that predicted by the Capital Asset Pricing Model, given the portfolio's beta and the average market return. It also takes into consideration the portfolio's risk-free rate (R_f), plus beta, relative to the benchmark.

$$Jensen's Alpha = (R - R_f) - (\beta \times (\overline{R} - R_f))$$

The expression R - R$_f$ is referred to as the *equity risk premium*. This formula is also referred to as Jensen's Index. This statistic is an indication of the professional manager's ability to achieve a superior return relative to the index.[34]

Tracking error

Tracking error measures the volatility of the excess return; that is, the variation around the average level of excess return. It measures the active risk – the risk taken by the manager, relative to the index. The math is quite simple – it's the standard deviation of the excess returns.

$$TrackingError = StdDev(Rp_i - Rb_i)$$

The larger the tracking error, the greater the volatility of the portfolio relative to the index. Table 10-9 shows the portfolio and index returns from above, along with their monthly excess returns.

Month	Portfolio	Index	Excess Return
1	3.00%	2.89%	0.11%
2	3.10%	2.99%	0.11%
3	2.80%	2.70%	0.10%
4	1.75%	1.77%	-0.02%
5	-0.14%	-0.10%	-0.04%
6	0.28%	0.90%	-0.62%
7	1.76%	1.80%	-0.04%
8	3.31%	2.80%	0.51%
9	1.75%	1.77%	-0.02%
10	1.21%	1.23%	-0.02%
11	1.14%	1.16%	-0.02%
12	-1.18%	-1.15%	-0.03%

Table 10-9: Input Data for Tracking Error

If we calculate the standard deviation of the excess returns, we'll get a result of 0.24 percent. Monthly tracking error is typically annualized by multiplying by the square root of 12.[35] Doing this, we get a result of 0.83%, which is very low.

An alternative way to calculate tracking error is to use the geometric view of excess return,[36] which is:

$$ER_G = \frac{R+1}{\overline{R}+1} - 1$$

where

R = portfolio return

$\overline{R}$ = benchmark rate of return

Instead of the arithmetic difference, we have a ratio. When this approach is used, our tracking error formula becomes:

$$TE_G = \sigma\left(\frac{r_i+1}{\overline{r_i}+1} - 1\right)$$

Tracking error is a measure of volatility. In this case, it's the volatility of excess returns over time.

Information ratio

The information ratio is another risk-adjusted measure. It is the "average excess return per unit of volatility in excess return."[37] Evidence suggests that it was developed by Treynor and Black (1973); they called it the "appraisal ratio."

One could also say that it is alpha divided by the standard deviation of alpha. Some consider this measure to be a variation on the Sharpe Ratio, with the numerator being excess return (portfolio return minus index return, rather than minus risk-free rate), and the denominator being the risk measure, tracking error (rather than standard deviation).

The formula:[38]

$$IR = \frac{\left(\dfrac{\sum\limits_{i=1}^{n}\left(r_i - \overline{r}_i\right)}{n}\right)}{\sigma\left(r_i - \overline{r}_i\right)}$$

We typically calculate this by using the annualized excess return, which we get by multiplying the average excess return by 12, and the annualized tracking error, which, as noted earlier, is arrived at by multiplying the tracking error by the square root of 12.

Using the information from above, we calculated the annualized tracking error to be 0.83 percent. You're invited to confirm that the average excess return is 0.0017%, which when annualized becomes 0.02 percent. The annualized information ratio is therefore 0.02.

Like many of our other statistics, the information ratio, by itself, yields little information. It is best when compared with other portfolio's information ratios.[39]

Modigliani-Modigliani[40]

"They stayed up late on Saturday night discussing such issues as the relationship between temperature and electrical conductivity."

From <u>Einstein</u>, by Walter Isaacoson, speaking of Einstein and Hendrik Lorentz

As I understand it (and has been confirmed by the measure's codeveloper, Leah Modigliani[41]) the late Nobel prize laureate Franco Modigliani and his granddaughter, Leah, were discussing the shortcomings of the existing risk-adjusted methods. For example, they found shortcomings in the Sharpe Ratio ("[M-squared] gives an answer in basis points that is readily understandable by non-experts, while Sharpe produces a ratio that is difficult for the average investor to interpret[42]"), the Treynor and Jensen measures ("these measures account for risk by adjusting the market portfolio to match the risk of [the portfolio], instead of adjusting [the portfolio] to match the risk of the market"[43]), and the information ratio ("[t]he ratio is essentially a measure of the probability that the performance of a portfolio will fall below that of its benchmark ... The information ratio is a useful concept, although its primarily relevance is for money managers (portfolio managers or pension fund managers) who are likely to be judged by their 'tracking ability,' i.e., performance relative to the market ... it includes the standard deviation in its denominator ... it is the standard deviation of the tracking error and does not take into account the overall risk ... the information ratio is *not* a risk-adjusted measure of performance"[44] [emphasis in original]).

M-squared is a measure that is "grounded in modern finance theory and yet easy for the average investor to understand."[45] I think that perhaps *this* is the greatest advantage this measure has: it is extremely intuitive.

We begin by finding the returns and risks for both the portfolio and benchmark. We'll refer to these values as:

R_p – Return of portfolio

R_b = Return of benchmark

σ_p = Portfolio risk

σ_b = Benchmark risk.

We want to *adjust* the portfolio's risk so that it equals the benchmark's. I would say that this is a basic concept of the measure ... the notion of adjusting the portfolio's risk to equal the benchmark's. How would we do this? Well, in reality, we're going to do this mathematically; we could accomplish this with a portfolio by reducing the portfolio's risk (if it's higher than the benchmark's) by increasing its exposure to cash or a risk-free asset, or increasing it (if its risk is lower than the benchmark) by adding more risky assets to it.

The simple explanation of this approach is that we calculate the M-squared for each month and then link the values as we would any return to arrive at a cumulative return. This results in what may be termed the "fully geometric approach."

In a note to this author, Leah wrote "With M-squared we are creating a 'risk-equivalent version' of our portfolio. In our example, the portfolio has more risk than the benchmark (as measured by standard deviation); therefore, the return has to be 'levered down.' We can accomplish this by, for example, putting more cash in until it matches the standard deviation of the benchmark. But how much cash? We determine this by calculating the ratio of the benchmark's standard deviation to the portfolio's standard deviation. This tells us how much should be in our original portfolio."

These ratios are two critical elements for our process. The first (the ratio of the benchmark risk divided by the portfolio risk) indicates how much we retain of the original portfolio. We already calculated the standard deviations and use them again here:

$$HowMuchOfOriginalPortfolio = \frac{\sigma_b}{\sigma_p} = \frac{0.0333}{0.0392} = 0.8505 = 85.05\%$$

The amount of cash (or in our case, of the risk-free return) is simply one minus this value:

$$HowMuchOfCash = 1 - \frac{\sigma_b}{\sigma_p} = 1 - 0.8505 = 0.1495 = 14.95\%$$

Now, we use these values to calculate the M-squared value for each month:

$$M^2_{Monthly} = \left[\left(\frac{\sigma_b}{\sigma_p}\right) \times r_{p_i}\right] + \left[\left(1 - \frac{\sigma_b}{\sigma_p}\right) \times r_{RiskFree_i}\right]$$

Before we proceed, we might ask what relationship this formula has with the version we showed earlier. Well, they're the same. We will leave it to the reader to apply the necessary algebraic tools to see this.

Our next step is to now apply this formula to each month (see Table 10-10). If we geometrically link these values we find a cumulative return for the period of 28.60 percent. And, if we annualize this our return is 26.13 percent.

Some have suggested that the M-squared method only uses the Sharpe Ratio or standard deviation as its risk measure.[46] This, however, is incorrect. The reason for this perhaps is due to the fact that so many examples are shown using standard deviation or the Sharpe Ratio. However, the authors indicated that virtually any risk measure may be used, "provided that it satisfies two more general conditions: 1) leverage changes the risk and reward of portfolios in the same direction, and 2) leverage does not change the ranking of portfolios at any level of risk."[47]

Month	Portfolio	Index	Returns R_f	M^2
1	7.00%	5.76%	0.43%	6.23%
2	5.00%	4.18%	0.46%	4.46%
3	-4.00%	-3.11%	0.47%	-3.47%
4	4.50%	4.00%	0.44%	4.02%
5	4.00%	3.87%	0.41%	3.58%
6	-3.00%	-2.36%	0.36%	-2.60%
7	8.00%	5.55%	0.39%	7.10%
8	0.10%	-3.12%	0.36%	0.13%
9	1.00%	-0.50%	0.38%	0.93%
10	-5.00%	-2.74%	0.41%	-4.36%
11	2.00%	6.33%	0.48%	1.82%
12	4.00%	2.03%	0.44%	3.58%
13	7.00%	5.89%	0.46%	6.23%
Avg	2.35%	1.98%	Cumulative M^2	1.3036
Std dev (ó)	4.3%	3.8%	Annualized M^2	27.73%
% of portfolio return	88%			
% of cash (R_f) return	12%			

Table 10-10: Calculating M-squared for each month

Now, why is it that I find this approach so good? Well, as the authors have said, it presents the information in the same format as our other returns: in basis points. Our Sharpe Ratio for this portfolio is 1.71, while the Sharpe Ratio for the benchmark is 1.88, meaning that the benchmark is getting 1.88 units of return for each unit of risk that it's taking, versus the 1.71 units of return that the portfolio is getting. While this is far superior to simply comparing standard deviations, does-n't the reporting of the result in a percentage format have greater value? We're showing what the portfolio's return is if its risk is adjusted to equal that of the benchmark: comparing apples-to-apples. We can then compare the returns with this value.

With the M-squared value we can report before and after risk returns, just as one might report before and after tax returns, or before and after fee returns. I could envision giving this client a report similar to what we show in Table 10-11.

In this example, we're showing that we clearly outperformed the benchmark on a *before* risk-adjusted basis, but that after we take risk into consideration we underperform. Another way to view this might be that the benchmark is getting a greater return for the risk it took versus the portfolio.

Portfolio (before adjusting for risk)	30.20%
Benchmark	28.60%
Portfolio (after adjusting for risk)	26.13%

Table 10-11: A Way to Report the Results

Contrasting the measures with our view of risk

As we discussed at the beginning of this chapter, it's appropriate to decide

	Volatility	Potential Loss	Not Meeting Objectives
Standard Deviation	x		
Beta	x		
Sharpe Ratio	x		
Treynor Ratio	x		
Sortino Ratio	x	x	x
Tracking Error	x		
Information Ratio	x		
M-squared	x		
Downside Risk	x	x	x

Table 10-12: How Measures Match Up with Risk Definitions

what risk means to you. And once this is done, we can look for measures that relate to our definition. Table 10-12 shows how the measures we discussed tie in with three views of risk.

As you consider what measures make sense for you, reflect on what your view of risk is. Clearly, one isn't enough. Risk measures, as David Swensen suggests, have a lot to be desired. So, the best we can do is to use a variety of them in order to gain as much insight as possible into what's being done.

The other two Ms of risk – Management and Monitoring

> "It's only when the tide goes out that you see who has
> been swimming with their trunks off."
>
> Warren Buffet[48]

Too often we only focus on the measurement of risk, but we should also pay attention to the management and monitoring of risk, too.

But risk management is, as Charles Ruffel stated, "in its infancy. Most pension pools have almost no awareness of what they need to be doing in terms of optimal risk management, and those sophisticated plan sponsors that have focused on risk find little in the market that they can buy."[49]

I heard about a survey where some plan sponsors were asked what they would do if their manager violated their risk policy. The majority apparently said that it depends on what the return is.[50] That's the wrong answer. We need to separate what the return is from risk when it comes to managing risk.

Some, however, might argue with this. Ineichen addresses risk management by contrasting hedge funds and active managers: "The main difference between risk management in a relative return setup versus an absolute return setup is that the term 'risk' is defined differently. In relative return space risk is defined as *active risk,* which is the possibility of deviation from the benchmark. Oversimplified, this means that an 18% return when the benchmark is up 20% is bad, whereas a 20% loss is okay as long as the benchmark is down 20%, too."[51]

An example of a risk management technique is the one employed by Goldman Sachs called "The Green Zone."[52] It's based on tracking error. An acceptable range is identified, which is called the "green zone." An additional broader band is next chosen, which is called the "yellow zone." Finally, anything beyond this will be in the "red zone."

The risk management team then monitors tracking error to ensure it remains within the acceptable or green zone. If it slips into either the yellow or red zones, the manager needs to figure out what's going on so adjustments can be made to return the portfolio to the acceptable range.

When you realize that tracking error does not indicate whether or not the excess return is positive or not, you see how that isn't the issue here – it's that the firm wants to ensure that risk is managed properly.

Not all agree that this method is acceptable. Muralidhar (2004, 1) argues that it limits the manager's ability to better manage the risk budget, to avoid periods where they feel they need to reduce risk (which might cause the tracking error to reduce significantly and hence enter the red zone) or take on added risk to exploit opportunities (again, entering the red zone). He feels this method can actually be detrimental to the client. Building on the work of the Modiglianis, he adds another M to the equation (his own) resulting in a concept he calls "M cube."

A problem with tracking error is that it is a measure of volatility, which some argue isn't risk. A manager who wisely avoids sectors that are underperforming will end up with high tracking error. A key of risk management and monitoring is to understand the source of the risk.

Frank Sortino tells a story of a plan sponsor who was looking for a manager for Japanese equities. They found one with exceptional returns over a ten-year period, but who also had a large tracking error. When they voiced their concern about tracking error, the manager explained that this was due to his avoiding the banking sector, which had not performed well. The plan sponsor was not satisfied, insisting that the tracking error had to be lowered. So, the manager asked "How many bad banks would you like me to purchase?" While this is perhaps a flippant response, it is what would have been needed to lower the tracking error. Knowing the source of the tracking error was probably all that was needed, for the plan sponsor to decide whether they were comfortable with this.[53] A better response, however, would have been for the manager to ask to run tracking error against the index without including the banking stocks; as long as the prospect was okay with the manager's decision to avoid this sector, then for tracking error purposes, this alternative might very well have been enough to confirm the acceptability of the manager's active risk.

Risk management is still a fairly new concept and there's bound to be controversy here, too – and hopefully new approaches to help.

We have seen too often where the high returns are applauded without taking into consideration the risk that was needed to achieve them.[54] And, unfortunately, it's often too late when we realize this, when significant losses occur.

Risk measurement is only part of the puzzle: you've got to make sure you properly manage and monitor the risks to avoid problems.

Summary

Return and risk are related in that we can't get good returns without taking on risk. But bad returns can come from risk, too. Measuring risk is therefore a practice which all investment firms need to do. Understanding the strengths and shortcomings of the various approaches, and what they accomplish, can be very helpful to the risk management process.

Exercises

1. Calculate the standard deviation for the portfolio in Table 10-E.

Months	Returns
1	3.15%
2	2.80%
3	2.60%
4	1.55%
5	0.24%
6	0.38%
7	1.26%
8	3.11%
9	1.55%
10	1.41%
11	1.54%
12	2.18%

Table 10-E: Monthly Returns

2. Using the information from 1, calculate the portfolio's Sharpe Ratio. (Risk-free rate = 0.17%.)

3. Using the information from above, along with the index data from this chapter, calculate the portfolio's tracking error.

4. Using the above information, calculate the portfolio's tracking error.

ENDNOTES

[1] I credit a variety of sources for providing clarity on the information contained in this chapter. Bruce Feibel's book (Feibel (2003)) offers quite a bit on risk, including helpful examples. Bruce also responds to various inquiries I've made. I've benefitted from hearing several of Frank Sortino's lectures over the years dealing with the Sortino Ratio as well as reading some of his articles, such as Sortino and Forsey (1996). Brian Rom provided assistance through e-mails, including confirming that it was actually he, not Frank, who developed the ratio which bears Frank's name (at Brian's request). I had the pleasure of interviewing Franco Modigliani, who provided some helpful insights into the measure he developed with his granddaughter, Leah. I may have missed a source or two, for which I apologize. Leah shared details regarding their model with me. Recently, Bill Sharpe and Jack Treynor provided me with some helpful information that's reflected here.

[2] Swensen (2000), page 309.

[3] Rosengarten (2003).

[4] Leong et al. (2002), as referenced in Ineichen (2003), page 171.

[5] Taken from *Men's Health* (2005), page 22, confirming that risk isn't limited to investing.

[6] See, for example, Schneeweis, et al. (2001), page 11.

[7] Rahl (2000), page 24.

[8] We will address *ex-post* risk measures; that is looking back historically to look at the risk we took. Although *ex-ante* (forward looking) risk is growing in importance, we elected to exclude these measures from this text, as they're more complicated and at a level beyond what we feel is appropriate with this material.

[9] TSG (2001), page 52.

[10] For example, see Flader (1994); and Rom and Ferguson (1994, 3).

[11] Rom and Ferguson (1994), page 32.

[12] Ibid, page 31.

[13] Dietz (2004), page 64.

[14] Ibid, page 64.

[15] Ibid, page 34.

[16] Meaning unusual things happen more frequently than you might expect.

[17] See, for example, page 36, Taleb (2007).

[18] In fact, most people consider themselves "above average" in many things, while only half of the population at a time can technically be "above average."

[19] Where the standard deviation would have to be zero – a very tight distribution, yes?

[20] We say a minimum of ten, but this is actually very low. We'd prefer 20 or more. Ideally, 36 or more.

[21] See Israelsen (2003) and Israelsen (2004).

[22] Lux (2002), pages 28-36.

[23] But even here we find disagreement. See, for example, Kaplan and Siegel (1994), Kaplan and Daugirdas (1996) and Rom and Ferguson (1994, 2).

[24] Rom and Ferguson (1997/1998), page 6.

[25] Feibel (2003), page 163.

[26] Rom and Ferguson (1997/1998), pages 6-7.

[27] In a recent e-mail with the author, Brian Rom and Kathleen Ferguson suggested that the simple term "target," represented by "T," is the preferred designation (Rom and Ferguson (2004)). In Sortino and Forsey (1996), the preference for MAR (minimal acceptable return) is stated. We'll use target for our examples.

[28] Feibel (2003), pages 199-200.

[29] Farrell (1983), page 40.

[30] Schneeweis et al. (2001).

[31] See Treynor (2005) and Farrell (1983).

[32] Interestingly, perhaps, Treynor disavows credit for this ratio and argues against the use of beta(Treynor (2008/2009)).

[33] See Jensen (1968), pages 389-416.

[34] Haight and Morrell (1997), page 184.

[35] We discussed annualizing returns in Chapter 5. Here, we're annualizing risk statistics. There are various ways to do this. Here, we use the square root of 12. In an c-mail conversation with me, Bruce Feibel explained, "Because the standard deviation is the square root of the variance, we are being consistent by multiplying the standard deviation by the square root of twelve to form the annual equivalent." For other measures, you'll see that we multiply by 12. Bruce explains, "When working with monthly data, we take the monthly return and multiply it by twelve in order to calculate the annual equivalent of the arithmetic mean (not the geometric mean). In the same way, we take the monthly variance and multiply it by twelve in order to calculate the annual variance." Feibel (2004).

[36] We discuss geometric excess return in Chapter 9.

[37] Goodwin (1997), page 2.

[38] Feibel (2003), pages 200-202.

[39] For further discussion on information ratio, we suggest Goodwin (1997) and Coggan (2004).

[40] For a comparison of this approach to the calculation with others, see Spaulding (2007, 1) and Spaulding (2007, 2).

[41] Modigliani and Modigliani (2006), page 70.

[42] Modigliani and Modigliani (1997), page 5.

[43] Modigliani and Modigliani (1997), page 6.

[44] Modigliani and Modigliani (1997), page 9.

[45] Modigliani and Modigliani (1997), page 3.

[46] See Bailey et al. (2007), page 769.

[47] Modigliani and Modigliani (1997), page 8.

[48] Ineichen (2003), page 17.

[49] Ruffel (1999), page 22.

[50] Source is unknown.

[51] Ineichen (2003), page 129.

[52] Litterman et al. (2001).

[53] See Sortino (2002).

[54] While the industry is replete with such examples, we suggest you read <u>When Genius Failed</u> by Roger Lowenstein, for an insightful look at one of the better known examples - Long Term Capital Management.

Chapter 11 –
The Performance Presentation Standards

Early on, we mentioned the three C words: confusion, controversy, and change. And for the performance presentation standards, confusion is probably the most appropriate of the three (although there's both controversy and change, too).

We'll touch on the most important aspects of the standards and hopefully address some of the more confusing points along the way. We'll also touch on some of the controversial points.

Before the standards

In 1986, I conducted a "mini-survey" of individuals from about 20 investment firms to find out how they presented their performance results to prospects.[1] At the time, I headed systems for a New York City (NYC) investment firm but also had oversight responsibility for our performance reporting, since I was the one who had designed the system.

We received quite a mix of responses; for example:

- a model – the problem with a model is that it isn't necessarily reality and can be difficult to validate.[2]
- a representative account – how truly representative is such an account? Does this account tend to get greater attention, knowing that this is what you use to showcase your performance?
- the average of top five portfolios for every quarter – in other words, these portfolios may change from period to period, and hardly represent the average of all the portfolios.
- a static group of portfolios – like the representative portfolio, these accounts will no doubt get special attention given their special role.
- a static group, across multiple styles – what does this represent? This firm used an average across a half dozen styles (from very aggressive to very conservative) to represent its return, but this represents nothing of any value.

Another NYC-based manager had begun a multi-million-dollar advertising campaign about this same time, touting their performance. The unfortunate thing was that their results mirrored that of the firm in our survey which reported that they always take the average of their top five portfolios; this NYC manager moved accounts in and out of their performance group because of "discretion." Apparently, performance and discretion seemed to be highly correlated.

An article in *The Wall Street Journal* bemoaned the absence of standards and the tendency of "Too many managers [who] use smoke and mirrors to make their performance look better."[3] As these advertisements began to get attention, other firms decided to follow suit by developing similarly misleading ads.

We also discovered that the calculations varied from firm to firm. For example, we reported our numbers net-of-fee (after the advisory fee was removed), while many others reported them gross-of-fee (before the removal of advisory fee). Thus, our returns would tend to be lower, on average, because the fee had been removed, putting us at a disadvantage when competing against a firm who used gross-of-fee returns.

We also didn't accrue for dividends or interest, while some other firms did. Returns with accruals tend to be higher than those without, thus another opportunity for differences and challenges when comparing results.

What's the point of a presentation?

When you hand someone your performance history, the message should be "these are the kind of results you would have expected to have gotten, had we been managing your money, in this given style, for this time period." That is what you are essentially telling your prospect. But, when you use a model, a representative portfolio, the average of your top five, etc., is this true? Probably not.

The birth of standards and a little history

In 1986, after seeing what was going on in the industry, the Financial Analyst Federation (FAF) decided to take action (before the regulators would).[4] They formed a "Blue Ribbon Commission" to come up with standards for presenting performance. These were published as a draft in the *Financial Analysts Journal.*[5]

In 1990, the FAF merged with the Institute of Chartered Financial Analysts to form the Association for Investment Management and Research (AIMR), and the FAF standards shortly became the AIMR standards: the AIMR Performance

Presentation Standards (AIMR-PPS).

During the next couple years, the draft standards were open for comment. Two groups (the Investment Council Association of America [ICAA] and the Investment Management Consultants' Association [IMCA])[6] voiced opposition to one point in particular: the way returns were to be calculated.[7] The standards called for them to be asset-weighted, but the ICAA and IMCA felt they should be equal-weighted.[8] While the AIMR was sensitive to these groups' concerns, the asset-weighting approach remained.

These standards went into effect in 1993. They were described as "a set of guiding ethical principles intended to promote full disclosure and fair representation by investment managers in reporting their investment results. A secondary objective is to ensure uniformity in reporting so that results are directly comparable among investment managers."[9]

The AIMR-PPS standards met with immediate success, as we saw later that year when we conducted our first survey of the industry. We found that over 90% of the U.S. firms had either become compliant or planned to be.[10] Since that time, we have surveyed the industry four more times and have continued to see similar results.[11]

Almost immediately after the standards went into effect, we saw some changes take place with the standards, partly in response to the particular needs of the banking industry. Two that come to mind are firm definition and taxable portfolios.

Because banks typically invested for both trust and institutional portfolios, and because many didn't feel that the trust side warranted becoming compliant, a change was made to allow firms to define themselves as "how they held themselves out to the public."

We also discovered that additional time would be needed for many of these institutions that wanted to bring their taxable accounts into compliance. Therefore, the effective date for compliance was shifted to January 1, 1994.

The standards were updated in 1997, when additional rules, as well as some clarification, were adopted.

The response from the global community and the creation of GIPS

Other countries saw what was happening in the States and decided to adopt standards, too. Some took the AIMR-PPS as it was written, while others decided to create their own. In response, AIMR created a global committee in the mid-90s to help with these efforts.

This led to the creation of the Global Investment Performance Standards (GIPS), which were published in 1999.[12]

Countries that had developed standards were encouraged to adopt the GIPS standards. This could be done in a couple ways: first, to abandon their standards completely; second, to accept GIPS but continue with those parts of their standards which represented past practices which were well established and they felt needed to continue (which we call a Country Version of GIPS, or "CVG").

Several countries almost immediately created CVGs or adopted GIPS; for example, Ireland, the United Kingdom, and Switzerland. In 2001, the AIMR-PPS became a CVG for both the United States and Canada.

Countries that hadn't developed standards were encouraged to adopt GIPS, either in English or by translating it to their local language (what we call a Translated version of GIPS, or "TG").

Revised standards / revised structure / convergence

As the Investment Performance Council (IPC) (the group previously responsible for the standards) began to work on the second edition, two major changes occurred, separate from what changed with the actual standards:

1. The decision was made to alter the organizational responsibility for the standards in order to increase the role of country sponsors
2. The decision was made to eliminate all individual country versions of GIPS and to *converge* onto the single global standard.

Two groups now exist that oversee the standards:

*   The Executive Committee (EC) is the group that's actually responsible for the standards
*   The Country Council provides input to the EC and is responsible for naming four of the seven members.

Convergence means there are no more country versions, including the AIMR-PPS. We have a single standard which (as of this writing) has been endorsed by roughly 30 countries: an amazing feat.[13]

The purpose of GIPS is to provide a standard which will allow firms to compete, on equal footing, as they seek business around the globe. It has been referred to as a "global passport," with the goal that a firm that complies with GIPS will be welcomed when competing in a market with a country version of GIPS.

What are these standards?

One of the confusing points of the standards is what they are exactly. Some think they're calculation standards, like the BAI and ICAA which we discussed in Chapter 2. Others think they're for client reporting.[14]

The standards address the way managers *present* their performance to *prospective clients*. There are three parts of the client presentation:

1. The presentation, which contains the performance returns, plus other statistics
2. The disclosures, which are essentially footnotes, providing additional details about the firm and the presentation.
3. Supplemental information, which is additional performance information to supplement the compliant presentation.

While the presentation and disclosures are mandatory for a firm compliant with the standards,[15] supplemental information is optional.

Now, let's get into some of the details of the standards.

Why become compliant?

When the standards were first introduced, firms could gain an advantage over their competitors by complying. Today, more than ten years after the standards went into effect, firms are at a disadvantage by not being compliant.

The institutional marketplace expects firms to be compliant. And even in the high-net-worth market, many prospects are now asking about compliance.

Another important, and possibly unanticipated, benefit to becoming compliant is that it helps firms enhance their controls over the performance measurement process, from the calculations to the dissemination of the information. Some firms have found that the controls are improved throughout the firm, perhaps most importantly in looking at the management of portfolios. While moving toward compliance, firms often discover problems they were unaware of (for example, how the returns are calculated). Naturally, clients in the same style or composite should have similar returns. If not, there may be a problem with portfolio management, the account may have certain restrictions, or perhaps some other factor is at work. Thus, there may be some unanticipated benefits from compliance.

The composite – the core of the standards

The key to the standards is the concept of a composite, which is a collection of portfolios into a single group that represents a particular style or investment strategy. This allows for an apples-to-apples comparison. We liken this to the various types of automobiles. If you go shopping for a car, you probably have a car type in mind (an SUV [sport utility vehicle], a van, a roadster, a truck) so that you can compare one company's offerings with others. The same thing holds true here: the consumer, who is looking for a manager of a particular style, will want to see how competing managers compare. The composite presentation facilitates this comparison.

The composite is a critical part of the presentation in that it allows for the comparability of results between managers.[16] While the definition of composites is up to the manager, we would expect them to follow the various products they offer, which probably are similar to many other firms, to at least some extent.

There are various criteria which can be used when creating a composite, including:

- Asset class – we'd expect composites to have a consistency of asset classes across its members (e.g., stocks, bonds, balanced)
- Investment style or strategy – e.g., growth vs. value, indexed vs. active
- Risk characteristics – if a manager uses risk as a way to differentiate clients (e.g., tracking error bands), then we'd expect this to carry over to the composite creation
- Type of portfolio – separate accounts vs. commingled or pooled portfolios
- Size of portfolio – where appropriate, composites can be constructed with asset sizes above or below a threshold
- Client characteristics – e.g., tax status or cash flow requirements
- Balanced account allocation ranges – we wouldn't necessarily expect all bal-

anced portfolios to be in the same composite unless they all have similar allocations to underlying asset classes

- Extent or use of derivatives, hedging, and leverage – while you're permitted to mix portfolios that have derivatives, hedging, and leverage with portfolios that don't, you're also permitted to use this as a criteria to segregate the portfolios

- Client type – in some cases, the type of client might mandate creating multiple composites; for example, in the States it's not unusual for the Taft-Hartley (union pension fund) clients to be segregated because of their unique requirements and also because many such funds only want to see presentations with other Taft-Hartley clients included

These are suggested but not mandatory guidelines. For example, some firms like to group their mutual funds with their separate accounts, while some don't – it's up to you.

A key rule of the standards is that all fee paying, discretionary accounts must be included in at least one composite. Accounts can be in more than one composite.[17] In addition, if a client has such unique characteristics that it doesn't fit with any of your composites, it can be in a single-account composite. Note: grouping these misfit accounts into a single composite isn't permitted.

Non-fee-paying portfolios may be included in composites, too; if they are, additional disclosures are required. Nondiscretionary portfolios may not be included in a composite. (Some firms will use composites as a way to group nondiscretionary portfolios as part of their management process. This is fine. But these groupings aren't technically composites for purposes of complying with the standards.)

Many firms believe that those products or styles they don't market don't require any work – that you don't have to bother putting the accounts into a composite and do the calculations. This isn't true. You still have to have composite presentations for these styles, although you're not obligated to undergo the same costly printing that you might do with those you are marketing. Just be prepared

> **Composite points of confusion**
> 1. You can group those portfolios that don't easily fit into other composites into a single, "catch-all" composite.
>   Wrong! Catch-all composites aren't permitted.
> 2. You don't have to worry about "nonmarketed composites."
>   Wrong! You still need to manage these and be prepared to present the results, although costly printed presentations aren't required.

to provide a presentation, if requested.[18]

Exceptions to the rule

We said that all fee-paying, discretionary accounts must be in at least one composite. There are some exceptions, however:

- Minimum asset size – you're permitted to create a minimum account size for your composites, below which you aren't required to include accounts. The idea behind this is that accounts that are below your minimum aren't able to represent your investment skill. However, this minimum must be a "real" minimum – you can't be marketing below the minimum: the minimum can be equal to or below the minimum you require for a client, but can't be above the minimum.
- New accounts – you're allowed time to get a new account invested before adding it to a composite.
- Terminated accounts – when an account announces they're leaving, you should immediately remove it from the composite (but retain the history through the last calculation period).
- Changes in investment style – if a client requests a change in investment strategy (e.g., from mid-cap growth to large-cap growth), you are permitted time to get the account's holdings converted to the new style.
- Large cash flows – you're permitted to establish a market value percentage for cash flows, whereby when an external cash flow exceeds this level you can temporarily remove the account from the composite.[19]

Portfolio returns

In general, the standards require the use of time-weighted rates of return for portfolios that are included in composites. The only exception at this time is for private equity investing, where the manager controls the cash flows. For these composites, since-inception internal rate of returns are required. We touch on this in Chapter 2.

Returns must include cash.

In addition to the returns being time-weighted, we require that the market values include accrued interest.

Gross-of-fee returns (i.e., returns before the removal of fees) are recommended but not required. The alternative is net-of-fee returns (i.e., after the removal of fees). Gross-of-fee are preferred because it's common for there to be a mix of fees within a composite, and the net-of-fee return will therefore not necessarily reflect the fee that a prospect would pay. With a gross-of-fee return, the prospect can always back-out the fee to determine their approximate net-of-fee return.

Composite returns

We said that these standards are not "calculation standards." But they do have some calculation rules. The return, as noted earlier, has to be asset-weighted, using the beginning period market values. There are three ways to do this.

#1 – Use the beginning market value only. Here, we use each portfolio's beginning period market value and multiply it by that portfolio's return. These values are then summed and divided by the sum of the total beginning period market values. The formula:

An example might help. In Table 11-1 we show the returns for a composite's

$$ROR = \frac{\sum_{i=1}^{n} BMV_i \times ROR_i}{\sum_{i=1}^{n} BMV_i}$$

portfolios, along with their respective market values and the application of this formula.

#2 – Use beginning market value plus weighted cash flows. To increase the accuracy of the composite return, we can include the cash flows that take place during the period. In Chapter 3, we addressed ths issue of weighting cash flows. Recall the idea of the weighting factor:

where

$$W = \frac{CD - D}{CD}$$

CD = number of calendar days in the period
D = day of cash flow

The formula looks a lot more complex, but it isn't really – we're just including the cash flows:

Portfolio	BMV	ROR	BMV x ROR
1	100	2.00%	2.00
2	120	2.20%	2.64
3	130	2.10%	2.73
4	100	2.30%	2.30
5	105	2.20%	2.31
6	110	2.10%	2.31
7	120	2.15%	2.58
8	135	2.10%	2.84
9	500	2.20%	11.00
10	600	2.30%	13.80
Total	2,020		44.51
ROR = 44.51 / 2,020 = 2.20%			

Table 11-1: Composite Return, Using Beginning Market Value Only

$$ROR = \frac{\sum_{i=1}^{n}\left[BMV_i + \sum_{j=0}^{m}\left(C_{i,j} \times W_{i,j}\right)\right] \times ROR_i}{\sum_{i=1}^{n}\left[BMV_i + \sum_{j=0}^{m}\left(C_{i,j} \times W_{i,j}\right)\right]}$$

We show two Riemann sums in both the numerator and denominator, because we have to sum the account's market value plus any cash flows that occurred. Table 11-2 shows an application of this approach to our composite.

Two things you might notice: first, the 10th portfolio's level of participation in the return has dropped significantly (from a weight of 600 to 426.67) because of its large cash flow early in the month; second, the return has dropped slightly.

#3 – Aggregate Method: The final approach is to have the composite look like a single account by aggregating all of the values and calculating a single return.

In Table 11-3 we show the aggregation of our ten portfolios by summing their beginning and ending market values and cash flows. The formula we're using is the Modified Dietz, treating each of the weighted flows as if they occur to this aggregated portfolio.

Portfolio	BMV	ROR	Cash Flow	Day of Flow	Weight (CD =30)	BMV + Weighted Flow	(BMV +Wtd Flow) x ROR
1	100	2.00%	+50	18	0.40	120	2.40
2	120	2.20%				120	2.64
3	130	2.10%	− 20	15	0.50	120	2.52
4	100	2.30%				100	2.30
5	105	2.20%	− 5	20	0.33	103.33	2.27
6	110	2.10%				110	2.31
7	120	2.15%				120	2.58
8	135	2.10%				135	2.84
9	500	2.20%				500	11.00
10	600	2.30%	−200	4	0.87	426.67	9.81
Total	2,020					1,855.00	40.67
ROR = 40.67 / 1855 = 2.19%							

Table 11-2: Composite Return, Using Beginning Market Value + Weighted Flows

Portfolio	BMV	ROR	Cash Flow	Day of Flow	Weight (CD =30)	BMV + Weighted Flow	EMV
1	100	2.00%	+50	18	0.40	120	152.40
2	120	2.20%				120	122.64
3	130	2.10%	− 20	15	0.50	120	112.52
4	100	2.30%				100	102.30
5	105	2.20%	− 5	20	0.33	103.33	102.27
6	110	2.10%				110	112.31
7	120	2.15%				120	122.58
8	135	2.10%				135	137.84
9	500	2.20%				500	511.00
10	600	2.30%	−200	4	0.87	426.67	409.81
Total	2,020		− 175			1,855.00	1,855.67
ROR = (1,855.67 − 2,020 − 175)/(2,020+50×.40+(−20)×.50+(15)×.33+(−200)×.87) = 2.19%							

Table 11-3: Composite Returns, Using the Aggregate Method

<u>Optional – equal-weighted returns</u>: Firms may optionally provide composite returns on an equal-weighted basis, as supplemental information. Table 11-4 shows the calculation of the equal-weighted return for our composite.

Carve-outs

On occasion, a firm may wish to take part of a portfolio and include it in a composite. This is perhaps most commonly done with balanced portfolios, where we want to take the equity portion and include it with an equity composite, and/or the fixed income portion and include it with a bond composite.

Portfolio	ROR
1	2.00%
2	2.20%
3	2.10%
4	2.30%
5	2.20%
6	2.10%
7	2.15%
8	2.10%
9	2.20%
10	2.30%
Total	21.65%
ROR = 21.65% / 10 = 2.17%	

Table 11-4: Equal-weighted Composite ROR

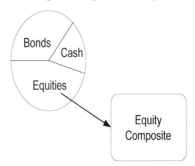

Figure 11-1: Carving Out the Equity Part of a Balanced Portfolio

Figure 11-1 shows what we're trying to accomplish with a carve-out. Since the returns must include cash, we're obligated to bring some of the cash along. But how much?

There are two general approaches to assigning the cash: cash allocation or having separate cash buckets for the segments.

A general rule for cash allocation is that we can't wait until the end of the period to figure out what we want to do – this might be called *cash allocation optimization*. Rather, our approach must be decided ahead of time. The method shouldn't be arbitrary, and we should be consistent in how we do it. We'll discuss two approaches.

First, we can simply select the ratio in advance: for example, at the end of this month, we'll assign 50% of the cash to bonds and 50% to stocks. This may seem arbitrary, but it's permitted.

The second approach we'll discuss relates to the allocation to the targets we've established for our balanced portfolio. We take the amount of cash we require to fulfill our allocation. The formula is:

$$Segment\ Re\ turn + Cash\ Re\ turn = \left(\frac{ActualAllocation}{T\arg etAllocation} \times SegmentROR\right) +$$

$$\left(\frac{\left(T\arg etAllocation - ActualAllocation\right)}{TargetAllocation} \times CashROR\right)$$

Table 11-5 shows an example.

Asset Class	ROR	Target Allocation	Actual Allocation
Stocks	2.00%	60%	50%
Bonds	1.00%	40%	35%
Cash	0.10%	0%	15%

Table 11-5: Portfolio Returns and Allocations

The equity segment is underinvested by 10%, so it's entitled to some of the cash. To come up with an equity-plus-cash return to allocate this segment to an equity composite, we can use the above formula as follows:

$$Equity\ Re\ turn + Cash\ Re\ turn = \left(\frac{50\%}{60\%} \times 2.00\%\right) +$$

$$\left(\frac{\left(60\% - 50\%\right)}{60\%} \times 0.10\%\right) = 1.68\%$$

A preferred method to allocation is to have separate cash buckets for the equity and bond segments. We can do this by having sub-portfolios, separate portfolios, or, if the accounting system can support it, different cash accounts for each.[20]

A key with carve-outs is that the carved-out portion resembles what an account would look like if it was invested solely in that asset class. So, the equity portion we carve out in the above example should be constructed in a similar fashion to the single asset class accounts which it will be joining in the equity composite.

The ability to allocate cash went away in January 2010. After this date firms that wish to use carve-outs must manage the cash separately for each carved-out segment.

Note that there are some additional disclosure requirements if you use carve-outs. Check the standards for the details.

Measure of dispersion

We said above that the returns of the composite should resemble the return that the prospect might expect to get had the manager been investing his money in the style of the composite for the period shown in the report. In order to give the prospect a sense of how likely this would have been, the composite presentation must include a measure of dispersion.

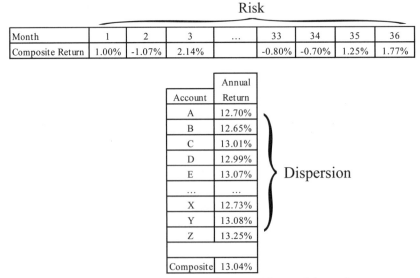

Risk

Month	1	2	3	...	33	34	35	36
Composite Return	1.00%	-1.07%	2.14%		-0.80%	-0.70%	1.25%	1.77%

Account	Annual Return	
A	12.70%	
B	12.65%	
C	13.01%	
D	12.99%	
E	13.07%	Dispersion
...	...	
X	12.73%	
Y	13.08%	
Z	13.25%	
Composite	13.04%	

Figure 11-2: Standard Deviation - Risk or Dispersion

If the dispersion is wide, the recipient of the report might question the consistency and discipline of the investment approach, as well as its construction; if it's tight, then the recipient would likely have greater confidence in the reported average return.

There are a variety of ways to calculate dispersion:

- standard deviation
- high/low returns
- range of returns
- quartiles, quintiles, deciles

Any of these are acceptable, although standard deviation appears to be quite common and is more appropriate when there are a sufficient number of portfolios to make the statistic significant or meaningful. A key in calculating these measures is that the portfolios that are included in the measure must have been in the composite for the entire period for which dispersion is being measured.[21]

Because we also use standard deviation as a risk measure, some are confused with this method. As a risk measure, we are looking at, for example, monthly returns over some time period (e.g., 36 months) to see how volatile our returns have been; as a measure of dispersion, we are looking at a single period (e.g., an annual return) and a group of accounts returns to see how disparate they are. (See Figure 11-2.)

Discretion

We say that all fee-paying, discretionary portfolios must be included in at least one composite. Fee-paying is easy to figure out; but what does "discretionary" mean?

It essentially has to do with the manager's ability to carry out their investment strategy. Often clients impose restrictions on managers. The manager needs to determine if the restriction is so imposing that they're being hampered in their investment approach so that the return doesn't truly reflect their skills.

The firm is free to decide their rules for discretion. A key is that the rules not be arbitrary and that they be carried out in a consistent manner. Also, the rules should be documented.

An example of a situation that might cause a firm to flag the portfolio as "nondiscretionary" would be a client who requires "no sin-stocks." The definition of sin may vary from institution to institution or individual to individual. For some, it means "no tobacco, alcohol, or gambling stocks." The manager would need to decide if this restriction impacts his or her performance. If it does, then they are free to call the portfolio a "nondiscretionary portfolio."[22] Alternatively, the firm might see this as an opportunity to create a new composite, with accounts with such a restriction. This way, they have something to show other prospects with similar restrictions.

Policies and procedures

The standards require firms to have written policies and procedures. We suggest they be created for all areas relating to compliance, including:

- timing for adding accounts into composites
- discretionary rules
- calculations (returns, measures of dispersion)
- treatment of large cash flows (for temporary removal of portfolios)
- how portfolio assignment to composites is handled (criteria)
- policies for distributing performance information to prospects

Verification[23]

Verification is a review of a firm's compliance with the standards by an independent, outside party. It is done at the "firm" level and involves a review of the firm's records.

Verifiers don't actually state that the firm "complies with the standards." Rather, the verifier will state that the composites were constructed properly and that the firm's processes and procedures are designed to calculate and present results in accordance with the standards.

While many of the firms that offer verification services are accounting firms, nonaccounting firms also perform this service.

Because the standards are relatively complex, many investment firms that believe they comply really don't. Consequently, we strongly recommend that firms undergo verification.

There are three general reasons why we favor verification:
- For peace of mind – again, the standards are complex; if you claim compliance, it's nice to have some confidence in this claim.

- For marketing purposes – the institutional market expects firms to (a) comply and (b) be verified.
- To avoid problems with regulators – many regulatory bodies (e.g., the SEC in the States) do their own "verifications" when a firm claims compliance – this is one verification you don't want to fail.[24]

It's important that the verifier remain "independent" so that their opinion isn't jeopardized. For example, if the prospective verifier was actively involved in bringing a firm into compliance, by helping write policies and procedures, assigning accounts to composites, validating returns, and/or preparing presentation materials, then they shouldn't verify the firm's compliance since they would, in essence, be verifying their own work.

Picking a verifier - due diligence. Some questions to ask
1. What experience does the firm have?
2. What experience do the individuals have who would do the verification?
3. What do their clients say? Have any later been found to be out-of-compliance, after the verifier issued their report?
4. How do they train their staff?
5. How do they keep up with the standards?
6. How active is the firm in the industry?
7. What's the cost?

Because verification can be costly, we encourage firms to undergo a thorough due diligence effort when selecting a verifier. There are no standards for verifiers; no one "verifies the verifiers." Verifiers can make mistakes, and you want to pick one that has a good reputation for thorough and accurate assessments.

Examinations

Firms that have undergone a verification may also want to consider an examination. This is an audit of their numbers. Unlike verification, which is done at the "firm" level, examinations are done at the "composite" level. You can have one or more composites *examined.*

Here, the independent, outside party validates the returns by checking security prices, portfolio holdings, and other details that typically aren't checked during the verification.

The verifier might compare the firm's records with custodial statements, independent pricing sources, and other records to ensure that what's reflected in the portfolio and the presentation materials is valid.

Examinations may not be done if the firm hasn't been verified (although they can be done in concurrence with a verification).

Examinations give the prospect some confidence that the numbers that are being reported are accurate (i.e., that the manager isn't "cooking the books"[25]).

Other areas of confusion

Let's touch on a few other areas where there's confusion about the standards:

- Mutual funds aren't included in composites – the last time I checked, mutual funds are both fee-paying and discretionary; so, if they're in the firm's definition, they need to be in a composite. Whether they're in a stand-alone (single-account) composite or grouped with individual portfolios is up to the firm, but they have to be somewhere.
- We can report that we're compliant, except for... – you're either compliant or not. If the firm isn't fully compliant, no reference to the standards should be made (other than saying "no, we don't comply").
- Software can't comply – software is a tool which can help a firm comply, but the software itself cannot be compliant with the standards.
- The calculations – composite returns are asset-weighted, and we've gone over the math in this chapter. However, some firms use the *ending* period market value rather than the *beginning* period market value. This yields a distorted value, as the ending market value already reflects the period's return and would inflate (in the case of positive portfolio returns) or deflate the composite return (in the case of negative portfolio returns). You must use the beginning period market value for these calculations.
- Inconsistent application of your policies – firms must be consistent; for example, with the timing on bringing portfolios into a composite, in how they define discretion, and in how they handle the minimum asset size. When they're not consistent, their compliance is in jeopardy.

Roadmap to compliance

We'll finish this chapter with an overview of an approach you may want to take to become compliant with the standards.

1. Get senior management support – without such support, compliance will be a challenge. Getting into compliance is costly and time consuming, although it can also be very rewarding.

2. Assemble a team – compliance isn't done by one individual. We recommend that a team be created, consisting of representatives from:

- marketing
- portfolio management
- performance measurement
- compliance / legal
- information technology

Someone needs to head up the effort – we generally suggest that this be someone from the performance measurement group. All members of the team should be familiar with the standards.

3. Define the firm – for many smaller firms, this is a "no brainer." But, for larger firms, especially global ones, some thought is required. This exercise can take months in some cases. Once the firm is defined, the scope of the effort is better understood.

4. Define the initial list of composites – these will typically be related to the products the firm offers and the styles they invest in.

5. Define discretionary and other rules for portfolios – this is an important step because these rules are used to decide whether or not a portfolio is included in a composite. Other rules include minimum asset sizes for composites.

6. Review portfolios / assign to composites – depending on whether the firm is complying with GIPS, *per se,* or a country version, they may have to go back five or ten years to gather records. Portfolios that existed during this period but that have since terminated must still be reviewed. As a result of this step, additional composites may be identified.

7. Get the required portfolio data[26] – at a minimum, portfolio market values and returns are required. This also includes the books and records to support what's reported.

8. Decide on the system to house the composites – many firms have used spreadsheets for their compliant data. While this is very tempting, given its cost and apparent ease of use, we strongly discourage this because spreadsheets are time consuming, error prone, cumbersome, and aren't databases. Today, there are many powerful composite systems available that will make compliance much simpler.

9. Put materials together   this includes the presentation and disclosures for all

composites and, optionally, supplemental information.

10. Get checked out – initially, we suggest an internal review of "self-check" be done to gain some confidence that you're compliant. Afterward, we strongly recommend a verification.

11. Stay compliant – this means keeping the records straight and keeping up with the standards, as they do change.

The future of the standards

The standards underwent a fairly major revision in 2005 (effective 2006). Subsequent reviews are planned every five years. The next major series of changes takes place in January 2011. Changes have (or will) occur in 2005, 2006, 2008, 2010, 2011, and 2012. Thus, keeping up with the standards is an important step to assure continued compliance.

Resources for the standards

There are numerous resources available for firms that wish to comply with or maintain compliance with the standards. Hopefully it's obvious that you need to have a copy of the GIPS standards, as well as your country version or translated version, if applicable. AIMR published a handbook for GIPS[27] which has since been completely replaced by the CFA Institute (the successor organization). This is a great reference book you should have in your library. The Spaulding Group was the first to publish a handbook, but it's virtually out of print. An update is being considered. We also offer a monthly newsletter (*Performance Perspectives*) which often includes updates on the standards (as well as commentary).[28]

The EC periodically issues "guidance statements" to enhance the material about the standards. These are typically made available for public comment before they go into effect. They are available on the GIPS web site and should also be added to the GIPS handbook.

You can sign up for the GIPS "e-mail alert list." This way, when there is any news about the standards, you are automatically e-mailed. And, as noted previously, you can attend the EC meetings and conference calls.

Summary

The presentation standards have helped to elevate the role of the performance measurement team. For institutional money managers, it's virtually a requirement to comply. But, it's not easy. And, once you've taken your firm into compliance, the job isn't over as you'll have to continue to report performance and manage the portfolios and composites. Also, you need to keep up with the standards, which include changes and new materials.

Exercises

1. Calculate the return for the composite in Table 11-E.

Portfolio	BMV	ROR
1	100	1.20%
2	110	1.40%
3	120	1.30%
4	110	1.40%
5	110	1.20%
6	130	1.10%
7	200	1.20%
8	140	1.30%
9	400	1.80%
10	600	1.70%

Table 11-E: Composite Data

2. In this chapter, we presented an example of a portfolio that had its equity portion carved out (see Table 11-5). Refer to it and carve-out the fixed income portion.

ENDNOTES

¹ I was unaware at the time that the Financial Analysts Federation was embarking on standards.

² We did analysis of a manager's model with their clients' portfolios; none of the portfolios matched the model. This was due to a few reasons, including the fact that the model rebalanced quarterly, while the actual portfolios didn't. Also, changes to the model were

not implemented at the same time as the actual portfolios. The returns were close, but definitely not the same.

[3] White (1989). Other examples are cited by McConnell (1989).

[4] In this case, the "regulators" are the SEC – the Securities & Exchange Commission. In the States, the investment industry likes to be as self-regulating as possible. Here was an opportunity to take action, to demonstrate that they saw a problem and were addressing it.

[5] Rosenberg et al. (1987).

[6] IMCA went so far as to develop their own standards (IMCA (1992)). However, as our 1995 survey showed, there was little interest from money managers in these standards (TSG (1995)). IMCA has since endorsed the AIMR standards.

[7] IMCA (1992), page 2; I no longer have the letter from the ICAA which addressed this.

[8] A concern with asset-weighting is that the larger accounts will get greater attention because their returns count for more. The attractiveness of asset-weighting, however, is that the returns better represent those of a single portfolio, which is the intention of the standards.

[9] AIMR (1993), page ix.

[10] TSG (1994), page 4.

[11] TSG (1994); TSG (1995); TSG (1997); TSG (2000); TSG (2002,1); TSG (2009).

[12] AIMR (1999).

[13] My favorite example of the lack of standardization is electrical outlets, where each country seems to have adopted a unique configuration with differing voltages, requiring the global traveler to equip herself with various adapters.

[14] The EC has discussed adopting client reporting requirements or guidelines, but to date nothing has surfaced.

[15] From this point forward, when we refer to "the standards," we mean GIPS and any CVGs, collectively.

[16] For further information on composite construction, we invite you to read the Composite Guidance Statement (IPC (2002, 2)).

[17] For example, a Taft-Hartley client could be in a Taft-Hartley-only composite, as well

as an institutional composite.

[18] The real key here is that these accounts are in composites and that you're maintaining them. If you're asked for a presentation, then you should be able to provide one within a reasonable amount of time (figure a day or two as a guideline).

[19] AIMR (2002), section 5-5, pages 1-5.

[20] Effective January 1, 2010, firms MUST use an exact approach to manage cash if they wish to use carve-outs; the allocation approach is no longer permitted as of this date.

[21] For example, if we're calculating dispersion for a year, then the portfolio must be present the full year and therefore have a return for the year in order to be part of the measure.

[22] Note: when we say "nondiscretionary" here, we're speaking only for purposes of the presentation standards. From a regulatory or client perspective, the portfolio is still considered discretionary.

[23] The most challenging and confusing area of the standards has been the issue of verification. We won't discuss the sordid history of this topic but will simply address what we have today, which is much better than the past.

[24] By no means is what the SEC does equivalent to a GIPS verification; however, they may conduct a review to see if they can determine if the firm isn't actually compliant.

[25] This is a phrase which means that the numbers are being altered so as to present a picture which is other than reality.

[26] Firms should have sufficient records to back up any returns they use for calculating composite statistics. This data should be independently generated (e.g., custodial and/or brokerage statements), although if the firm regularly reconciles their portfolio.

[27] AIMR (2002)

[28] To sign up contact info@SpauldingGrp.com

Chapter 12 –
Controls, Policies & Procedures

Given the enhanced role of the performance measurement function within investment management, it's critically important that the organization implement controls, policies, and procedures. In this chapter, we'll touch on some of these areas.

Controls

Returns are used to attract new business. But these returns must reflect reality. A student in one of my classes once remarked that "It's everyone's responsibility in the firm to *present the best possible picture*." In January 2009 a reporter asked me how managers might make their 2008 returns "look better." Such attitudes suggest that we can somehow manipulate the data. Wrong. We present reality. To do otherwise would be a mistake and could lead to problems. There are numerous cases where individuals did things to "present the best possible picture," only to be eventually found out and punished.

Controls are therefore needed within the organization to limit access to critical data and to ensure that the picture presented is reality. Tools have been developed to assist in this effort. But the organization should have formal systems of controls, policies, and procedures in place to avoid problems from arising.

Such tools include performance systems which often provide the ability to have controls, by providing audit trails and security features, that limit access to certain information. But manual systems are also needed to manage the performance measurement and reporting process.

There are many areas that need to be addressed, including the following.

Data

Our returns rely on data, and the much worn-out cliche "GIGO" (garbage in, garbage out) continues to be valid, regardless of how tired we might be of hearing it. It applies here. And given the massive amount of data, the frequency (often daily) in which it comes in, and the potential for changes to occur, getting it right can be quite a challenge.

Firms need controls to avoid unauthorized changes to be made and should have an audit trail to reflect changes. Firms need policies on when changes can be made, when they'll alter previously reported returns, and when clients, prospects, etc., will be informed of changes.

Some firms employ "data scrubbing" to provide a level of assurance in the data's quality. Techniques such as reasonability checks, comparisons with prior values, and comparing items with multiple sources can help have higher quality data. At times a firm may need to put in checks to ensure that they can reconcile results across time periods (e.g., to take a starting month's positions, incorporate intra-period activity, and then confirm that the result matches the ending month's positions). In addition, it's important that the firm reconcile their information. We worked with a client once that NEVER did reconciliation as they felt that the custodian was the "official books and records" and so why check it? Once we implemented a performance system they quickly realized why: many of the returns were in error.

Price changes

While there may be reasons why prices might be overridden (in the fixed income market, for example, where many issues aren't traded on a regular basis), controls are needed to monitor and track these overrides.

Ideally, the firm should record the identity of the individual making the change, security identification, the date of the change, the original price, the revised price, and the reason for the change. If other prices were obtained during the process, these should be recorded, too.

Changes to returns

On occasion, there may be a need to change rates of return. This may be because of large cash flows, missed trades, problems with corporate actions, reconciliation issues, or for other reasons. Access to returns must be limited, and any changes should be tracked with a documented audit trail (e.g., record the original return, the revision, the reason(s) for the change, the date of the change, and who made the change).

I recall a firm that allowed one of their managers to calculate her return herself. They had a performance system for everything else, but her return, which she calculated using a spreadsheet, would be the one used for her portfolios. Definitely an opportunity for controls.

Presentation materials

Oversight is needed over any materials that are used to present to both prospects and clients to ensure the materials are accurate and adhere to the appropriate standards, rules, and regulatory requirements.

If the firm complies with the presentation standards, then someone needs to sign off on the materials. As noted in Chapter 11, there are three parts of a compliant presentation:

- the presentation (the composite's returns and other statistics)
- the disclosures (footnotes)
- optionally, supplemental information

Someone needs to make sure that all of this information is prepared properly. In addition, anyone who provides performance information to prospects must be aware of firm policies, such as the requirement to present a fully compliant presentation to any prospect.

Advertising materials

Review and oversight is needed over any materials which reflect the firm's performance information; for example, responses to requests for proposal (RFP) to ensure that the information is accurate and complete. Often, the institution that issued the RFP will ask for information that goes beyond what's required by the presentation standards, and which may, in some ways, not even reflect the standards. For example, a firm may be asked for a "representative account," equal-weighted composite returns, or returns without cash. Presenting such information isn't in violation with the standards. However, the firm must ensure that the institution requesting the information still obtains a fully compliant presentation, even if they don't request one. Also, when asked for returns from a "representative account," procedures should be in place to ensure that this account is truly representative. Overseeing the RFP process is important to avoid problems.

The firm also needs controls, policies, and procedures over printed advertising materials and any performance information which would appear on the firm's Web site. A system should be in place to ensure that such materials comply with the presentation standards and any regulatory requirements.

Case study

We can't overstate the importance of controls. The press is replete with examples of firms that didn't have the proper controls and later suffered. One of my favorite examples dates to mid-1993. The article addressed a situation where a manager's returns were significantly overstated. The article stated that the money manager involved "flunks the grade school exam for basic math. After stating that his accounts had gained 22.1% in1990 ... [he] was forced to revise his figures and report that he'd actually lost 6.6% that year." Why did this occur? "The mix-up over the 1990 numbers came in part because one of Mr. Yu's employees put plus signs where there should have been minuses next to the returns on his stocks. As luck would have it, the employee did not put minuses where there should have been pluses, making her boss look spectacular in a bad year for the stock market."[1]

Policies and procedures

We suggest that firms have written policies and procedures for virtually every area of the performance measurement process. If you comply with the presentation standards, you're required to have them, as they related to the standards. And you should have policies that go beyond the standards.

Here are several examples of where you should consider having such policies and procedures:[2]

1. *How you calculate performance* – your formula(s); how you handle cash flows (start-of-day; end-of-day); if overrides are permitted; this is applicable for both portfolio and composite returns.
2. *Composite construction rules* – the rules to create composites; who makes the decision; who reviews these decisions; what happens if you discover a portfolio was in the wrong composite; if a form is used, a copy along with instructions.

3. ***Process for handling new accounts*** – who makes the decisions as to what composite(s) they go into.

4. ***Process for termination / portfolios*** – what occurs when a relationship ends; tracking; removal from composites; timing.

5. ***Change in styles / strategy*** – how handled when a client requests a change; timing; required documentation.

6. ***Discretion*** (your rules for discretion).

7. ***Minimum account size*** – if they exist, what happens when an account falls below / goes above; what the limits are for each composite.

8. ***How you calculate gross-of-fee returns*** – the formula, the rules, especially for mutual funds.

9. ***How you calculate net-of-fee returns*** – the formula, the rules, especially for mutual funds.

10. ***Pricing procedures / sources*** – it's not unusual for a firm to use multiple pricing sources, depending on the asset type; this documentation will include the sources of security pricing and foreign exchange rates, as well as the timing you use for pricing; also, if there are known differences between these sources and the composite's associated benchmark.

11. ***Treatment of cash flows*** – how the firm handles them from a return perspective (touched on in #1 (start-of-day, end-of-day) as well as temporary removal (#12 below)).

12. ***Temporary removal of portfolios from composites*** – circumstances that would warrant removal; include, if appropriate, for large flows (criteria; timing).

13. ***Policy on reporting*** – what you give to clients, prospects; how you handle special situations.

14. ***How you handle as-of adjustments to returns*** – for example, when a situation arises that may require a change in the originally published number(s); see appendix for further discussion.

15. ***Portability issues[3]*** – how were mergers/acquisitions handled (where applicable)? Should retain a list of any such events and how they were handled.

16. ***Corporate action processing*** – how handled; this can be an issue when, for example, there's a spin-off and you don't have all the details for some time, meaning you may have to revisit a previously processed action.

17. ***Carve-outs*** – if you use them, how you do the carving out (what method you employ; if it's changed over time); that is, how cash is allocated to the carved

out segments.

18. *Measure(s) of dispersion* – what measure(s) is(are) used; under what circumstances you might use one (e.g., standard deviation) rather than another (e.g., high/low).

19. **Initial composite construction** – the process that was used to create the composites initially.

20. **Document retention** – how long different documents are retained, both originals and copies; where copies are stored; how document destruction is handled.

You may also want to consider having a **policy on policies**. That is, how policies are created: what's the process, who authorizes them, etc.

Summary

Performance measurement isn't just about calculating portfolio returns anymore. It's so much more, and its role in the investment organization has grown, too. And just like any important area of the investment firm, controls, policies, and procedures are necessary.

We've touched on part of what you want to consider. But each organization is different, so you might have some unique needs. Make sure they're addressed.

Appendix 12-A: Adjustments to Prior Period Returns[4]

One problem that is common among all money management firms is the need to address adjustments to prior period returns. We'll discuss some of the reasons for these problems, alternative ways people are dealing with them, and a set of "proposed standards" for handling adjustments. It is our hope that these standards will become universally accepted and agreed upon.

Why we have to make adjustments

Each month, money managers use their portfolio accounting data as the basis for the rates of return they publish and report. Prior to initiating the reporting cycle, however, the portfolios typically go through a reconciliation process with the account's "official books and records." These records are typically maintained by the account's custodian or clearing broker, who is responsible to ensure complete integrity of the data.

For a variety of reasons, there are often exceptions discovered between what the money manager believes the portfolio looks like and what the custodian shows. There can be a variety of reasons for this, including:

- Missed trades. Perhaps a trade was processed against the wrong account or wasn't correctly registered on either system.
- Mishandling of corporate actions. On occasion, a corporate action may have been missed completely or simply not processed correctly.

Missed cash flows. Perhaps the client added or withdrew funds from the account; while the custodian may have recorded these actions, the manager may not have been aware of them and therefore didn't record them on the portfolio accounting system.

- Pricing problems. This is especially a problem for securities that aren't actively traded or for which market prices aren't available. We may have overridden a price, only to learn later that our manually applied price was incorrect. Pricing inconsistencies can lead to erroneous rates of return being reported. This is especially problematic when the problems are related to capital flows.
- Exchange rates. Differences in the sources for exchange can also cause differences. Sometimes huge differences.

Once the reconciliation is complete, the money manager confidently moves forward and produces rates of return which will appear on client statements, in their GIPS and AIMR-PPS presentations, and in the firm's marketing brochures.

Unfortunately, the story doesn't end here. On occasion, we will learn of problems that occurred in a prior period, after the reconciliation has been done, which may cause us to reconsider the accuracy of previously reported rates of return. What can cause these problems? Well, they are often similar to the problems we identify during the reconciliation process:

- Failed trades. Perhaps a trade that was booked wasn't able to settle, necessitating the trade being cancelled.
- Incorrectly processed trades. Trades may have been recorded and reconciled, but later found to be in error.
- Problems with corporate actions. Often, all the details necessary to properly process a corporate action may not be available for several weeks, possibly

months, following the announcement. For example, with a spin-off, there may be shares plus cash issued, but the specifics may not be known for some time. Once they're known, backdated adjustments may be needed.

- Pricing problems. Perhaps as a result of misapplied corporate actions or trade problems, we may also have pricing problems.

On occasion, our custodian may have made an error that they haven't discovered for some period. When they do, they adjust their records. Should we?

Another source of potential errors is benchmarks. On occasion, a benchmark provider will go back and adjust a previously reported index. Perhaps they had mispriced a security or failed to process a corporate action; or, there may have been some other cause for their error. If we've used the benchmark data in our attribution analysis, we may want to go back and recalculate our numbers.

Once the money manager becomes aware of these as-of adjustments, they must decide what to do from a reporting point of view. Do we recalculate our previously reported returns and inform the client of changes? Do we change our returns in our GIPS presentations?

The problem with changed returns is that the client normally notices them, especially if calendar year or fixed-period returns are shown. Showing rolling period returns (e.g., rolling year) can reduce this risk, but this kind of reporting is not in line with the GIPS or the AIMR-PPS. In addition, most clients want to see returns reported by calendar years.

Reasons not to make the changes

One reason firms often don't want to tell their clients of changes is they feel this will suggest that the firm doesn't have the correct controls in place to catch these problems before the reports are issued. They feel that these adjustments will only raise concerns about their processing and the new results will have little benefit to the client. This is the same reason why indexers do not want to communicate recalculated index data to their clients. While we can understand the basis for this position, we don't feel it's justified. Clients need to be aware that there will be occasions when prior period results will change. Our clients should be pleased that we are willing to go back and make the necessary adjustments to ensure the highest quality of our reported data.

The change will be captured in a subsequently reported return. This often does happen. For example, perhaps we missed a trade; thus our ending period market value may be incorrect. However, the correction will be made in a subsequent period, and we expect the numbers to be adjusted in the next period. While this may be true, it doesn't take away from the fact that a prior period had an erroneous return.

Another reason firms may not wish to make changes is because they have little impact on the previously reported numbers. Changes that may be considered minuscule may not be felt worth addressing. We don't necessarily disagree with this notion and have included it in our proposed approach. We refer to this as "materiality," which you'll see below.

How firms handle retroactive adjustments

We have discussed this topic at a few meetings of the Performance Measurement Forum and have some insight into what the process may look like. In general, this is what seems to occur.

#1 – Ascertain the materiality of the correction. In order to do this, we must calculate the return after the correction is made and compare it with the previously reported number(s). Firms will often establish (perhaps not formally) some cutoff, below which nothing will be done. Criteria such as the change relative to the published return or how far back the change would have to be made will be considered.

#2 – Freezing of time periods. Many firms will "freeze" a time period, after which no change will be applied.[5] While we can understand the reasoning behind this, depending on how recent the freezing may be applied, we may be creating some problems. For example, if our policy is to freeze any returns reported prior to the last quarter, we're not allowing much of a window for adjustments. Freezing may be applied to the previous calendar year with a lagging period of six months (after verification). If a material return error does not wash out over time, then the firm has no choice but to recalculate. Investment advisors cannot knowingly report incorrect returns.

Proposed approach

1. Written Policies and Procedures

We feel that firms must have written policies and procedures on handling prior-period adjustments and they should be strictly adhered to.

Clearly, the presence of controls is of utmost importance, as they will help minimize the need to make adjustments; for example, to avoid distributing returns until after the reconciliation process has taken place. Unfortunately, the pressure to reveal numbers is often so great that we issue returns prior to the reconciliation being completed. We recommend that any numbers published in such a manner carry notation such as "preliminary numbers; changes may occur as a result of reconciliation" to alert the recipients that the numbers haven't been finalized. Following the reconciliation, subsequent reports can carry the notation of "final." Of course, we realize that "final" doesn't always mean "final." Example: for a GIPS or AIMR-PPS report, we may want to use a phrase like "figures have not been verified yet and are therefore subject to change."

Another matter, which should be part of the firm's policies, is *when* the books should be "closed." And, if they are closed, under what circumstances can they be reopened?

Let's now address *when errors are truly errors.* Do people expect their reports to be *estimates,* in which case adjustments are merely finalizing the previously estimated reports? Under this approach would it be necessary to announce a correction, since the recipient should understand that what they received was an estimate?

A lot depends upon the level of sophistication of the recipient. It's difficult, if not impossible, to know how performance-savvy our clients are. The reality is that the knowledge level probably varies considerably from client to client. We may want to consider having a policy with each client which outlines *when* we will notify them of changes. Education is important as (a) the returns, in many cases, are only approximations of the "true time-weighted rate of return" and (b) because individuals who are knowledgeable about the investment industry know that changes do occur.

2. Definition of Materiality

Our decision as to whether to apply a change or notify recipients of changes will be tied to the materiality of the correction. For example, if we reported a year-end return of 23.16%, but found that it should be 23.15%, is a one basis point change worth disseminating? Perhaps not. So, what will the cutoff be?

Something to consider: report returns to ten basis points (one decimal place). This would mean that both 23.15% and 23.16% would be reported as 23.2%, meaning no notification would be needed. This may be easier said than done, however, as many people expect to see returns shown to the basis point, as if this level of detail really shows the true accuracy of the information.

Table 12-A shows an example of the factors that you might consider when defining your level of materiality. We believe there may be one set of rules for portfolios and another for composites. Also, we might have rules based on security types. Other factors we're considering are the length of the reported time period (month, quarter, year). Finally, we have one set of rules for republishing and another for restating. For example, we might recalculate our returns based upon a certain degree of error but won't actually republish (i.e., notify the recipient) of

			Time Periods		
			Month	Quarter	Year
Portfolios	Equities	Restate	1 bp	2 bps	3 bps
		Republish	3 bps	4 bps	5 bps
	Fixed Income	Restate	1 bp	2bps	3bps
		Republish	1 bp	2bps	3bps
Composites	Equities	Restate	2 bps	3 bps	4 bps
		Republish	3 bps	4 bps	5 bps
	Fixed Income	Restate	2 bps	3 bps	4 bps
		Republish	2 bps	4 bps	6 bps

Table 12-A: Sample Materiality Table

the change unless it's of a higher degree of materiality. These rules may be defined on product level because depending on the underlying data (for example, emerging markets) one or two basis points may be nothing.

Another issue is if we have accounts which are valued only once a month and for which the account value is only available three weeks after month end (e.g., hedge funds). In these cases, other rules may be applied because it makes no sense to send a letter for correction every month to the client.

Our rule may be based upon the magnitude of the correction. Two possibilities: *absolute* and *relative*. While our table shows the changes in absolute terms, we might want to consider materiality based upon relative magnitude as well.

An absolute change of 10 basis points or more, for example, may trigger a correction.

From a *relative* standpoint (relative to the benchmark), a change which would cause the portfolio or composite to move in relationship to the benchmark (e.g., from outperforming to underperforming), regardless of the absolute magnitude, might trigger a correction. Or perhaps the test will be the degree of change relative to the size of the return. Or perhaps from an *absolute* perspective (if the change is more than a certain number of basis points), a correction might be made. We think this is not an option that should be employed.

The investment advisor must present their returns accurately. In a year where the index is up 30%, can the manager report returns that are off by 2 percent? I think the answer is no. The threshold used for recalculating ought to be absolute.

3. Freezing Time Periods

While we feel that it's appropriate to "freeze time periods," we should be prepared to "open" a previously closed time period should the magnitude of the correction warrant it. For example, if our policy is to close a prior year once we're at least six months into the new year, what happens if we discover an error that would result in a change of 500 basis points (5%)? Wouldn't this warrant a reopening of the period (books)? We believe it would.

The policy should state when time periods are "frozen" and what would be done if a very large change had to be applied.

4. The Process

Some firms will go through the following process when an error is identified:

- Step 1 – recalculate the returns.
- Step 2 – compare degree of correction to the materiality table. If the magnitude warrants action, provide to a responsible party (individual or committee) for review. This may also go through the firm's legal or compliance department for review.
- Step 3 – decide on what action to take. Document the original number, the corrected figure, and the action taken.

Figure 12-A-1: Decision Tree for Portfolio Changes

Figure 12-A-1 shows a "decision tree" that you might employ for handling corrections. As you can see, the first step is to determine whether or not a report has been sent to the client; if it has, then a change would be needed (providing the magnitude exceeded our threshold).

Note: Ideally, the client contract has a section on performance measurement and a disclaimer or understood policy with respect to corrections.

Figure 12-A-2 provides a similar approach but with respect to changes in composite returns. In this case, we not only need to address notifying the prospect but also clients, verifiers, and others.

Ideally, clients should be able to identify their rules for materiality (i.e., at what level they want to be aware of changes to prior periods). Alternatively, they would default to standard firm policy.

Performance-based fees

It's important that the firm's policy be sensitive to situations involving per-

238 The Handbook of Investment Performance

formance-based fees. There's a belief that if an adjustment is made it will be caught up in a subsequent period. If this is true, perhaps an adjustment isn't needed. But this needs to be assessed.

Another issue occurs if the custodian provides the return which is used for the fee and the error occurs there. A review should be performed to determine the magnitude of the error and how the change should be handled.

What if the problem is with the index provider? If the provider makes an adjustment, then a review is in order. If the provider didn't make an adjustment, then the firm may elect to recalculate the index's return as they believe it should be and, if appropriate, report and take the appropriate action to ensure the correct fee is assessed. However, this option is clearly not available to all firms; in addition, the firm would have to explain why they did this. So, caution needs to be exercised if this action is taken. Perhaps a better step is to simply make it known that the index is in error.

Educating the client

As noted earlier, it's important for clients to be aware that errors do, on occa-

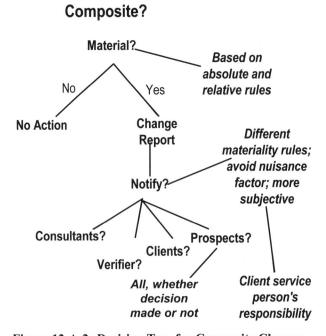

Figure 12-A-2: Decision Tree for Composite Changes

sion, take place. How this is communicated may vary, depending on the size or sophistication of the client. However, if the portfolio is subject to prior-period adjustments, it's important that the client be aware of this and what may cause an adjustment.

This educational exercise is not only important for clients but also for consultants.

A similar issue is adjusting the return of an attribution software to the official return calculation.

All users of returns should realize that the correctness of a return figure is dependent upon the quality of lots of input data for which the money manager doesn't control and is not responsible for.

Proposed standards

Now, to the standards we discussed early on.

We've had calculation standards since the late 1960s and presentation standards since the early 1990s. The Performance Measurement Forum developed proposed standards for attribution,[6] which are fairly extensive. Handling corrections is yet another area where standards should exist.[7]

Regarding handling corrections, we propose some fairly basic standards which we feel the industry should follow. As you'll see, they're rather brief:

#1 Develop and maintain a written policy: All firms (who are subject to as-of adjustments, [and who isn't?]) should develop and maintain written policies and procedures that outline what steps they take in the event of changes to prior-period returns. Any as-of changes (whether or not action is taken) should be documented (the change, the reason for the change, the action[s] taken).

This is in line with GIPS, which now mandates the development of policies and procedures. This is just one of those policies which a firm should have.

#2 Make available upon request: Written policies must be made available to clients and prospects, upon request.

We don't propose that there be one universal set of standards and that everyone adopt them. However, we realize that changes occur and that it's important that investment firms outline how they handle them. This is also in line with the spirit of GIPS: consistency, disclosure, and fair representation.

Everyone is subject to the problem of having changes occur. The question is "What do we do about it?" We've attempted to outline the reasons, issues, and some suggestions on how to deal with these problems.

ENDNOTES

[1] Antilla (1993).

[2] This list is taken from our firm's Web site (www.SpauldingGrp.com). It's periodically updated, so you may want to visit it occasionally to see if there are any changes.

[3] "Portability" refers to how "portable" the performance history is. That is, when two firms merge, one firm acquires another, or portfolio managers move from one firm to another. For further information, refer to the guidance statement on portability (AIMR (2002), section 5-2, pages 1-4).

[4] This appendix is based on an article I originally wrote with Stefan Illmer, which appeared in *The Journal of Performance Measurement*. (See Spaulding and Illmer (2003).)

[5] Some firms refer to this as "closing their books." But "closed books" can be opened again under certain circumstances (analogous to unfreezing time periods).

[6] Spaulding (2002/2003).

[7] The IPC developed guidance on error corrections (see IPC (2004, 2)).

Chapter 13 –
A First-class Performance System

We're occasionally asked what the criteria is to have a "first class performance system." While there are no set rules, I'll share with you some of my thoughts.

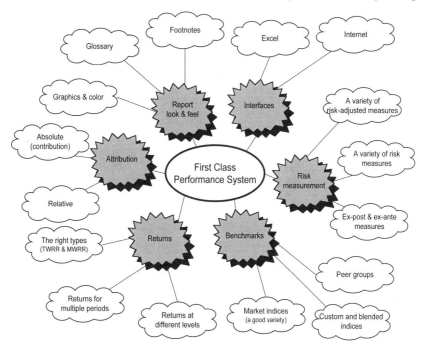

Figure 13-1: Characteristics of a First Class Performance System

Figure 13-1 provides an overview of what such a system will include.

System overall

<u>Returns</u>

- <u>The right type(s) of returns</u>. As we discussed in Chapter 6, there is a time for time-weighting and a time for money-weighting. You should ensure you're using the right approach. Being able to support both is important; in addition, being able to calculate both approximation as well as exact methods, and having additional flexibility (such as how cash flows are treated (start-of-day vs.

end-of-day) is also important.

*   <u>Returns for multiple time periods</u>. Ideally, variable periods should be permitted. Rolling and/or stationary periods. This obviously means the ability to calculate cumulative and annualized rates of return for a variety of periods.
*   <u>Returns at different levels</u>. Portfolio, sub-portfolio, and superportfolio (e.g., composite, family, or other groupings) should be supported. Although we favor money-weighting for sub-portfolio returns (see Chapter 6), we recognize that not everyone does, so you should have the flexibility to do either.

Benchmarks

*   <u>Provide access to a variety of market indices</u>. Ideally, all the major indexes are supported so that returns are shown in line with the indexes that are most appropriate.
*   <u>Support custom and blended indices</u>. Custom indexes have value and ideally can be utilized, when appropriate. In addition, the system should support the blending of two or more indexes.
*   <u>Support for peer groups</u>. The system should provide access to various peer groups for reporting and analytical purposes.

Attribution

Because attribution can be a complicated topic as well as a costly process to employ, one would expect that some discretion be exercised in determining which clients to provide attribution to. As we discussed in Chapter 9, there are two forms: absolute (contribution) and relative. The retail market is often best served with absolute, while both may be appropriate for institutional clients. A lot of flexibility is important, such as the support of various models, support for both arithmetic and geometric and both holdings- and transaction-based attribution. The more flexibility and options, the better.

Risk measures

As we discussed in Chapter 10, risk is a controversial and challenging area. Not everyone agrees on what risk is (e.g., is it volatility, the potential for loss, uncertainty, the inability to meet the client's objectives) or how to measure it. You should be prepared to:

- Provide a variety of risk measures, such as standard deviation, beta, downside deviation, and tracking error.
- Provide a variety of risk-adjusted measures, such as Sharpe ratio, information ratio, Jensen's alpha, and M-squared (Modigliani-Modigliani).
- Support both *ex-post* and *ex-ante* risk. While most are satisfied with *ex-post* (backward looking) measures, many find value in seeing *ex-ante* (forward looking) risk reported.[1]

Report Look & Feel

Systems exist to report. But what are some of the characteristics of exceptional reporting? Good reporting includes the following features:

- Valuable information: throughout the report the information that is provided has value for the recipient. Providing lots of reports that won't be read serves no purpose.
- Presented in a logical fashion: Think about how information is grouped and the order in which it appears (often we start with more general or higher level information (summary-level) and then *drill down* to lower level details.
- That's intuitive; easy to comprehend: the recipient can understand what they're given. Overwhelming users with how smart you are doesn't help if *they don't get it*. It's better to leave some of the details out if you can communicate the essence of what's of value to them.
- That's meaningful: the information should have meaning to the recipient.
- That's accurate: providing inaccurate information serves no purpose. Controls should exist to ensure the highest degree of accuracy. And when errors are discovered, your policies should dictate how they're handled, including when individuals are notified that errors had occurred.
- That's precise: the appropriate level of precision. Having flexibility here is important as some don't care to see very low level details and are satisfied with getting information summarized.
- That's presented in a top-down fashion: part of the logical format idea.
- That's well organized: again, falls under the concept of being logical.
- That allows for drilling down to lower levels, if desired: flexible to support gaining access to lower levels of information.

- That's attractive: laid out in a manner that's eye catching.
- Colorful, as necessary, in order to grab attention: color helps convey special information and draw attention. Most firms have access to color printers: take advantage of this option for both tabular and graphical presentations.
- That's presented in both tabular as well as graphical format, when appropriate: suits different needs or preferences. Some people prefer pictures, others tables: having flexibility is important.
- That's consistent: layout should be consistent and values should be identical throughout. Ideally, all reports should be titled for easy reference. And, ideally, if reports are produced in packets, pages should be numbered sequentially.
- Flexible: allows for altering look and feel.
- Customizable: can customize to meet certain needs. While many want to limit the degree of customization, having some degree available is important.
- Timely: available when needed. Many will issue "preliminary" reports in advance of their reconciliation to meet client and internal needs: as long as reports are so noted, then this is usually fine. Where appropriate, follow up with revised reports that reflect adjustments following the reconciliation.
- Appropriate: the right information to the right person in the right way.
- Accessible: the person who needs the information can get to it.

In addition, it's ideal to minimize the amount of customization and manual involvement: as much as possible should be automated. The system should be able to identify which reports go to which clients, and the options (e.g., periods) that are to be employed. The frequency of reporting should be table driven and automated so that minimal manual effort is needed to know what reports go to what clients at what time periods.

It is important that in addition to providing valuable information that reports are also attractive and well constructed.

- The use of colorful graphics. Graphics are an excellent adjunct to a presentation; they translate data that's shown in a tabular fashion into a picture. While graphics can be shown on separate pages, ideally they should be incorporated on the same page as the tabular information.
- Glossary: a glossary of terms can be helpful, especially given the variety of interpretations for terminology.
- Footnotes: footnotes serve as a way to provide additional details about what's

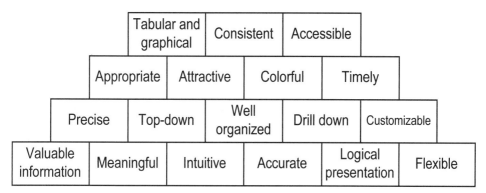

Figure 13-2: Report Building Blocks

reported.

ENDNOTES

[1] Forward looking (ex-ante) risk is beyond the scope of this book; however, we realize that many firms want to be able to report risk this way, so having this flexibility (or access to such systems) is important.

Chapter 14 –
The Performance Measurement Profession

I like metaphors and believe that we can use books as a metaphor to show the growth of our industry. Figure 14-1 lists the books that have been published since 1980.

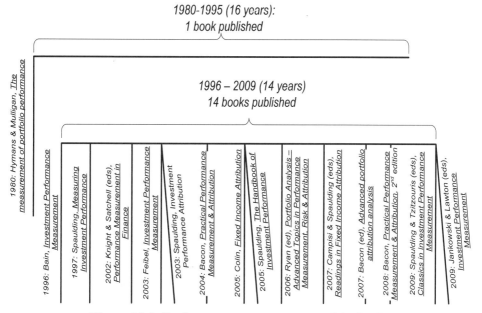

Figure 14-1: Performance measurement and its books

From 1980 to 1995, a span of 16 years, only one performance book was published; but from 1996 to 2009 (a span of 14 years), 14 books have been published (with more in the works). This is quite impressive, yes? I believe it shows how the industry has grown.

In the mid-80s, performance was typically relegated to the back office of a money management firm, with a clerk being responsible for it on a part-time basis. Today, whole teams oversee this area.

Performance measurement used to be *calculating the returns of the portfolios.* Today, it most likely includes:

- slicing and dicing the portfolio returns (i.e., calculating returns at the sector

and security levels)
- performance contribution or absolute performance attribution
- relative performance attribution
- risk measurement, management, and monitoring
- benchmark selection and management, including market indexes and peer groups
- presentation standards
- preparing marketing materials
- preparing client reports
- responding to requests for proposal

These groups are organized in various fashions. Some have a single department with no specialization; rather, team members work in all areas of performance. Other firms have created teams that specialize in one or two of these functions. In some cases, the risk function is separate; in other cases, it's part of performance, and sometimes performance is part of the risk function.

While many of the performance teams report to either marketing or portfolio management, we favor having them report to compliance, the chief operating officer, or chief executive officer.

The systems' role in performance

There's no question that technology is needed to accomplish performance measurement properly. And while portfolio accounting systems have traditionally played a major role in providing these tools, specialized software seems to be pretty standard today, as each area's requirements have grown in complexity.

We still see spreadsheets used quite a bit but recommend that this be done on an *ad hoc* basis rather than for "systems," as spreadsheets tend to be error prone, cumbersome, and time-consuming. And since they're not databases, getting the data out and into other systems isn't trivial.

Keeping up with the profession

The third C-word we mentioned early on is change, and that's what we've got plenty of. Performance measurement is truly a dynamic area. But keeping up with it can be a challenge.

Attending industry conferences is one way. There are plenty to choose from, so due diligence is needed to make sure the ones you attend provide you with the best information possible.

Formal training classes is another. Again, there are various groups offering training.

Having a library of reference materials is also important. We appreciate you obtaining a copy of and reading this book. There are other books available which you should consider getting, too. We recommend Carl Bacon's recently published <u>Practical Portfolio Measurement and Attribution</u> and Bruce Feibel's <u>Investment Performance Measurement</u>. Although you'll find some overlap with this book, you'll also find different views and material, which will serve you well. My book on attribution goes well beyond what we provided in Chapter 9, so if this is a subject you require more information on, you'll no doubt appreciate the additional focus provided by it. Other reference materials worth having access to include Peter Dietz's <u>Pension Funds: Measuring Investment Performance</u>, the GIPS and, if appropriate, your country version of GIPS standards (e.g., the AIMR-PPS, U.K.-IPS, SAAJ-IPS), the GIPS handbook, the calculation standards (e.g., the BAI and ICAA standards), and, if you're involved with global attribution, the Karnosky-Singer standards. Our Web site (www.SpauldingGrp.com) provides a list of other references you may want to acquire.

Participating in performance measurement groups is also advantageous. The Performance Measurement Forum is an interactive group which meets semiannually to address current issues, challenges, and topics. Some areas have informal luncheon groups for performance measurement professionals.

If the presentation standards are important to you (and hopefully they are), make sure you're included in their e-mail service so that you're kept up-to-date with the changes and publications.

In addition to understanding all aspects of performance measurement, we encourage you to understand the investment process, especially as it relates to your firm. The more you know, the more you can contribute and the more you can grow. Obtaining an MBA and CFA® can also be greatly beneficial in providing you with a better understanding of the industry and enhancing your opportunity for growth.

Certification

In 2004, The Spaulding Group created The Foundation of Investment

Performance Professionals. This is a nonprofit membership group supporting individuals who are actively involved in performance measurement.

We also formed a Blue Ribbon Committee ("BRC") to work on a formal certification program. The members of the BRC came from North America and Europe and volunteered their time to develop this examination. The purpose of the CIPA (Certified Investment Performance Analyst) program was to distinguish those professionals who had obtained broader and more extensive knowledge of investment performance measurement. It was to serve as a way to enhance the presence and visibility of those engaged in investment performance measurement and analysis.

The certification examination was to address all aspects of investment performance, including:

- rates of return
- attribution
- presentation standards
- risk measurement
- benchmarks
- industry basics

However, in late 2004 we learned that the CFA Institute had embarked on a similar effort to develop a certification program for investment performance measurement professionals. Rather than continue with our program and have a competing examination, we decided to terminate our project and to turn over our materials to the CFA Institute to help them with their development efforts. In addition, several members of the BRC have been appointed to the team that will further develop the CFA Institute's examination program. This program, originally named "CGIPS," was renamed "CIPM" (Certificate in Investment Performance Measurement) to better express the broad aspect of this program.

Certification is important for the investment performance professional, whether it's done by The Foundation of Investment Performance Professionals or CFA Institute. It's a way to further signify that this area has grown considerably in its importance to the investment industry and warrants such attention. We support their efforts and continue to wish them much success.

Industry volunteers

In addition to the volunteers who are working on the development of the certification program, we have volunteers involved in other aspects of performance. In Chapter 11, we touched on the Investment Performance Council (IPC). As noted previously, IPC members come from various parts of the industry and throughout the world. In addition, there are several subcommittees supporting the IPC. These groups are comprised of volunteers.

Various local groups have also been created. In North America, we have the NAIPC (North America Investment Performance Council, formerly the AIMR-PPS Implementation Committee); similar groups exist elsewhere. These groups are actively working to enhance the knowledge base of the industry and to develop new standards, enhance existing ones, and address other areas of performance measurement.

These groups are always looking for professionals who are prepared to contribute their time, energy, and talents.

The future

Given the dynamics of our industry, it's difficult to predict what we'll be looking like in five or ten years. We've seen the elimination of boundaries when it comes to software, and we're also seeing the same when it comes to hiring management and staff, as the demands of the industry are creating tremendous opportunities for knowledgeable professionals.

ENDNOTES

[1] Chartered Financial Analyst - for more information, contact the CFA Institute (www.CFAInstitute.org).

[2] Crawford, 2004, 1.

Bibliography

AIMR. 1993. *Performance Presentation Standards.* Association for Investment Management and Research.

AIMR. 1997. *Performance Presentation Standards Handbook.* Association for Investment Management and Research.

AIMR. 1999. *Global Investment Performance Standards.* Charlottesville, VA: Association for Investment Management and Research.

AIMR. 2001. *AIMR Performance Presentation Standards (AIMR-PPS).* Charlottesville, VA: Association for Investment Management and Research.

AIMR. 2002. *Global Investment Performance Standards Handbook.* Charlottesville, VA: Association for Investment Management and Research.

Antilla, Susan. 1993. "This Money Manager Can't Count." *The New York Times.* (June 20). 15.

Bacon, Carl. 2002. "Excess Returns – Arithmetic or Geometric?" *The Journal of Performance Measurement.* Spring.

Bacon, Carl. (2004). <u>Practical Portfolio Performance Measurement and Attribution</u>. John Wiley & Sons.

Bacon, Carl. 2007. "Money-weighted Versus Time-weighted Attribution." *The Journal of Performance Measurement.* (Supplement): 21-27.

Bacon, Carl, 2007/08. "Measuring performance returns." *Professional Investor.* Winter.

Bacon, Carl. 2008. <u>Practical Portfolio Performance Measurement and Attribution</u>. 2nd Edition. John Wiley & Sons.

BAI. 1968. *Measuring the Investment Performance of Pension Funds.* Bank Administration Institute.

Bailey, Jeffery V., Thomas M. Richards, and David E. Tierney. 1990. "Benchmark

Portfolios and the Manager/Plan Sponsor Relationship." *Current Topics in Investment Management*. Frank Fabozzi and T. Dessa Fabozzi, eds. New York: HarperCollins.

Bailey, Jeffery V., Thomas M. Richards, and David E. Tierney. 2007 "Evaluating Portfolio Performance," Chapter 12 in John L. Maginn, Donald L. Tuttle, Dennis W. McLeavey, and Jerald E. Pinto, eds., Managing Investment Portfolios; A Dynamic Process (CFA Institute). Pages 717–782.

Bain, William G. 1996. *Investment Performance Measurement*. Cambridge, England.

Brinson, Gary P. and Nimrod Fachler. "Measuring Non-U.S. Equity Portfolio Performance." *Journal of Portfolio Management*: Spring 1985.

Brinson, Gary P., L. Randolph Hood, and Gilbert L. Beebower. 1986. "Determinants of Portfolio Performance." *Financial Analysts Journal*: August.

Sanford C. Bernstein & Co. (Date unknown). "Performance Measurement Techniques."

Campisi, Stephen. 2000. "Primer on Fixed Income Performance Attribution." *The Journal of Performance Measurement*. Summer.

Campisi, Stephen. 2002. "Creating and Managing Custom Benchmarks – A Practitioner's Guide." *The Journal of Performance Measurement*. (Summer 2002): 14-26.

Campisi, Stephen. 2004, 1. "The Case for Money-weighted Performance Attribution." *The Journal of Performance Measurement*. (Spring 2004): 31-41.

Campisi, Stephen. 2004, 2. "De-bunking the Interaction Myth." *The Journal of Performance Measurement*. Summer. Fall.

CFA Institute. 2005. "Global Investment Performance Standards."

Chapra, Steven C. & Raymond P. Canale. 2005. *Numerical Methods for Engineers*. (McGraw-Hill: New York).

Chernoff, Joel. 2004. "Arnott challenges conventional wisdom with new stock index." *Pensions & Investments*. (September 20): 53.

Christopherson, Jon A., David R. Cariño & Wayne E. Ferson. 2009. *Portfolio Performance Measurement and Benchmarking*. (McGraw-Hill, New York).

Coggan, Phillip. 2004. "Not so Clever Information Ratio." *Financial Times* (December 13): 28.

Copeland, Thomas E., J. Fred Weston, & Kuldeep Shastri. (2005). *Financial Theory and Corporate Policy*. (Pearson Addison Wesley).

Crawford, Gregory. 2004, 1. "Standardizing performance measurement." *Pensions & Investments*. (June 28).

Crawford, Gregory. 2004, 2. "Ron Ryan quits to start new firm after his buyout offer is rejected." *Pensions & Investments*. (July 26).

deSilva, Harindra, Steven Sapra, and Steven Thorley. 2001. "Return Dispersion and Active Management." *Financial Analysts Journal*. (September/October).

Dietz, Peter O. 1966. *Pension Funds: Measuring Investment Performance*. New York: The Free Press.

Dietz, Peter O. 2004. *Pension Funds: Measuring Investment Performance*. Somerset, NJ: TSG Publishing.

Dietz, Peter O. & Jeannette R. Kirschman. 1983. "Evaluating Portfolio Performance." *Managing Investment Portfolios*. The Institute of Chartered Financial Analysts.

Dorfman, John. 2004. "Stocks are Hurting More Than the Averages Show." Bloomberg News. (August 26).

Dvorak, Phred. 2009. "Poor Year Doesn't Stop CEO Bonuses." *Wall Street Journal*. March 18, page B1.

Eadie, Dugald M.. 1973. "A Practical Approach to the Measurement and Analysis of Investment Performance." *The Investment Analyst*. 12-18.

Eling, Martin, and Frank Schuhmacher. 2007. "Does the choice of performance measure influence the evaluation of hedge funds?" *Journal of Banking & Finance*. 31, 2632-2647.

Farrell, James L., Jr. 1976. *Guide to Portfolio Management*. New York: McGraw-Hill.

Feibel, Bruce. 2003. *Investment Performance Measurement*. New York: John Wiley.

Feibel, Bruce. 2004. E-mail conversation with the author regarding annualizing risk measures.

Fisher, Lawrence. 1966. "An algorithm for finding exact rates of return." *Journal of Business*. XXXIX, 111-117.

Flader, Alan. "'Standard Deviation' is False God." *Financial Planning on Wall Street*. (May): 53.

Fulman, Ricki. 2004. "Money managers praise S&P for float-adjusted index weightings." *Pensions & Investments*. (March 8): 2 & 38.

Goodwin, Thomas H. 1997. "The Information Ratio: More Than You Ever Wanted to Know About One Performance Measure." Russell Research Commentary. (November.)

Green, S.J.. 1989. "Another look at portfolio performance measurement." *The Investment Analyst*. 92, 6-10.

Greynolds, Elbert B., Jr., Julius S. Aronofsky, and Robert J. Frame. 1979. *Financial Analysis Using Calculators: Time Value of Money*. McGraw-Hill.

Haight, G. Timothy and Stephen Morrell. 1997. *The Analysis of Portfolio Management Performance*. New York: McGraw-Hill.

Harlow, W.V. 1991. "Asset Allocation in a Downside-Risk Framework." *Financial Analysts Journal*. (September-October): 28-40.

Hayes, Michael. 2000. "Conquering 'Performance' Anxiety." *Registered Rep Magazine*. February 1.

Hazen, Gordon B. 2003. "A New Perspective on Multiple Internal Rates of Return." 48,1. 31-51.

Hymans, Clifford and John Mulligan. 1980. *The measurement of portfolio performance*. (Kluwer, Brentford).

ICAA. 1971. "The Standards of Measurement and Use for Investment Performance Data." New York: Investment Council Association of America.

IFIC. 2000. "Personal Rates of Return." *IFIC Bulletin Number 21*. The Investment Funds Institute of Canada. (Number 21).

IMCA. 1992. "The Consultant's Performance Standards." The Consultant's Performance Standards Task Force.

Ineichen, Alexander M. 2003. *Absolute Returns*. New Jersey: John Wiley.

IPC. 2002, 2. "Guidance Statement on Composite Definition." Investment Performance Council.

IPC. 2003, 1. "The Addition of Venture Capital and Private Equity Provisions to the Global Investment Performance Standards." Investment Performance Council.

IPC. 2003, 2. "The Addition of Leverage & Derivatives Provisions and Guidance to the Global Investment Performance Standards." Investment Performance Council.

IPC. 2003, 3. "Real Estate Provisions for GIPS Standards." Investment Performance Council.

IPC. 2004. "Guidance on the Use of Leverage and Derivatives." Investment Performance Council.

IPC. 2004, 2. "Guidance on Error Correction." Investment Performance Council.

Israelsen, Craig. 2003. "Sharpening the Sharpe Ratio." *Financial Planning*. January.

Israelsen, Craig. 2004. "A refinement to the Sharpe ratio and information ratio." *Journal of Asset Management*. November.

Jean, William H. 1968. "On Multiple Rates of Return." March. 187-191.

Jensen, Michael C. 1968. "The Performance of Mutual Funds in the Period 1945-1964." *Journal of Finance*. May: 389-416.

Kaplan, Seymour. 1967. "Computer algorithms for finding exact rates of return." *Journal of Business*. 40, 389-392.

Kaplan, Paul and Larry Siegel. 1994. "Portfolio Theory is Alive and Well." *Journal of Investing*. Fall.

Kaplan, Paul D. and Marius Daugirdas. 1996. "Traditional vs. new forms of risk measure." *Pensions & Investments*. (November 25.) 12.

Karnosky, Denis and Brian Singer. 1994. *Global Asset Management and Performance Attribution*. Charlottesville, VA: The Research Foundation of the Institute of Chartered Financial Analysts.

Kelly, Gary, and Mark Tippett. 1989. Estimating returns on financial instruments - deterministic analysis. *Accounting and finance* 29, 59-71.

Kritzman, Mark. 1993. "About Return and Risk." *Financial Analysts Journal*. (May-June).

Leong, Clint Tan Chee, Michael J. Seiler, and Mark Lane. 2002. "Explaining Apparent Stock Mark Anomalies: Irrational Exuberance or Archetypal Human Psychology." *Journal of Wealth Management*. Vol. 4, No. 4 (Spring).

Lerit, Steven J. 1996. "Measuring the Impact of Cash Flows and Market Volatility on Investment Performance Results." *The Journal of Performance Measurement*. (Winter.)

LIFFE. 1992. *Recommendations for the Reporting and Performance of Financial Futures and Options*. London International Financial Futures and Options Exchange.

Litterman, Robert B., Jacob Longerstaey, Jacob D. Rosengarten, and Kurt Winkelmann. 2001. "The Green Zone...Assessing the Quality of Returns." *The Journal of Performance Measurement*. (Spring.)

Longbottom, David and Linda Wiper. 1978. "Necessary Conditions for the Existence of Multiple Rates in the Use of Internal Rate of Return." *Journal of Business Finance & Accounting*. 5,4. 295-303.

Lux, Hal. 2002. "Risk gets riskier." *Institutional Investor*. (October): 28-36.

Mao, James C.T. 1969. *Quantitative Analysis of Financial Decisions*. (The MacMillan Company: Toronto).

McConnell, Nancy Belliveau. 1989. "Can phony performance numbers be policed?" *Institutional Investor*. (June.) 91-104.

Menchero, Jose. 2002/2003. "Performance Attribution With Short Positions." *The Journal of Performance Measurement*. (Winter): 39-50.

Menchero, Jose. 2004. "Multi-period Arithmetic Attribution." *Financial Analysts Journal*. (July/August): 76–91.

Men's Health. 2005. "The best things said about ... risk management." (March): 22.

Modigliani, Franco and Leah Modigliani. 1997. "Risk-Adjusted Performance." *The Journal of Portfolio Management*. (Winter: 2-9)

Modigliani, Lcah. 2001. "Risk Isn't Bad – M², the Basics." Morgan Stanley Equity Research. November 6, 2001.

Modigliani, Franco 2001/2002. "The Journal Interview." *The Journal of Performance Measurement*.

Modigliani, Leah. 2006. "Risk-adjusted Performance: How to Measure it and Why." *PMAR Conference Proceedings, 2006*. The Spaulding Group, Inc. (70-82).

Muralidhar, Arun. 2004, 1. "When the Green Zone Could Land You in the Red Zone." *The Journal of Performance Measurement*. (Summer): 8–13.

Muralidhar, Arun. 2004, 2. "A Few Currency Performance Myths." PMAR Conference

Plender, John. 1999. "What a performance." *Financial Times*. (March 27/28): 7.

Rahl, Leslie. 2000. "Risk Budgeting: The Next Step of the Risk Management Journey – The Veteran's Perspective." *Risk Budgeting – A New Approach to Investing*. Leslie Rahl, ed. London: Risk Books.

Reddy, Sudeep, John McKinnon, Michael Crittenden, & Kelly Evans. 2009. "Congress Looks to a Tax To Recoup Bonus Money." *Wall Street Journal*. March 18: pages 1-2.

Reniers, Corné. 2004. E-mail message to the author.

Rom, Brian M. and Kathleen Ferguson. 1994, 1. "Post-Modern Portfolio Theory Comes of Age." *The Journal of Investing*. (Fall): 11–17.

Rom, Brian M. and Kathleen Ferguson. 1994, 2. "'Portfolio Theory is Alive and Well': A Response." *Journal of Investing*. (Fall): 24–44.

Rom, Brian M. And Kathleen Ferguson. 1994, 3. "Lord, What Have we Begun." *Financial Planning on Wall Street.* (October): 6.

Rom, Brian M. and Kathleen Ferguson. 1997/1998. "Using Post-Modern Portfolio Theory to Improve Investment Performance Measurement." *The Journal of Performance Measurement.* (Winter): 5-13.

Rom, Brian M. and Kathleen Ferguson. 2004. E-mail conversation with the author.

Rosenberg, Claude, Jr., R. H. Jeffrey, Robert Kirby, Dean LeBaron, and John J. F. Sherrerd. 1987. "A Report on Setting Performance Presentation Standards." *Financial Analysts Journal.* (September-October): 8-11.

Rosenberg, Robert J. 2001. "How the Dow Hides the Bear." *Business Week.* (April 23): 98.

Rosengarten, Jacob. 2003. "Risk and Performance Evaluation and Decomposition Using Factor Models." Performance Measurement, Attribution and Risk Conference (PMAR.)

Ruffel, Charles. 1999. "Understanding Risk." *Plan Sponsor.* (March.)

Ryan, Ronald J. 1997. "The Journal Interview." *The Journal of Performance Measurement.* Fall 1997.

Schneeweis, Thomas, Hossein Kazemi, and George Martin. 2001. "Understanding Hedge Fund Performance: Research Results and Rules of Thumb for the Institutional Investor." Lehman Brothers. (November.)

Seiff, John. 1966. "Measuring Investment Performance: The Unit Approach." *Financial Analysts Journal.* (July-August): 93-99.

Sharpe, William F. 1966. "Mutual Fund Performance." *Journal of Business.* 39, 119.

Sharpe, William F. 1992. "Asset Allocation: Management Style and Performance Measurement." *The Journal of Portfolio Management.* (Winter): 7-15.

Sharpe, William F.. 1994. "The Sharpe ratio." *Journal of Portfolio Management* 21, 49.

Society of Investment Analysts. 1972. *The Measurement of Portfolio Performance for Pension Funds.*

Solnik, Bruno. 1996. *International Investments.* Addison-Wesley Publishing Company.

Sortino, Frank. 2002. "Looking only at return is risk, obscuring real goal." *Pensions & Investments.* (November 25.) 12.

Sortino, Frank and Hal J. Forsey. 1996. "On the Use and Misuse of Downside Risk." *The Journal of Portfolio Management.* (Winter.)

Spaulding, David. 1998. "When Performance Numbers Don't Make Sense." *The Journal of Performance Measurement.* (Summer.)

Spaulding, David. 2002/2003. "A Case for Attribution Standards." *The Journal of Performance Measurement.* (Winter): 13 – 21.

Spaulding, David. 2003, 1. "Is the Modified Dietz Formula Money-weighted or Time-weighted? *The Journal of Performance Measurement.* (Spring): 37–41.

Spaulding, David. 2003, 2. *Investment Performance Attribution.* New York: McGraw-Hill.

Spaulding, David. 2003/2004. "Demystifying the Interaction Effect." *The Journal of Performance Measurement.* (Winter).

Spaulding, David. 2004, 1. *Performance Perspectives.* (June.)

Spaulding, David. 2004, 2. "Uncle." *Performance Perspectives.* (August.)

Spaulding, David. 2004. "Geometric Attribution and Interaction." Performance Perspectives. August.

Spaulding, David. 2005, 1. The Handbook of Investment Performance. *TSG Publishing.*

Spaulding, David. 2005, 2. "Contrasting Time- and Money-weighted Returns: When Each Should be Used." *The Journal of Performance Measurement.* Fall.

Spaulding, David. 2005, 3. "Mind the Gap." *Performance Perspectives.*

Spaulding, David. 2007, 1. "M-Squared: A Double-Take on Three Approaches to a Primary Risk Measure." *The Journal of Performance Measurement*. Summer.

Spaulding, David. 2007, 2. "Getting to Know M-Squared a Bit Better." *Performance Perspectives*. (February)

Spaulding, David. 2008, 1. "The Confusing World of Modified Dietz." *Performance Perspectives*. (March).

Spaulding, David. 2008, 2. "A Blackbox Approach to Interaction." *The Journal of Performance Measurement* (Spring).

Spaulding, David and Stephen Campisi. 2007. "A Case for Money-weighted Attribution." *The Journal of Performance Measurement*. (Supplement): 8-20.

Spaulding, David and Stefan Illmer. "Adjustments to Prior Period Returns." *The Journal of Performance Measurement*. (Summer).

Stannard, John. 1996. "Measuring Investment Returns of Portfolios Containing Futures and Options. *The Journal of Performance Measurement*. (Fall): 27-33.

Stempel, Jonathan. 2009. "Merril may have misled congress on bonuses." Reuters. May 11.

Swensen, David F. 2000. *Pioneering Portfolio Management*. New York: The Free Press.

Taleb, Nassim Nicholas. 2007. *The Black Swan*. (Random House: New York).

Tam, Pui-Wing. 1999. "Study Finds Risk Adjustment Is Necessary for Tech Funds." *The Wall Street Journal*: February 26, 1999.

Treynor, Jack L.. 1965. "How to Rate Management of Investment Funds." *Harvard Business Review*. 43, 63-75.

Treynor, Jack L. 2008/2009. "Reader's Reflection." *The Journal of Performance Measurement*. Winter.

Treynor, Jack L., and Fischer Black. 1973. "How to Use Security Analysis to Improve Portfolio Selection." *Journal of Business*. 46, 66-86.

TSG. 1994. "Performance Measurement Survey, Detail Results." The Spaulding Group, Inc.

TSG. 1995. "Performance Measurement Surveys, Summary Results." The Spaulding Group, Inc.

TSG. 1997. "Performance Measurement Surveys, Summary Results." The Spaulding Group, Inc.

TSG. 2000. "Performance Presentation Standards Surveys." The Spaulding Group, Inc.

TSG. 2001. "Performance Measurement Technology Survey." The Spaulding Group, Inc.

TSG. 2002, 1. "Performance Presentation Standards Survey." The Spaulding Group, Inc.

TSG. 2002, 2. "Performance Measurement Attribution Survey." The Spaulding Group, Inc.

TSG. 2005. "Performance Measurement Attribution Survey." The Spaulding Group, Inc.

TSG. 2009. "Performance Presentation Standards Survey." The Spaulding Group, Inc.

White, James A. 1989. "How a Money Manager Can Pull a Rabbit Out of a Hat." *The Wall Street Journal*. (March 16.) C1 & C24.

Williams, Arthur III. 1992. *Managing Your Investment Manager*. Homewood, IL: Irwin.

Zhang, Duo. 2005. "A Different Perspective on Multiple Internal Rates of Return: The IRR Parity Technique." *The Engineering Economist*. 50. 327-335

Zuckerman, Gregory. 2004. "Float-weighted S&P 500 Likely to Pressure Some Stocks." *The Wall Street Journal*. (September 10): C1.

Index

86

CFA Institute, xviii, xx, xxi, xxii, 37, 40, 67, 220, 250, 251

Composite, 206-223, 227-230, 235-237, 242

    Creating/managing, 206

    Returns, 209-219, 227, 237

    Controls, 225-243

    Country Version of GIPS, 204-205, 249

    Cumulative returns, 72, 82

Day-weight, 37, 40, 64, 65, 93

Dietz, Peter, xx, 5, 11, 40, 85, 86, 249

Dietz mid-point method

Discretion, 87, 90, 202, 207, 208, 215, 216, 218, 219, 223, 229, 242

Dispersion, 128, 174, 214-216, 223, 230

Examinations, 3, 217

Excess Returns, 168, 180, 187, 188

    Arithmetic, 158-160

    Geometric, 158-160

FAF, 202, 221

Feibel, Bruce, xxii, xviii196, 198, 249

Ferguson, Kathleen, 197

Future value, 12, 13

Geometric linking, 9, 69-72, 74, 77, 78, 82, 102, 155, 156, 158, 160

GIPS, xii, xvii, xix, xxi, xxiii, 36, 59, 64, 82, 86, 203-205, 219, 220, 222, 223, 231-234, 239, 240, 249, 250

Indexes, xiv, 120-128, 130, 131, 133, 134, 242, 248

    Custom, 122, 130, 131, 242

    Free float, 124, 125

    Liability-related, 121, 122

    Providers/Intellectual property, 123, 124, 134

    Shortcomings indexes, 126, 127

ICAA, 27, 36, 44, 86, 203, 205, 222, 249

IPC, 28, 117, 204, 222, 240, 251

IRR, 5, 7, 11-29, 38, 39, 48, 49, 55, 60, 63-65, 78, 85-88, 90-99, 104-108

IMCA, 203, 222

Karnosky, Denis, xxi, 155, 157, 170, 249

Leverage and Derivatives, 109, 114

Linked IRR, 38, 48, 49, 60, 63-65, 93

Menchero, Jose, xxi, 66, 110, 112, 117

Modified Dietz, 6, 7, 9, 11, 21, 22, 24-26, 39-44, 49, 50, 52, 58-61, 64-66, 90-97, 99, 104-108, 210

Modigliani, Franco, 189, 196

Modigliani, Leah, 189

Money weighting, xviii, 6, 27, 28, 31, 43, 85, 86, 88, 91, 96, 116, 163, 241, 242

Muralidhar, Arun, 117

Myners, Paul, 132

Original Dietz, 34, 36, 37, 40, 41, 44, 51, 64

Peer groups, 120, 127-131, 241, 242, 248

    Advantages, 128

    Construction, 129

    Disadvantages, 128

Performance measurement profession, xix, xx, xxii, xxiii, 247-251

Performance presentation standards, xix, 201-222

Policies and procedures, xxiii, 216, 217, 225-240

Present value, 11-13, 18, 19, 64

Reniers, Corne, 147, 169

Risk, xii, xvii, xxi, xxii, xxiii, 9, 55, 115, 117, 120, 121, 125, 130, 146, 165-167, 169, 171-199, 206, 214, 215, 232, 241-243, 245

Beta, 185, 186, 192, 198, 243

Definition, 112, 127, 172, 175, 192, 193, 203, 206, 215, 218, 234

Downside risk, 181, 185, 192

Information ratio, 180, 188, 189, 192,

About the author

David Spaulding is the Founder and President of The Spaulding Group, Inc. He's also the Founder and Publisher of *The Journal of Performance Measurement*. He is an internationally recognized authority on investment performance measurement. He and his wife, Betty, live in North Brunswick, New Jersey.